LOVE'S
APPRENTICE

LOVE'S APPRENTICE

SHIRLEY ABBOTT

HOUGHTON MIFFLIN COMPANY

BOSTON   NEW YORK

1998

For information about permission to reproduce selections from
this book, write to Permissions, Houghton Mifflin Company,
215 Park Avenue South, New York, New York 10003.

Library of Congress Cataloging-in-Publication Data
Abbott, Shirley.
Love's apprentice / Shirley Abbott.
p.   cm.
ISBN 0-395-67369-0
1. Abbott, Shirley. 2. Man-woman relationships — United States.
3. Women — United States — Biography. 4. Love — United States.
I. Title.
CT275.A1494A3   1998
306.7 — dc21   97-44865   CIP

Printed in the United States of America
QUM 10 9 8 7 6 5 4 3 2 1

The author is grateful for permission to reprint excerpts from the following
works:

"I Got It Bad," by Duke Ellington. Reprinted by permission of Warner
Brothers, Inc.

"Unchained Melody," lyric by Hy Zaret, music by Alex North. Copyright © 1955 (renewed) by Frank Music Corp. All rights reserved.

The Identity of France, by Fernand Braudel. English language translation copyright © 1989 by Sian Reynolds. Reprinted by permission of
HarperCollins Publishers, Inc.

Intercourse, by Andrea Dworkin. Copyright © 1987 by Andrea Dworkin.
Reprinted with permission of The Free Press, a division of Simon &
Schuster.

LOVE'S
APPRENTICE

1

PRELUDE

*L*ong ago in the city of Paris, in the time of Louis XIII
and the young Louis XIV, there lived a woman named
Madeleine de Scudéry, a learned woman, it's said, and the
author of formidable, thick, preposterous, very successful romance
novels. What she's remembered for now, if at all, is her map of
love, or map of tender feelings, la carte de tendre, which still
sometimes shows up in old texts or dictionaries of French literature.
It is a sketchy, earnest little thing, like a child's drawing, showing a
great continent bisected north to south by a river and dotted with
castles and villages. Maybe she got the idea of mapping love's terri-
tory from the equally tentative maps of North America that French
explorers sent home to the kings of France: maps of conquest in
another sense.

Madeleine de Scudéry's map was a board game for a sport the
French call gallantry. You might start from New Acquaintance, follow the treacherous road leading toward the Castle of Love, and
end up at the bottom of the Lake of Indifference. The town of Sin-
cerity was a stop on the road to Tenderness by Esteem. Unless you
watched your step, you might drown in Inclination River, or be
swept off toward the Dangerous Sea and Uncharted Lands. You
had to beware of false lovers, one of whom might be you.

The object of the game was to find a lover obsessed with the
forms and formalities of love. A person in love with love, a man of
wit. Nowhere on the map was there a way station called marriage.

The salons of Paris oohed and aahed for a time about la carte
de tendre, but eventually they turned to other celebrity authors and

began calling Madeleine a précieuse, *which was not a term of en-
dearment. I ran across her years ago, in a schoolbook, and decided
she was on to something with her map. Like LaSalle or Champlain,
Marquette and Joliet (grand names from my childhood geography
books), Mlle. de Scudéry was a navigator of the unknown. Love
needs guidebooks and road signs, since it is forever terra incognita,
the new world, the unmapped land of each heart. I ask her blessing
on this undertaking. Go with me, Madeleine, be my Saint Christo-
pher in the chartless wilderness of love.*

~

I am an ordinary American woman, a wife, mother of two adult
daughters, signatory to a mortgage, possessor of an insurance
policy — universal life. I vote, give to the community chest,
make soup stock and banana bread, put little packages into the
freezer, gather up and do the wash, look after my mother-in-
law. I have not lived the life of a rake.

Yet I am a libertine, if the word still retains any of its old
subversive juice. For I know that love is the destroyer as well as
the giver of life, a game of power as much as affection, a game
of self. Most of us — men and women alike — are eternally
deceived about love. It is not what we believe it to be. Most
marriage, and indeed the institution of marriage, is not founded
on love but rather is a bargain as to bank accounts and inheri-
tances, surnames and how to educate the children — a struggle
over who rules and who obeys. Politics, in a word. The pursuit
of romantic love, some say, has undermined marriage, and this
might be true, if romantic love were ever given a chance. Yet
who marries for love? People marry their opposites, in order to
look better themselves, or marry their twins, because they fear
any variation. We marry for beauty, which is worse than marrying for money, though we marry for money too. Or just because
love is like musical chairs: the music stops, and we rush to sit
down before somebody beats us to it. And contrary to the conventional wisdom of our half-century, sex is not liberation. It is

dangerous, though hardly any more so than it ever was — an efficient method, as one scientist recently noted, of transmitting viruses. Besides that, it runs the gamut from boring to destructive, sometimes with no intermediate stops.

Of course, none of that matters, not in the least, nor has this hard-earned knowledge cured me of loving, or even of the romantic dreams of my girlhood. I am not cynical, let alone embittered. The songs still set me dancing. ("How deep is the ocean, how high is the sky?" I warble off-key at the kitchen sink, even when I've no particular person in mind.) You won't find me blaming my troubles on men. The battle may have been unequal, and I have emerged with all the wounds and welts, guilty secrets, and sins to expiate that characterize all but the most angelic lives. Yet I can say of myself what Casanova said when, having found work as a librarian in his last years, he began to write his memoirs: "Feeling that I was born for the sex opposite to mine, I have always loved it and done all that I could to make myself loved by it."

The old boy added, "If anyone calls me a sensualist he would be wrong, for the power of my senses never drew me from my duty when I had one." (He is lying, of course, as we all lie in such matters.)

And he wrote as well: "By everything good or bad that I have done throughout my life, I am sure that I have earned merit or incurred guilt, and that hence I must consider myself a free agent."

No more than he am I an innocent victim or a dupe. When I was a little girl, "out-of-wedlock" was spoken in a whisper. Childbirth was a function that women still occasionally died of. Virginity was one's dowry. Dreary messages! But I heard other messages. I was ready, at a young age, to launch my raft on love's dark rushing river, eager to swim in the waters.

Gullible, easily seduced, a roundheels for every crooner and show-tune lyric coming out of the radio or TV and every movie star of the silver screen, every book and poem. Keats and Shelley, Elizabeth Barrett and Robert Browning, and Emily and Charlotte Brontë, Sand and Chopin (oh, they more than anyone, the powerful woman, the male genius doomed to die), Ginger and Fred, Bogie and Bacall, Betty Grable and Harry James, Freud and Jung, D. H. Lawrence and Lawrence Welk, and later the Marquise de Merteuil and the Vicomte de Valmont, not to mention a hundred screen lovers. I have marched with the whole regiment of love-devisers, sonneteers, soothsayers, pattern-makers, and novelists, scissoring the fabric of love from the dawn of time until now.

As a small child I used to sit on the floor and run compulsively through my father's edition of Casanova's *Memoirs*, pleased by the odd language, my childish brain heated up by the delicate allusiveness: ". . . we unlaced, we unbuttoned, our hearts throbbed, our hands hurried to calm their impatience . . . our arms opened to clasp the object they wished to possess." From all this, I derived some notion of what grownups in foreign lands — Venice, for example — did after midnight.

But all that was mere delight. I did not know that love had its dark side. Only later did I come across Don Juan, and his menacing brother the Marquis de Sade, as he has come to be called, who occupies the hellish underside of love. A rape was better than a seduction, a woman's tears and agony more intoxicating than her pleasure. And one woman, for such a man, is pretty much like another: orifices, skin, a reputation to be ripped asunder, blood to be shed. In Sade's day as in our own, as we have come to recognize, some of us merely wish to sodomize the body of love itself, to lash its bleeding backside, pour hot wax in its wounds, feed it on Spanish fly, see it beg for more, see it crave permission even to die. This man, we now know, is the author of a kind of love that lasts as long as the human will and human compliance, as long as power and evil and muscle and sword, which is to say forever. Longer than "till death do us part." And that is as much a thread in love's fabric as sweet kisses and bouquets.

Love in our time has many strands. Is it even the same word, the same thought, the same act as it was when the world was younger?

I was determined that love should conform to my image of it. I now know that wisps of love, the encounters that emerge from recollection, are more powerful in the end than a lifetime of matrimony, and that the passions in your head — *amours de tête*, as the French call them — are perhaps more usable, more enduring than any. My sins are therefore less interesting than my ambitions. I quested for a holy grail, an absolute. I believed, in the beginning at least, that I might find it.

Memory is a knave. To re-collect means to pick one thing and abandon another, and to embroider one's selections, perhaps leaving the truth untold. I'll try, like my mentor Casanova, to tell truth. He didn't tell it, to be sure. The mere act of narration distorts. I wish that I could begin in that surefooted, I'm-all-innocence way that novelists begin: "Any resemblance between living persons and the characters in this book is purely coincidental." But novels seize the real, just as memoirs seize fantasy. Perhaps both novelists and memoirists should begin by saying, "Some of this is true, but I mean all of it as truth." I have labored to disguise and protect the models for characters herein, to allow them very deep cover, as though they had been secret agents. This book, if it is a memoir, is a shaped memoir, a coming-of-age book for the last sixty years, a recollection of heart and mind, of fantasies as much as fact. Above all, this is a book about books, about music, about other romances, as all romances are. My hope is not to set down the facts but to tell a story — never identical undertakings.

May readers find their own stories here, some piece of the *carte de tendre*.

2

IMAGE WORSHIP

I first encountered love one July afternoon when I was six and my mother announced that she was taking me to the picture show. We bathed, dressed in the mother-daughter dresses she had made for us, identical, except that mine had a sash and hers a belt with a pearly buckle. (I had wanted one of those enchanting belts, but she pointed out that I had no waist and must wear sashes until my waist somehow created itself.) Her shoes were my favorites, made of clear plastic with multi-colored polka dots and very high red heels — alas, how I coveted them! But she at least permitted me to wear my new patent leather shoes, and then wound my hair around her fingers like Shirley Temple's. We took the bus to the Paramount Theater.

We lived in a little town in the South, and the Paramount was the only picture show decent people went to, because the Central and the Roxy showed double features and Gene Autry shoot-'em-ups and had gospel quartets and hillbilly music live onstage Saturday mornings and other fare my father said was junk. Also, the Central and the Roxy smelled funny. The Paramount had first-run pictures, Movietone News, and the *March of Time*. The best that Hollywood could devise, served up with serious, patriotic news. And Donald Duck or Bugs Bunny or Mickey and Pluto, though not always. Also, the Paramount was air-conditioned, the only place in town.

I spotted the glass case of chocolate kisses and all-day suckers and Hersheys and jawbreakers ("Mama, I want a . . ."), but she marched me right on past ("No, it would spoil your supper, it would rot your teeth") and I thought that one day, far in the future, I would buy my own all-day sucker when I came to this place. Leading me into the dim, chill aisle, Mother picked our seats as carefully as peaches from a basket. Not behind somebody in a hat, not near that boy smacking his Beeman's pepsin, nor close to any lone male, whatever he might be chewing. You never knew. And not too close to the front, because it would ruin your eyes. We had to be on the aisle, because what if we needed to go to the ladies' room and had to crawl over people.

The ladies' room was where you went to act like a lady. Straighten your stocking seams, pull up your slip strap, check your teeth for smears of lipstick, the way I loved to watch my mother do, and I imagined how it would feel one day to have those thin little fall-down strings for slip straps, rather than secure wide underwear straps or flat-chested camisoles with no straps to flop alluringly down your upper arm, needing to be retrieved at the end of an index finger. How it would feel to have the dark lines running straight down the back of your legs. Seams had to run straight, had to bisect the symmetrical curves of the calf. This was a constant worry, because other women noticed your stocking seams. My mother was always twisting her neck around, or imploring me to see if they were straight. I never got to wear seams myself, because seamless came in before I was allowed nylons. (Sometimes, even today in aerobic shoes, I am tempted to track down a pair with seams.)

She finally found the right places and we sat in them. I'd never seen a flip-up theater seat, and my weight would barely hold it down. I let it fold me up, knees under chin, then forced it down, then up again, and down, for a higher bounce. Mother laughed at first, but soon took steps to control me. "Do I need to take you to the ladies' room and give you a good spanking?" Then the lights went down and the curtains opened like a huge chenille bathrobe. My rambunctious tendencies disappeared. The enormous screen absorbed me, canceled me out, made me cower in my seat, as the multitudes outside the great Gothic cathedrals must once have cowered before the intricate, rich carvings on the walls, the saints and gods and the virgin mother in the glowing stained glass, for images are truly terrifying to those who've never seen them, and they symbolize the world.

The film was *Gulliver's Travels*, a cartoon, brilliant yellows and browns, blues and reds slashing across the screen, and I fell for the handsome Gulliver at first sight, this dark-haired, muscular illustration of a man in a doublet and hose and wide belt. I loved his brown eyes with their precisely rendered lashes, and the way they turned into little black slits when he closed them. I loved his vast smile, so vast I could have fit inside his mouth. I loved his power, even as he lay tethered to the ground by tiny threads, laced to the ground like a shoe tongue in a pair of oxfords, bound by the same hard threads my grandmother crocheted into doilies and was teaching me to tether around my fingers just as Gulliver's splendid limbs were tethered, and then you took the sharp little needle and knotted the threads into antimacassars, also a device for controlling men or at least keeping their hair oil and tobacco crumbs off the furniture.

I loved the way Gulliver broke the threads and outsmarted the Lilliputians. He was tiny among the Brobdingnagians, but smarter than them as well. A man of a perfect size. I was tall for my age. I had been photographed at kindergarten, one of eight kids, and I was already a head taller than the others. I had drooped and slouched in the photo, trying to shorten myself, my face twisted by a sun grin, my hands knotted at my skirt tail.

Gulliver, up there before my eyes, had some other quality that I could not name, that tugged at my throat, my thighs. I wanted to be forever in his presence, to be dwarfed by his hugeness, I wanted the picture not to end, and when the music stopped and the lights went on, I pleaded to see it again, to remain in the air-cooled cavern that we had reached by ritual magic. But Mother led me out to reality. The white sunshine bashed me over the head, blinded me, and the summer heat shimmered from the sidewalks where you could fry an egg, because last week someone had got his picture in the paper doing it. He really ate the egg, only that was in the state capital, many miles to the east.

"Well, that was a pretty good show," she said.

I said my head hurt.

"You always come out of the picture show with a headache."

When the bus eventually lumbered to a halt at the bus stop and opened up, I stumbled up the steps, and once again my mother chose the right seats for us, two together in the middle where the windows were open; you couldn't sit at the back with colored women, everybody knew that, though Mother said it made no sense for them to have to sit back there. They should sit where they pleased, she said, their dime shone just as bright as anybody else's in the fare box.

As the bus rolled through town, I squinted out the window, sickened less by the pain in my cranium than by the substantiality of things. On a dozen front porches, fat women in flowered housecoats sweated in their rockers, flapped their funeral-parlor fans, and touched their slippered toes to the floor to keep on rocking. Oh, they made me sick. So did the squatty bus and its drab passengers. So did the tarpaper on the sides of the icehouse, where some folks still purchased ice by the fifty-pound slab, stowing it in their iceboxes, which we had done when very poor but now we had an Electrolux, not electric at all but gas with two metal trays that gave you ice by the cube, although Mother could get nearly as aggravated trying to loosen the cubes as she had chipping ice off the block with a pick. The instant we got home, she would make me put on my old play clothes and scuffed sandals, and she would change her new dress for a faded one, get into a clean apron, and begin to peel potatoes. Gulliver, oh Gulliver.

I dreamed of him for many days, imagined myself on the screen with him, myself a cartoon character, my eyelashes precisely rendered, my skirt blowing around my legs, my slip straps thin, my shoes high-heeled, my seams straight. I'd no idea what anybody would want with a man or do with one, but I pretended he was in my room, floating blimplike above my small bed, occupying all the airspace.

I had no idea what love was like. It seemed to be wholly contained in married life, which was mostly drudgery. My bedroom was next to my parents', with only a door between, which they usually left open in case I coughed or had a bad dream in the night. They observed every law of decency. If they ever made love while I slept so near them, they must have waited until I was dead asleep. I imagined that they lived together in order to take care of me. Or so that my father could earn money while my mother cooked and washed and mopped, because that's what grownups did, the law of life, or at least that's the way it was in every house I knew.

It was a question of us against the world; there was an "us" in every little house, holding out against the sleet of January and the heatstroke of August, against the car not starting, against worn-out shoes and holes in socks and thin hand-me-down coats and no money for the utility bill and the terrifying recollection of no job and not even a can of beans in the cupboard, the memory that still, on the eve of World War II, threw off dangerous particles like radium from a watch dial and had a half-life of a thousand years. That's what these little hard-knot units in the houses were all about: enough to eat, work shirts ironed without any monkey faces, the light bill paid on time — not about kisses and hugs and cuddling up in bed, not about love. A man with a steady job and a mother fixing up the lunch pails, thanking her stars for something to put in them, and hanging wash on the line.

Gulliver was the purest of all my loves, I see now, for I could imagine no life with him, no useful role for him or me. Such a one would surely not go out to work while I scrubbed. What I felt for him, I concluded, surely had never been felt before. "Penny for your thoughts," Mother would say when she caught me sighing and singing a little song from the film. She looked mockingly at me as if she were reading my mind, and I would cringe and hide behind some door in my mind, because I knew my thoughts were inadmissible, knew I must not mention the image that warmed me, caused an odd sensation between my legs, made me want to see myself naked, to see what was happening there. Actually, I knew she would laugh. I did try, at the height of my passion, to describe it to my best friend, Jo-ella, who was four years older and had seen a lot of movies. She stayed at our house often because her daddy didn't earn enough money, unlike my daddy, and her mother had to work (a terrible sadness in those days, a font of unending anger for the mama).

"I want him to come and stay with me," I told Jo-ella. "I want him to be with me always. See if they'll let us see that picture show again, and I'll reach up with my hand and lead Gulliver home with us."

"You love Gulliver! It's only a cartoon, dumbbell. Next thing I know, you'll say you love Bugs Bunny. How do you feel about Elmer Fudd? No, you can't get Gulliver to come and stay with you, you can't have anybody from the picture show. You can't lead him off the screen. It's just a picture. It's just pretend."

I tuned up and cried — that was Mother's term for it, to show her impatience with all whining — and Jo-ella went into high gear, the way she always did when she had me cornered.

"You goose, I think I'll tell your mother on you."

I wiped my eyes and stopped sniffling. Mother would never stop laughing if she knew I was in love with Gulliver, if she knew I thought an image could be coaxed off the screen. I don't think Jo-ella told: it must have slipped her mind.

As time passed, my passion cooled, my heartache subsided. I forgot Gulliver. Later it embarrassed me to recall being in love with a cartoon. My father had told me that there was a book by the same name as the picture show and that one day I must read it, and much later, after I learned to read, I did read *Gulliver's Travels,* eager to see if the Gulliver in the book would be as seductive as the one onscreen. He was not: Jonathan Swift's Gulliver was too much a creature of the brain to suit me, at least in those years when the only hero I sought was a love hero. He could not readily convert into a moving image, was not soft and enormous like the screen Gulliver, and though he was clearly as imaginary as that other Gulliver and engaged in the same fabulous, impossible adventures, he was boring and rational, concerned with social justice and whether people suffered or did not suffer, and whether they made sense when they talked or were knaves.

Not me. I cared nothing for good sense and justice. I had learned to love in a certain way, to love the image, to love my own love for the image. I had acquired a knack for the crush — which calls up "mush," or "mash," and makes you think of pimples and adolescent love tunes, but is also what you do to beetles with your boot or to your finger with a hammer.

3

PIANO MAN

At ten I was not yet obsessed with love. My childhood was filled with the pleasures proper to it — trees to climb, swings to fall out of, toys and books, standing rib roasts and fried chicken, a dog, a crowd of self-replicating cats that lived in the garage. My father, at least during World War II, brought home the money. When I was seven or eight, my parents felt they could afford a bedroom set for me. My mother repapered my walls herself in blue and yellow flowers. I had a double bed, and a matching comb and brush and nail file set (useless, to be sure, but sets always came with a nail file), a knee-hole dressing table, twin yellow ruffled lamps, a Martha Washington white chenille bedspread, and a blue floral carpet I'd picked out myself. Plus a drawer full of Sunday-to-Saturday embroidered panties, and I always wore the right day.

On summer evenings we sat outdoors in our lawn chairs, and sometimes got together with the neighbors, and the daddies would take turns doling out ice cream money, and then we would set off in groups of three or four for the ice cream parlor and triple dips of chocolate that ran down to our elbows, left ineradicable brown circles on our shorts and shirts.

We spoke little of the war. I believed, along with most other safe and secure American children, that a Japanese plane with those terrible red suns on the wings would any day come screaming out of the sky to strafe my house, picking it out of all other houses in the United States, or that a German pilot in a parachute would be entangled in the topmost branches of our cherry tree one morning when I awoke. Nevertheless, the night sky remained untroubled by dogfights, in spite of my hopeful vigils past midnight. The war reached me mainly through movie newsreels (which I avoided, whenever possible, by visiting the candy counter) and through the mournful voice of a commentator called Gabriel Heatter on the Mutual Network. ("Bad news tonight!" And I would listen to the casualty figures, composing my face as though visiting a funeral home with my mother to gaze into the casket and sign the book.) Only one of the daddies in the neighborhood had had to go in the service, the rest being 4F or too old. Not a single window in the vicinity bore one of those little purple banners with the stars for dead sons, though across town there was one with three stars. Three! We hastened past it as if it had been a mortuary. With just me, a girl, fortunately, my mother would never have stars in her window.

We had to put up with rationing, and our shoes fell apart quicker than they used to, which I thought was splendid since I loved being fitted for shoes, and Mother had to buy sugar from a mysterious man who came to the back door after dark with a hundred-pound bag instead of at the grocery store. And Mother had had to lie to the Rationing Board in order to get enough stamps for an extra gas heater. But wartime shortages weren't all that terrible. No matter how blatant the lie, the Rationing Board never said no. The fellows who ran it were always your second cousin, or married to your neighbor's daughter, or had known your granddaddy personally and certainly weren't about to deny you a few extra stamps for this and that. If you said you were doing home canning, you could get nearly anything — extra sugar, extra meat, extra butter. My father muttered about hardship, but it seemed more like a game to me.

The war, I supposed, was being waged so we could live exactly as we were living, without having to do more than fantasize about bombs or a Japanese coming through the front door to spear us with a bayonet or some Nazi rounding us up for torture. We were what those men were fighting for, so people could sit on the lawn on a summer evening and kids could go to the ice cream shop. Since I wasn't the one who had to die, our way of life seemed worth dying for. But even as I ate my ice cream cone from the bottom, contrary to my mother's orders, and reveled self-consciously in the things of childhood (for life was never real to me; rather, it was a story I told myself every day), I knew that the childhood idyll would end and that unless I found some trap door in my pathway I would end up a house-coated denizen of ordinary life, like my mother — ironing organdy curtains, turning berries into cobblers, sighing over the state of my ragged cuticles, middle-aged at thirty, old at thirty-five.

Ever since Gulliver, I had been on the lookout for the trap door, which I knew had something to do with love. I looked for signs of love, for clues to what it was, like a scout in the woods searching for bent twigs, the indentation of a leather moccasin on a pile of leaves, the pressed-down place in the grass, the nick of a knife on a tree trunk. None of the grownups I knew, obviously, had any idea about it. There were, of course, songs on the radio. Some had a certain tug to them, a sense of the darkness, of the mystery I knew was there. "Begin the Beguine," for instance: what moment divine, what rapture serene, but what the lyrics really insisted on was loss. "Now when I hear people curse" — and the voice would stop way up high, like a real curse — "the chance that was wasted, I know but too well what they mean." Or, "Like the *beat beat beat* of the tom-tom, when the jungle shadows fall." I liked those things. They were exciting. However, most of it was "Always" and "My Blue Heaven" and "Surrey with the Fringe on Top," tinkly little tunes with no dark patches in them. Sunshine. A fellow who adored you and danced all around you but who seemed determined to set you on the road to housecoats and vacuum cleaners, broken finger-nails and middle age.

The picture show sometimes hinted at the sort of thing I

meant. I now went to the Paramount insatiably, every time the feature changed. But movies too had that trap in them. Pure, wholesome June Allyson and Margaret O'Brien. Goody-goodies. Saints. Judy Garland had hard times, but things always worked out just fine for her before the end. And the fellow she picked was always a good fellow. Fred Astaire swirled around with Ginger and other svelte ladies in feathery white skirts and high heels, the two of them fighting and pouting and kissing and making up and dancing. Or Betty Grable singing and kicking her luscious, perfect legs, and finding happiness with some guy wearing a straw boater. All sunny, cheerful, and happy-ever-after.

Ginger and Betty made me feel shut out. They were nothing compared with Rita Hayworth and her provocative stare, Rita sitting on her haunches in a satin nightgown with black lace on the bosom, the pinup picture soldiers carried into battle with them and looked at while they died. No matter how many glasses of milk I drank or green salads I consumed, I would never have legs or hair or lips like that. I could see that it was the wondrous bodies of these women that brought about so many happy endings, and I didn't have the equipment. By age ten I knew I would never have it, at least not the luscious, delectable kind they had. You can't hope to shed your knobby knees, sharp elbows, freckles, your thick hair that refuses to lie down and shine like a satin dress in the moonlight, your peculiar nose.

There was Spencer Tracy, who looked like my father and always seemed to be married to somebody like Teresa Wright or Myrna Loy. The Nazis shot down his plane in one movie and he came back as a ghost, but it all ended up the same for Teresa, because he was such a good guy that he made sure she found happiness with another good guy. I cried a little when Spencer whispered in her ear and guided her to the new good steady man, but Abbott and Costello were really better, and no sillier than Betty Grable, although my parents said Betty was first-class and they couldn't stand Abbott and Costello. At least with Abbott and Costello you could laugh till you hurt, till you cried, till you rolled on the floor. On the Saturday after Good Friday, you got a chance at passionate, self-denying tears: the heavenly choirs of *King of Kings,* in which Jesus with the long fingers and blond locks and mild eyes got crucified, though all you saw was the base of the cross and a long view of Gethsemane when the storm broke, and you came out with red eyes and wads of snotty tissues. At least you didn't sit there wondering how you ever were going to get your hair into a pompadour or grow a body with S curves. My father loved the music of the band-leader whom the real Betty Grable was married to, and some-times, for a joke, he would go around the house singing, to the tune of "Dear Old Dad," "I want a girl just like the girl that married Harry James." All men, it seemed, wanted such a girl, the million-dollar legs, the smile, the flaxen hair, the feet in three-inch heels with bows on the toes.

And then, on the screen at the Paramount, love struck again, disabled me emotionally for months, unhinged my mind, changed my life. I had never had a blow this severe. Luckily, I had gone to the show with my friend Jo-ella, not my mother, because I was sure the film would only have made my mother giggle, whereas Jo-ella really liked it. The movie was about Frédéric — in three syllables, and something funny about the *r*'s — Chopin, and a woman they kept calling George, but not like George Raft: Jeorj, or Madame Sawng. Sand, it really was. She was gorgeous and bad. When she first came in, she was wearing pants and riding boots (a sure way not to have to worry about your stocking seams) and a top hat, and one of those cut-away jackets and a tie, though she sported dark red lipstick and plenty of curves. Even in the long dresses she wore later (any of my fanciest dreamboat paper dolls could have worn them), she acted as if she wore the pants. She was the boss. Fred-a-reek, as I heard it, was a Pole and played the piano — not only played it but wrote music for it. And suddenly, booming out of the tinny sound system of the Paramount, which heretofore had echoed with the sweet voices of Fred or Judy, the roar of Spencer Tracy's plane or the fury of Donald Duck, came piano music of a kind I'd never heard. This couldn't be music, I thought. It was too beautiful, too full of some odd brand of authority and self-assuredness that made my scalp tingle. If this was music, what would you call that stuff they played on the radio all day? I went for it as if it were a double banana split. I spooned it up, gulped it down, ate it from the bottom, let it run into the creases of my elbows. Truly, this film was an open work. I was its collaborator, its ultimate creator, its perfect reader.

I quickly caught on that this was biography, not just another made-up hero. This was about a real piano player. A composer, as Madame Sand kept calling him. A genius, not just Cornel Wilde dressed up like a genius. And she was a real woman too, not just Merle Oberon. How strange it was, this Frédéric with the girlish Ipana toothpaste smile and the lace cuffs and the ruffled shirtfront, the sweet demeanor, unlike any man I had ever seen, though indeed he had the tall, muscular body of a man. At least, he had a man's body after the part where he was a little boy in Poland taking piano lessons. But then he put on his lace cuffs and black velvet jacket and got into the little boat in the fog and ran away to Paris and met George. Ran away — what an idea! If you wanted to do something, you had to run away from home. You couldn't do it in Poland. I made a note of it. Paris, France, was where you did it, plus assorted chateaux in the environs and charming little islands off the coast of Spain.

So here was George, tough as one of her riding boots, running the world, including Chopin, of whom she swiftly took charge after one thrilling kiss (he bent her backwards, doubled her right over, which I had seen before in pirate movies and liked a lot, and wanted desperately to happen to me). George herself was a writer. You knew this because of a shot of her at a desk with a feather in her hand. Shocking novels were what she wrote, and my heart quickened, like the *beat beat beat* of the tom-tom, as I imagined writing shocking novels. In one scene George was at her desk while Frédéric was at his piano, he dipping his quill pen in ink, she dipping hers. That's what they did all day. All he had to do was play the piano and please his woman.

Clearly she was keeping the wolf from the door — a benevolent wolf it was, too, not like the wolf that hung around our neighborhood, sending kids to school with nothing but a sweet potato in their lunchbox, keeping Santa Claus from coming. As long as this wonderful man wrote elegant music, she liked it. Ah, but what was this? They were squabbling over politics. He was for Polish independence, and she wanted him to forget all that. Don't think about politics, darling; make music, make money, make love! She got furious when she heard him play that polonaise like a steam engine coming down the tracks. He had to sneak around to play it behind her back. No good, George, a sure way to lose your man.

But as long as he did what she told him, this adorable fellow never had to go out and drive a truck or sit behind a desk at an insurance company or cut cloth from a bolt in the dry-goods store, will there be anything else, ma'am? Though the love angle was muted after that first backbreaking smooch, it had been sufficient for me. I knew these two did something besides write and compose, they did all the things Casanova and his ladies did, unbuttoning, grasping, feeling, or else why were folks back in Paris constantly fussing about how this nice young man was ruining his reputation living with this bad woman? Yet never did he shout, "What's for dinner?" or tell her she had it easy compared to him. He never got drunk, never listened to baseball, never smoked a Lucky or left his dirty BVDs on the floor or a ring around the bathtub. He just thanked her for all her kindness and played the piano.

Then, inexplicably, he got sick. His face kept getting paler in scene after scene, and his eyes darker, and circles came under his eyes, and all of a sudden he would sweat a lot when he played and have to use his lace-trimmed hanky. Once some red blood splattered right on middle C. Where did it come from? I didn't know.

"What's he sick from?"

"TB, nitwit, can't you tell it's TB!" Jo-ella exclaimed, and the lady behind us hissed for silence. Well, pretty soon he left George, who didn't care about Poland and in any case deserved to lose her man because she was so bossy and mannish, and went off on a concert tour to raise money for the Polish patriots. She said it would kill him, and sure enough it did. There he lay at the end in a great big ruffly dollhouse bed with a draped canopy and satin pillows, just the kind of bed I dreamed of having for myself, and his face was green and the circles darker than ever. He asked for George but she wouldn't come, and then he did that little thing with his head, dropped it over on the pillow, and they knew he was dead. Just the same "I'm dead" gesture I used when playing dress-up.

I fell in love with this sweet androgynous man who lived for art and died so daintily on a lace-encrusted pillow. And in love with the notion that it took that sort of man to make that kind of music. And though, if someone had queried me at that moment, I would have stoutly maintained that women should not wear breeches, smoke cigars, or try to control their lovers' politics, I was just as smitten with George Sand as with Frédéric Chopin. More so. Ah, she could dip her quill pen in ink and have a lot of money and run the world. And keep that beautiful, talented, lace-cuffed, ruffled-bosomed man around to bend her backwards and kiss her lips when she wanted kissing. Never, never would she set off on some road leading to drudgery and boredom.

Yet in some deep crevice of my prepubescent soul, I knew that the love that had so captivated me in this film did not reside in either Frédéric or George but in the fingers (not belonging to Cornel Wilde) plying the keyboard, in the music that had emerged from this dying piano man.

I played dress-up out of this movie for weeks, at least when I could get any privacy. Sometimes I was George, in my long skirt, left over from when I was a gypsy in the Halloween pageant; sometimes I wore my dad's old jacket over my jodhpurs (bought only to please my childish fantasies — we couldn't afford even a rental horse) and was Fred. I had a velvet ribbon that passed for a cravat. It had seen service at the neck of various cowboys and Jean Lafitte, and now did okay for a tubercular gentleman of the nineteenth century. A blouse I had wheedled from my mother had a frilled bosom and was okay for either Fred or George. My wardrobe was sparse, but I wasn't fussy. Either way, my life-size dummy, constructed out of a mop handle and a wig, took the opposite role. I tried to work it out so that they married, had kids. He'd go off to work at the concert hall, she'd stay home with the babies. He'd turn out not to die of TB. But it was impossible. At least one of them had to die, maybe both. Yes, she should have died too.

I tried out one script like that. But George was too tough to die. She could cry a lot over Fred, but she insisted on living into the next chapter. I couldn't find a thing about her in the local library, except a few lines in the encyclopedia, but I resolved to track her down when I could.

4

BLUES

He don't love me like I love him, nobody could . . .
I got it bad and that ain't good.
　　　　　— Duke Ellington

At age twelve I developed a crush, specific and serious, on a real boy named Joey Cash. Unlike Gulliver, he was neither gigantic nor strong. Like Chopin he was frail, but scarcely handsome. He had thin arms that hung out of his shirtsleeves and pale blue eyes. He was a musician — third clarinet in the junior high marching band. Our active, quantifiable relationship consisted of two events. When I was turning thirteen, Joey accompanied me to a party, a "first date" supper dance — meaning we were to go to a local motel coffee shop in long dresses and the boys in jackets and ties, eat hamburgers, and then dance to a jukebox if we had the nerve, and a photographer would come and take our pictures. The party was given by a girls' club I belonged to, so the girls had to ask the boys. Joey's mother and mine actually made all the arrangements.

That morning my mother took me to the beauty shop. With a chain mail of bobby pins on my head, I sat under the dryer for an hour and emerged, roasted, with a tidy pouf of frizz beginning at my ears and going all around my head, topped off with meticulously waved bangs down to my eyebrows. No tendril was left to chance, no lock allowed its seductive, slow-curling escape down the nape, and anyhow, I didn't have that kind of hair. My great-aunt in her coffin had worn a coif similar to this, but I actually liked it, called it cute, and asked for spray and a hairnet to preserve the corpselike effect. I was allowed my first beauty-shop manicure, so my fingernails were now light pink, red not being suitable for a young virgin: "You don't want that! Look like a tramp!" I bought my first lipstick (besides Pongee Natural, which was like paraffin and didn't even make your lips red) plus a tiny box of dry mascara with a brush. In the bathroom at school I had seen the big girls spitting on their mascara brushes.

Later, as I sat in the front porch swing, not swinging, simply admiring my painted fingers and protecting them from harm — love's own creature embalmed in the mild October air — a florist's truck pulled up and parked. Yes, exactly what a lady expected, needed, deserved, when she got home from the beauty parlor. The box contained a gardenia corsage and a card that struck like a blow: "Love, Joey." His own handwriting, which I knew well from school. He hadn't had to say "love," I reasoned, he could have said "sincerely." Hadn't had to, but had. Love. He loved me. Zing went the strings of my heart. It seems that we have stood and talked before, but who knows where or when? I'm all for you, body and soul.

These were the songs I sang in my swing, one after another, holding the card, adoring his handwriting, adoring my nails. The same porch swing, sheltered by trellises of red and white roses, where so recently I had sat rereading *The Secret of the Old Clock* or *Heidi* for the eighth time, waiting until Mother left for the grocery store so I could gulp a pint of milk from a bowl — for in the real world you could only drink from a glass, not like in the Alps with the health-giving bread and cheese. Heidi and Peter and the wildflowers and the goats, and me singing in the wilderness beside them, and wilderness were paradise enow! However, now I was a woman, my price beyond rubies. I had put away childish things. I would yearn no longer for milk in a bowl but for coffee in a cup. I would worry about my weight. I would put all my dolls away except the new bride doll that sat in state upon my bed, and I never played with her, just fluffed her veil. Goodbye Johanna Spyri, Omar Khayyám, and

Nancy Drew! My childhood story was over. I was embarking for France.

Later that afternoon I put on my floor-length dress of flowered lawn trimmed with a white eyelet yoke and ruffled cap sleeves. My mother had made it. I had to wear socks with my white flats. Before you got any nylons, you had to become a woman, which I hoped was not about to occur that night. For there was a catch to all this primping. "Something happens to girls at about your age," my mother had told me a year or two before, her hands shaking as she spoke. I steeled myself for what I knew was coming. "And it will happen to you, but you mustn't be afraid when it happens, you must come right to me and I will give you a pad and belt. One of these rigs." And she showed me an oblong of white cotton and an elastic band with metal clips. Of course I had looked at hers a hundred times in the back of her closet.

Horrible, not like slips with thin straps and garter belts and nylon stockings and high heels. Not like earclips and perfume and eye shadow and the other seductive paraphernalia of grown women. Years later I finally understood the courage my mother had displayed in showing me, telling me. Her own mother, like most mothers of that time, had allowed her daughters to discover menstruation all by themselves, to believe it the onset of an incurable illness until they confessed or were found out. My mother, perspiring from nervousness, asked me if I knew about "this" already, and I swore it was the first I'd heard of it, but I lied, as all children lie on such occasions. "Nope, I never asked myself how babies get born, Mama. Why do you mention it? Thought never crossed my mind."

Indeed, when Jo-ella had wised me up on Santa Claus a while back, she had also told me about the bleeding. I told her she was full of baloney, but in due time I did further research. I noticed an offer for a free, plain-brown-wrapper booklet in a Kotex ad, sent off for it. My hair might get dry and brittle at that time of the month; showers would be daintier than tub baths, and since I was certainly a dainty girl, I would prefer showers. Swimming in public pools was inadvisable unless you were wearing a tampon, and you wouldn't be wearing one until much later — news I definitely welcomed, as the idea of "internal protection" made me feel faint. Tennis was out of the question, except perhaps mixed doubles, where the boys expected to do all the playing, and horseback riding should be postponed until the waning days, if not given up altogether. Oh, and you could expect cramps, sometimes disabling. They would get you in the abdomen and back, and a heating pad would help some but not much.

Tennis and horses did not apply to me, so maybe cramps wouldn't either. As I put on a new pair of panties I had been saving for this occasion, I resolved not to turn into a woman tonight, because I imagined a sea of unmanageable blood, which would spoil my new panties and perhaps even my formal. Then they'd all know. Did the whole world have to know this nasty thing was happening to a person? Did it happen to George Sand? Rita Hayworth? Evidently.

Mother and I picked up Joey in our car and drove to the motel coffee shop at the appointed time. He sat in the back seat. The two of us ate supper together, me jealous of every word he said to anybody else. He said lots of words to other girls, while I felt bleaker and grimmer. Actually, it was more like the school cafeteria than the date I had imagined. I was scared he'd go sit by somebody else. We may have danced, though I actually have no recollection of his touching me, not that evening or ever. I still have the photograph of him and me crowded into a booth with four other youngsters. He could be ten years old. I look thirty. With the gardenia pinned to my shoulder, I am as tightly sprung as my curls. My eyes are hollow with anxiety, like the women in the Farm Security Administration photos, clutching their babies in their bony arms and staring into the distance. Except for my butterfly sleeves and flat chest, I am as seriously dedicated to the womanly ideal as my mother, capable of entering into holy matrimony on the spot. With that look, I could have stood at the kitchen sink for all eternity. At least, however, I did not get my period that evening.

That was the first event. The second occurred a year later, when I again asked Joey to be my date, this time for a hayride and picnic sponsored by another girls' organization I belonged to. This was the Rainbow Girls, daughters to the Eastern Star, sisters to the Demolays, who were junior Masons, a perfect, four-cornered model for the world, as orderly as the Trinity: religion and life founded on squares and triangles. It was pervasive, Lions and Junior Lions and their female auxiliaries, Bible study classes at church organized along exactly the same lines. White people had their triangles and squares, and so did black people. The menfolks got the robes and rites and odd hats and the womenfolk brought the food, though in Eastern Star they did a little dress-up too. I was only too happy to have become a part of it. It seemed right and proper that groups should contain only girls, or only boys, or only whites or only Jews or only Catholics or Baptists. Like sex, the various ethnic, religious, and racial divisions of polite society were scarcely alluded to. They were no more to be discussed in public than bowel movements. Northerners may imagine that southerners sat around talking all day about lynchings, or even attending them, but we did not. Any more than we walked into school every day and said, "There are no black people in here and never shall be, and the Jews had better sing 'Silent Night' in school in December and wear angel wings in the Christmas pageant, or we'll be terribly offended." For the moment, they took our orders and sang our songs, or so it seemed, for my father wondered what they said about us behind our backs.

Joey was a Demolay and his dad a Mason, so he was better off than I was, because my parents wouldn't join anything, not even the church: Daddy said organized religion was hypocritical — "Bunch of do-gooders" — and Mother wouldn't go without him. This did not keep them from sending me off to Sunday school, and they urged me into the Rainbow Girls and saw to it that I took part. I was the only one of us in an organization. Joey agreed to be my date for the hayride. I was smoldering, ready for kissing. Almost every waking moment, in fact, was filled with thoughts of his kisses, of his lips on mine, the way the song said: your lips pressing on mine. Lying in my bed, about to fall asleep, I could feel those lips. I would wear a blue gingham dress, which I began badgering my mother to sew for me; I would make my hair uncurl, somehow, so I could wear braids like Judy Garland; Joey and I would meet at six, exchange promises during and after kissing; the moon would shine. Then love notes and adjoining lockers, me wearing his band jacket, the junior prom, the senior prom, and us picking out the washing machine. I practiced my signature, *Mrs. Joseph Cash*, a hundred times a day and tore the notebook paper into little bits.

By now I had become a woman according to the Kotex definition. I tried to take it in stride, as Kotex advised, and to keep a positive attitude about bleeding once a month. My mother had received the news of my first bout of womanhood with anxiety and tight lips, but she had equipped me as promised. The elastic belt with its little metal sliders cut into my abdomen. The bleeding was unpredictable: in that first year, it sometimes happened every two weeks and then not again for six or eight. I hated it. The only good thing about it was it got you off PE, which was stupid anyway because all the teachers did was warn you about hurting yourself. In softball, you couldn't slide into a base, which didn't apply to me because I couldn't hit the ball with the bat. In track, you couldn't compete with boys, because you would lose. It was agony anyway, and I dropped out because I overheard a group of boys making fun of my long, gangly legs and the knobbiness of my knees in shorts. In basketball, you had to play by girls' rules, which meant pivoting on one toe to pass, and you were forbidden to dribble the ball — just one bounce and pass the thing. During basketball I had my period all month.

And instead of thinking about Julius Caesar or compound interest or comma faults in class, I sat worrying about telltale red stains on the back of my skirt and detoured to the bathroom four or five times a day, checking. Fearfully, I carried the belt and pad around with me, and they made my purse bulge. Surely Joey Cash or any other boy could not know about anything so disfiguring as menstruation — a word I loathed and never said. Maybe males found out just before they got married. Maybe after, for otherwise, why would they ever hook up with a woman in the first place? I hoped I would never betray the terrible truth by appearing at school with a spot of blood on my clothing. I bargained peremptorily with God against having my period on hayride night. How would I manage if that happened? (Cramps, it turned out, did apply to me, though my mother had no sympathy about them and never allowed me to stay home from school, no matter how badly it hurt. You shouldn't gripe about something normal, she felt, and complaining about it meant you had to speak of monthly bleeding.) Also, there'd be no place to go and change the pad. How did girls ever get through life?

Three days before the hayride, I got a headache and fever at school and was sent home. By morning I had broken out in chickenpox, so ferocious a case that the doctor thought it might actually be smallpox, though like all children in those days, I had been vaccinated at age six. I was sick for three weeks — feverish, weeping, itching, and pestilential, trying not to scratch, because Mother said it would make scars and I would be so sorry when I was older and wanted to wear a bathing suit, would be pockmarked and ugly, and she tied white gloves on my hands with ribbons, but sometimes the itching overpowered me and I clawed myself savagely, as if to lay bare my bones, which also itched. If what it took to get Joey to love me was not to scratch this itch, then the hell with him and all men. The hell with beauty, this was torment, who could care about beauty or the future with a seared skin? I wept like Job with his boils, and my mother smeared me with ointments and bathed my hideous, runny blisters with calamine. "She even broke out under her tongue," I heard her tell a neighbor. "She even broke out between her legs and on the bottom of her feet. I never in all my born days . . ."

The first week a card came: "Get Well Soon, Love, Joey." Nothing else. After the contagious time passed, a girlfriend brought the news that Joey had gone to the hayride with Betty Sue Sykes. Yes, they had sat in the back of the truckbed and kissed, like everybody else, and had been seen exchanging notes in the hallway since. They were sweet on each other, boyfriend and girlfriend. That was that. I lay on my flabby stack of pillows at least a week afterward, feebly practicing *Mrs. Joseph Cash* on notebook paper. After six weeks I returned to school, as thin and weak as a garter snake, with crusts and scabs still on my arms and legs and a permanent scar, a small moon crater, on my brow, though I had scratched almost every place but there.

Joey spoke politely to me but looked right through me. No doubt his mother had forced him to write me the get-well note. "Love, Joey," I told myself murderously, in the same spirit that you make a wound bleed or dig at an infected place on purpose. I slumped at my desk, refused to eat my lunchtime hamburger, wiped the tears from the pages of my anthology of great American poetry. Grieving as I was, I turned to poetry, the ancient vice of the lovelorn. (At times of deep sadness, I still turn to it, have recited it to men who scarcely wished to hear it, have copied out Shakespeare's sonnets and included them in love letters to lovers who were surely not in the mood for high culture and may not have known an iamb from a trochee.) I had a huge anthology of American literature, which I was supposed to be reading anyhow, and I quickly learned to like most of the American poets, with their puzzling triple nomenclature (Ralph

Waldo Emerson, John Greenleaf Whittier, Henry Wadsworth Longfellow, James Russell Lowell, Edward Arlington Robinson) and was starting to cozy up to Amy Lowell, Imagist poetess — "In my stiff brocaded gown, up and down, bright blue squills, a pattern called a war, Christ! what are patterns for?" — until the teacher revealed that this one female who had so far made it into the History of American Literature, Semester I, smoked a cigar. This must be what it took to be an intelligent woman and get admitted to the three-name club, even when you had only two names and no cravat.

5

LIEBESTOD

By now, in eighth grade, I had grown obsessive about love. What is this thing, this crazy thing, I saw you there one wonderful day, you took my heart and threw it away. Unless forced by school requirements to read something that was not about love, I chose only books about love, sang songs about love, went to the cavern of the Paramount Theater and studied it, Plato's lessons flashed upon the cave wall. The ideal, the pure ideal, stripped to its essence. And some of these lessons stuck.

> *One beautiful, expensively dressed young woman to another:* "Did you ever love a man so much that all you wanted was to sacrifice your whole life for him?"

Or,

> *Van Johnson in pilot suit to girl (he's leaving on a dangerous bombing mission against the Japs):* "You're so cute. How did you get to be so cute?"
> *Girl:* "I had to be, to get a guy as good-looking as you."

And off he went, and there she stood, staring out the curtained window, tears of pride and anxiety in her eyes, as his squadron took off over the trees. If only I could develop enough "cute," I would have that look of serene pride in my eyes. I could belong to such a man. I slurped all this up like a cherry Coke at the soda fountain, believed it the way I believed my Sunday school lessons. Blessed are the meek. Blessed are the pure in heart. Blessed art thou among women. George Sand and Casanova, along with Chopin's fingers on the piano keys like the hooves of a thoroughbred flying around the racetrack, became specters and spirita non grata, banished to the attic of my mind. Craziness, craziness.

I cultivated the mutually exclusive impulses that have tormented me all my life. On the one hand, I yearned to be a radical, a subversive, a woman who broke all the rules. On the other, I was compelled to be ordinary, to conform to every possible demand society could make of me. Incapable of articulating this, I vacillated back and forth without once perceiving that my impulses were schizophrenic. In adolescence I had visions of myself jitterbugging in a skirt that whipped around my waist, revealing knees no longer knobby, or one-stepping down the aisle after the soprano had successfully tonsilled all the high notes in "Because God made you mine, I'll cherish thee" — a pure-hearted, fulfilled young bride-to-be ("was honored by a tea yesterday afternoon at the country club; looked lovely in a pale blue dressmaker suit, with dyed-to-match pumps, chosen from her trousseau . . . her princess-style ecru satin gown and cathedral train were adorned with seed pearls, and she chose a Juliet cap with a traditional veil of tulle . . . For traveling she selected a pale green frock with matching coat and pillbox hat, accessorized with white gloves and black patent leather pumps and matching clutch bag"). The brides in the papers — I read the society page threadbare, as if it were a novel — were always being honored at this or that social event, always looked lovely, were adorned with seed pearls and dyed-to-match, and did a lot of choosing and selecting.

But the subversive side of me never quite retired. On Saturday afternoons I should have been at social events myself, or watching the boys at football practice, but instead I listened to operas, falling for the music as well as the plots. I began to understand that sex was mixed in too. Not all male-female relationships were pure and sweet, like Van Johnson and June Allyson, nor were they dedicated to keeping the wolf from the door and sending the kids to Sunday school. On the opera stage, a lot of male-female relationships resulted in death, a peculiar kind of death that seemed infinitely preferable to life.

Carmen, for instance: *l'amour, l'amour,* just a gypsy lass who never could and never would play fair, la la, and then the tenor stabs her behind that fence because she went off with the toreador. I'd have done the same thing — gone off with the bullfighter. In spades, twice over. Why stick to your mooning soldier boy when you can have the most-wanted? But loving Escamillo had nothing to do with getting meals on the table and paying the light bill and going to prayer meeting Wednesday nights. It was what you did instead. And also, I could understand Don José. Being he, I would definitely have stabbed that gorgeous Carmen and faced the electric chair or whatever they did to you in Spain. I would have abandoned poor Michaela, the hometown girl, who probably was dreaming of seed pearls and dyed-to-match, of picking something from her trousseau to wear on the honeymoon. I accepted the tragedy with a kind of vicious pleasure. Hooray for you, sweet Carmen, stamp your wicked gypsy feet and tell them you're the boss, even if your lover stabs you. Michaela made me want to vomit, the way June Allyson did when she came twittering on the screen, all goodness and trustworthiness. And when Don José sang "O ma Carmen" and his voice rose up to that high note that made your eardrums vibrate, I fancied I knew precisely how he felt.

But the best plot, and the music I loved to delirium, was Princess Isolde going to Cornwall, in England, to marry some old king who was waiting for her; they were betrothed. She was promised to him, the way princesses were in those days, with no say-so in the matter at all. And this king had no more sense than to send this handsome young knight Tristan to fetch his bride. What did he expect? And there they were on the deck of the boat, singing loudly in German, as the waves crashed all

around them in the dark night, and they had drunk the love potion, and nothing could stop them now. Oh, that music, that
enormous orchestra, those enormous voices, spilling out of our
floor-model cathedral-styled RCA, causing the empty candy
bowl on top to rattle and quake, that music modulating and
moiling and moaning like a squall in the Irish Sea, boiling up to
a climax that erupted right out of the speaker cloth, and I would
crank the volume on up to match the music and sing along,
aware that whatever the two of them were doing on the deck of
that boat was well worth doing in spite of the death penalty so
clearly attached to this activity. A capital crime, to betray the
king, your fiancé, with another man. I could see them there on
that boat deck as plain as day, grappling with each other, both of
them blond and lithe and muscular, he in a kind of Prince
Valiant suit and she in diaphanous princess veils — all this in
spite of knowing that Lauritz Melchior and Helen Traubel were
fat as hogs (television, had it existed, might have saved me from
this fatal seduction) and in spite of Mother hollering from the
kitchen, "For the Lord's sake, would you please can that stuff, I
can't hear myself think!" But even with two massive opera stars
before my eyes, I'd have known it was something in the music,
that the notes themselves were love, or some affirmation of
love's melodiousness.

I was as systematic as I knew how to be in my quest for
enlightenment. Children my age were not supposed to know
about sex, were not supposed to take an interest in adult love,
and were ridiculed even for cultivating a bit of puppy love. The
public library consisted of one small room, under the supervision, six afternoons a week, of a bright-eyed, half-starved
young woman wielding a rubber stamp on the end of a pencil,
seated behind a metal desk amid metal shelves containing
mostly mystery stories and certainly nothing pornographic,
erotic, or even suggestive, because she would have been fired or
lynched if any works of this nature had taken up space at tax-
payers' expense where children could be exposed to them. Her

name was Cora Lena Brown; she was pretty enough to attract a man, everybody agreed, but for unknown reasons had instead grown up to be our librarian. She seemed always to know exactly what I was looking for.

Filed alphabetically among the murders were a few works that seldom left the shelves: George Eliot, Sir Walter Scott, Shelley and Keats and Byron, Dickens, Nathaniel Hawthorne, and F. Scott Fitzgerald. Cora Lena also had *Anna Karenina, Madame Bovary, Jane Eyre, Wuthering Heights* — books powerful enough to blow the library to bits, if anybody had read them or taken them seriously. (We were the only family I knew with books in the *house* — my father's small collection of literary standards, including some of the same ones Cora Lena planted so judiciously on the shelves, plus some bestsellers.) Cora Lena called me a "good little library patron," and I was less terrified of her than most children — for she would tolerate no noise in her temple of books and had been known to eject brawny young boys who dared try her patience or speak aloud.

But she always had something set aside for me. Stacks of hoop-skirt and pirate novels. *Trilby,* George du Maurier's novel about a lovely young singer under the power of Svengali. Stories by de Maupassant (who always seemed so dry and bloodless to me after a stack of Frank Yerby novels). *Idylls of the King,* which I ransacked looking for Lancelot's adventures with Elaine, or Guinevere. A ruiner of women, Lancelot. No doubt it had been worth it, when Guinevere and Lancelot brought down Christian Camelot, put an end to that smug little men's club of the Round Table, pale British knights preoccupied with holy quests, destroyed by the lovers' passion. Hooray for Guinevere! With such subversive emotions in my bosom, lusting after descriptions of royal embraces, the smallest word or hint, I would watch Cora Lena ink the stamp at the end of her yellow Ticonderoga and press it lovingly, firmly, under "Date due" as if she were planting an approving kiss on my cheek.

Since naughty bestsellers were barred from the library, we

got them elsewhere — from the drugstore, from under our parents' beds. Junior high school girls formed a true literary underground. Our appetite for pornography was insatiable, and nearly anything qualified as a dirty book. We passed notes from hand to hand: "Look on page 89 of *God's Little Acre*"; "Start with page 56 in *Forever Amber*."

I was momentarily smitten with Charles II, read up on him, imagined myself as his mistress. Every girl I knew had memorized the staircase scene in *Gone With the Wind*, the staircase up which Rhett carries Scarlett, rending her gown and then doing whatever he did to or with her. This was absolutely thrilling, but even words like "compromised," which Rhett had done to some girl in Charleston, brought up visions of lust for me. I was titillated to learn, in a biography of John Wilkes Booth, that he had slept with a lot of girls, which seemed far more interesting than assassinating President Lincoln. Why hadn't he just stayed out in the Virginia countryside and rolled in the hayloft? Why didn't the biographer tell more about that?

Part of my instruction came from the Bible, which as all children who've been raised in the Christian church know is unsurpassed as a source of sexual fantasies, or even smut. As an observant member of a Methodist and then a Baptist Sunday school class, I was urged, prodded, and enticed to read the Bible on my own — to read the whole thing, to plow, awake or sleeping, through the New Testament and the Old, and when you claimed you had read through the whole thing, they gave you (surprise) a Bible. In addition, the principal read the Bible over the loudspeaker each morning, as was required by law, usually a psalm or something from Ecclesiastes or the Book of Ruth, and you had to stop and listen, to hear of Ruth's loyalty to her mother-in-law, who said to Ruth, "Behold, thy sister-in-law is gone back unto her people and unto her gods: return thou after thy sister-in-law." And dear virtuous Ruth replied, "Entreat me not to leave thee or to return from following after thee: for whither thou goest, I will go: and where thou lodgest, I will

lodge: thy people shall be my people and thy God my God."
Well, I thought, if I ever get Mrs. Cash for a mother-in-law, I'll
be good, sure I will stay and be among her people and go to
her church, only it would be awfully inconvenient and a bore if
Joey weren't there.

And the good woman of Proverbs, her price far above rubies, who is trusted by her husband's heart, who "seeketh wool
and flax and worketh willingly with her hands, who buyeth a
field and planteth a vineyard, girdeth her loins with strength,
whose candle goeth not out by night" — oh, that sort of
woman I shall be because it says here that the woman who
seeketh, worketh, buyeth, and girdeth is the only truly admirable kind.

There were, of course, better parts than that. Like multitudes of children before me, thumbing through the four brief
pages headlined "Christ and his church," "The mutual love of
Christ and his church," "Description of Christ," "The love of
the church to Christ," I knew the Song of Solomon had nothing
to do with Christ and his church. Jesus had the sexless, touch-
free love, the kind that landed you in church listening to an interminable sermon. Actually, the Song of Solomon made good
reading while the sermon went forth, and they could hardly rap
your knuckles for reading the Good Book, no matter what page
you were on.

"His eyes are as the eyes of doves by the rivers of waters,
washed with milk and fitly set, his cheeks are as a bed of spices,
as sweet flowers, his lips like lilies, dropping sweet smelling
myrrh, his belly is as bright ivory overlaid with sapphires, his
mouth is most sweet; yea, he is altogether lovely" was the sort
of thing never said of the Lamb of God, the Savior, or trum-
peted from the pulpit of the Methodist or Baptist church, not
this stuff, not this poetry of the flesh, these words that made
your mouth water, made you want to touch yourself, dilated the
pupils of your eyes. And when the poet said of the prince's
daughter, "The joints of thy thighs are like jewels, the work of

the hands of a cunning workman, thy navel is like a round goblet, which wanteth not liquor, thy belly is like an heap of wheat set about with lilies, thy two breasts are like two young roes that are twins," he was certainly not speaking of Perfect Attendance Sunday and "The Old Rugged Cross" and the collection plate making the rounds, and me sitting there in a hat and white gloves (take them off, put them on, maybe this will soon be over) and my face composed in a proper church snurl.

That poet was speaking of some ancient drive beyond propriety or legitimacy, indeed an emotion that stamped out propriety and legitimacy, the same thing that Tristan and Isolde sought on the boat deck, willing to give their honor and their lives for whatever it was, the same thing that made Carmen defy Don José's knife or that made sweet Lucia of Lammermore melt into her lover's arms by the fountain and the next minute skewer her lawfully wedded spouse with a dagger. And what this was all about, I realized in the vague, wordless, adolescent furze that constituted my thought on the subject, was love so intense that it equated death.

Among the stacks of romances, historical novels, poems, and tales of love that I was reading, I now discovered *Jane Eyre*. Cora Lena slipped it to me. She was good to her few customers who were in need of entertainment beyond Sam Spade. "Read this first," she counseled. "Then you should check out *Wuthering Heights*." *Jane Eyre* became my textbook, a resource for proper female feelings that I have hardly abandoned to this day, though I now have written Charlotte Brontë onto my enemies list. Brought up by kind parents, I nevertheless mated at once with Jane, the baleful orphan, the abused child — in the house of her evil, treacherous aunt and her cousins, who specialized in brutal power plays, among the barbarians and torturers at Lowood School, where she was sent to be starved and exploited. If the blows that fell on Jane's poor back had fallen on me personally, I could not have experienced more indignation.

And then, at last, the stock-in-trade of all pulp fiction: the enormous dark house on the moor, Thornfield Hall, the enormous dark man on his horse, his black eyes, his sardonic smile, his cruel ways, his manner of humiliating his poor governess, his ward Adèle, who was a budding courtesan as her mother had been before her, the mystery, the flames in the night, the strange cries, the passion of Jane for Mr. Rochester. Though I was to lose my virginity in a variety of ways (since virginity is a thing of the mind as much as of the crotch, shedding it can be a major undertaking), I lost it first to Mr. Rochester, for I loved him at least as much as Jane Eyre. I wanted him for Jane. I wanted him for me.

Here was the master all women must wish for: the man booted and spurred and ready to ride and yet possessing a terrible secret that made him vulnerable. Here was the father of all the love tribe, and I bought it. So much was I the tool of Charlotte Brontë that when Jane in her bridal gown heard the voice from the back of the church — "The marriage cannot go on: I declare the existence of an impediment" — and the truth came out, that Mr. Rochester had been harboring a mad wife in his attic, I was crushed and began to weep aloud. According to Miss Brontë's simile, Mr. Rochester "moved slightly, as if an earthquake had rolled under his feet," and the same earthquake rolled me. When Jane was forced to confront the maniacal Mrs. R. with her shaggy locks, and when the "eddying darkness" swam around her, the same eddying darkness swam around me. Kill Bertha! How could she spoil my pleasure this way!

When, upon seeing the deep remorse in her lover's eyes and the manly energy in his manner, Jane forgave him but refused to become his mistress ("Mr. Rochester, I will *not* be yours") and went off into the night, crying "Farewell," I could not forgive *her*. Kill Jane! Stupid! Wrong! Of course she should stay with him! Dammit, she was supposed to be Isolde, since he was certainly Tristan. They must do whatever a man and woman did (I had more or less grasped the physiological details of love and was not convinced, after sober reflection, that it could possibly be anything but extremely embarrassing, but did that matter?) and then die in each other's arms. What was this self-denial for? What did it mean, this spurning of your dark lover, this running off, a virgin, into the night?

I grew distraught, hysterical. I buried my face in the unyielding cushions of what Mother always called the divanette — maroon, with hog-bristle upholstery — and sobbed until she herself grabbed me by my shirttails and threatened to slap my face if I didn't get hold of myself and explain why I was taking on so. "What is it? What is the matter with you?" She must have thought that here at age thirteen I had somehow managed to do the worst thing a girl could do (get pregnant), because otherwise why would I be sobbing and kicking on the divanette like a brat in a tantrum or an out-of-control teenager? ("Teenager" was a recent invention, linguistically and conceptually; my mother never pronounced the word without putting quotation marks around it. She believed that when you stopped being a little girl you turned into a young lady — that is, if you were lucky, because she herself had gone from little girl to household drudge for her mother and then wife at age nineteen, which wasn't much better; in her book, "teenager" was not steady work.) "For Lord's sake, straighten up and tell me why you're acting like this. Did you need to take a laxative?"

"This book is so sad," I sobbed. "Jane can't marry Mr. Rochester."

"Mr. Rochester my foot. It's past your bedtime and you didn't wash your hair today. Don't argue with me, I know you never got near the bathtub. At least wash your ears before you get in bed. First thing in the morning, you have a good scrub and wash your head. And you can run the vacuum cleaner tomorrow after you get yourself cleaned up, and keep your nose out of these books."

With a flashlight under my blankets that night I read on to the end, through the fire at Thornfield Hall that killed Bertha

Rochester and left Mr. Rochester blind but free to marry. I skipped impatiently ahead for Jane's return to her Samson, and was grateful to Miss Brontë for setting the universe to rights once more. Again I wept over Jane's account of married life:

> I have now been married ten years. I know what it is to live entirely for and with what I love best on earth. I hold myself supremely blest — blest beyond what language can express; because I am my husband's life as fully as he is mine. No woman was ever nearer to her mate than I am: ever more absolutely bone of his bone, and flesh of his flesh. I know no weariness of my Edward's society: he knows none of mine . . . Mr. Rochester continued blind the first two years of our union: perhaps it was that circumstance that drew us so very near — that knit us so very close! For I was then his vision, as I am still his right hand . . . Never did I weary . . . of doing for him what he wished to be done.

And then of course there was the matter of Jane laying his firstborn in his arms, a boy, with his father's large black eyes.

Thus, at age thirteen, had I been asked to write an industrious little two-thousand-word essay on the subject of love, drawing only on what I had read and heard and seen onscreen, it would have been an odd little exercise indeed. I might have spoken of the unattainability of the loved object. I might have observed that love was sometimes intricately connected with disease, such as chickenpox, for example, although I did not believe that loving Joey Cash had given me chickenpox. Chickenpox had merely been the misfortune that kept me from constructing the perfect evening. There was the curious way, in a hundred stories, that love led joyously to marriage, and then the door of art slammed shut. Too, there was that strange connection between love and death. Female corpses were draped all over the radio opera stage, which, along with the Paramount Theater, seemed the most active arena of love. Of course, there was Jane Eyre, who had managed, after some trouble, to get the blessing of society and the church, and to combine the ineffable passion she felt with the female ideal of domestic service. A very clever trick, for sure.

And then there was George Sand, about whom I knew little but the bits contained in a free-handed and (I would one day understand) ludicrous old Hollywood concoction. If I did not know it then, I would soon discover, digging into various books, that George Sand had marched out on the stage of life in pants, determined to create herself, to create some new form of love. She was headstrong, she would hammer love out to suit herself. And yet I shrank in fear from such a notion. If I must create myself, it should be as the good woman of the Bible, the sweet women of the silver screen, the lovely young women in the society pages of the Sunday paper, who attended dozens of kitchen showers and other prenuptial festivities and went down the aisle in satin.

From *Jane Eyre* I also learned that you should never, never give up. That you can have what you want, even though you must suffer to get it. And that the only way to manage a man is somehow to tether him to you, to make him dependent on you. Blind him, lame him, cut his Achilles tendon. Then you will be happy. He will be happy. You will never tire of serving him. If you both pay for your sins by getting married, you'll have a place to put your boundless desire. He won't be able to escape, and everyone will smile approvingly when you lay the baby in your former lover's arms. Nobody will have to die of rage and sin, at least not prematurely.

By the time I was fourteen or so, I had perfectly internalized all this. If some commissioner of romance had ground the whole mix into fragments and added it to the drinking water, or vaporized it and pumped it into the air, I could hardly have assimilated it faster or more thoroughly. It was as much a part of me as the fat in my daily serving of bacon, as the vitamin A in the cod liver oil I still swallowed, at my father's behest, to ward off colds. But the problem was that the love stuff added up to anarchy. It made perfect sense, at least some parts of it, but put all together, it was insane. I did not know this, nor that there was more to come. It was not yet as insane as it would be, nor was my belief in this vast, tangled mythology as deep as it one day would be.

❧

6

SWEET MYSTERY

I began reading *Seventeen* magazine to see how to get Joey Cash to adore me. I would do as they directed: put clear polish on my fingernails, shampoo every day, select demure shades of lipstick and apply it with a brush just outside the lipline, be content with my freckles since little could be done for them, spend money on freckle creams since you never knew when something might work, avoid vertical stripes or anything that emphasized my thinness and height, and remember, even as I penciled an arch into my eyebrows and applied a curler to my lashes, that personality was what mattered, not looks. Knobby knees, a Roman nose, and fuzzy hair could be disguised.

But what shade of lipstick, O *Seventeen,* makes up for knowing how to diagram a sentence with a noun clause in it, or for actually liking *Macbeth* when everybody else is dozing off or — worse — snickering when Lady Macbeth says she'd pluck her nipple from the boneless gums? Why did I think it was okay for Shakespeare to use such language when all my peers took him for an idiot? Oh, can all the perfumes of Arabia ne'er wash the stain from this white hand? No, they cannot. Would Revlon's Fire & Ice keep people from calling me a brain, a grind, a brownnose? Not likely.

Nevertheless, I lusted for the perfumes of Arabia, underarm deodorants, vanishing creams, facial "masques," depilatories, eyelash curlers, and metallic instruments for operating on pimples. I was now a person with needs, desperate needs that could only be satisfied when the cash register rang and the products were tucked into brown paper bags. These were the things of womanhood. *Seventeen* might never turn me into a beauty, but the child who had once gone into drugstores for limeades and chocolate sundaes now fingered bottles and jars and spent her whole allowance on cosmetics.

I had no explanation for loving Joey Cash. He was willowy, with pleasingly artistic hands, but even I could see that he was ordinary. His dad worked for the post office; they lived in a frame house with a slanty porch in an old part of town. His mama hung the wash on the line just like mine did, patched the elbows of jackets, and dried her dishes with hemmed flour sacks. They went to a different church from the one I was sent to, but they went. Joey made passable grades and continued to play third clarinet, which was a long way from Chopin. But the more mediocre he became, the more I craved him — for was he not to be my passport into mediocrity, into utter normality, into the life true women wished to lead? With him in it, the band stepped smartly down Central Avenue behind the football floats, tootling the Trojan fight song in junior high, and then the Spartan fight song. (Football teams are never named for the Athenians.) I worshiped Joey Cash as he marched past me in band parades, the love surging up in my throat until I could hardly breathe. Yes, yes, I would be the faithful young girl, waiting and watching from the sidelines.

A woman's magazine of this era ran a cartoon in each issue about a "watchbird," a creature who eyed naughty little girls. "This is a watchbird watching a grouch [for example]. Is this a watchbird watching you?" And there would follow a checklist ("Do you complain when your mother asks you to tidy up your room?" and so forth), so that you could tell if you really were a grouch. But I was a watchbird watching the boy I loved. I went to football games to watch him play the clarinet, not to watch the home team. I could pick him out all the way across a football stadium. I began to relish the role of rejected lover. Became content to have only a crush, proud of my loneliness and suffering, proud that I could wait it out like faithful Penelope.

Though the world in those days hoped to keep the information secret, I knew that sexual intercourse made babies. Still, I indulged in tormenting pregnancy fantasies, counting up days on the calendar, assuring myself that I had fabricated a fetus all alone out of the sheer force of my love. What I felt for Joey, I thought, was stronger than biology. Conjugation was for paramecia and Latin students. What I felt in my heart, the desire I had to merge myself in this boy, to obliterate my own ambitions and desires in his, had to be more powerful than protoplasm. And if my parents shipped me off to the home for unwed mothers, let them do it. I would go. I would give my baby up. With pleasure; that would be the easy part. My mother also said or implied that such a thing would kill her off, which seemed a greater burden for me to bear than an out-of-wedlock baby. Never mind; for Joey no sacrifice was too great.

Forgetting what I had learned from watching Chopin and Sand smooching in Majorca — that if you wanted a meaningful life you had to leave Poland and go forthwith to Paris — I allowed myself to be powerfully seduced by the banal, particularly the ads and editorial copy in such publications as *Life*, *Look*, *Woman's Home Companion*, and the *Saturday Evening Post*. Like the women in the ads, I would have gladly washed and ironed the shirts and underpants Joey wore, prepared his meals for him. Indeed, my vague ideas of sexuality — of his mouth on my mouth instead of on the clarinet, of his hands on my body, of what it might be like to see him naked, fantasies I could admit to only in my deepest dreams — were purified and sanitized, in my thoughts, by the notion of service. Being a wife required heavy machinery. Washing machines and mangles, refrigerators, kitchen ranges, peelers, choppers, and making the agonizing choice between gas and electric. (I would choose gas.)

I was determined to be Mrs. Joey Cash, Mrs. Joey Anybody (on some days), a proper wife in apron and high heels, beaming with pride as she extracted a pair of her husband's khaki pants from the dryer. By four-thirty the rib roast would be crackling in the oven, the carrots and potatoes pared. When Joey came through the door at five in the evening, I would, of course, snatch off my apron. I would pat my neatly coifed hair, my curly bangs, I would be there in full makeup. After he got home and kissed my cheek and sat down with his paper, I would set the vegetables to steam in vitamin-conserving waterless cook-ware. I would be the sort of housewife who had her work done by noon every day, so that she could put on a fresh dress and be-gin thinking of dinner. And though I saw little enough love in the lives of the properly married, properly aproned wives I knew, it seemed the only choice, the only way to get some sort of love and be permitted to hold your head up and drive a car and have clerks wait on you in stores and possibly become a mother. To live, in short. Live a woman's life.

So I would put myself to sleep with uneasy, unsatisfactory fantasies of shiny kitchens and beds made with clean sheets, and in the dresser drawer a tube of spermicidal jelly and an ap-plicator, and in the bathroom a feminine syringe, hidden in its plain white bag behind the stack of towels. And then, waking in the middle of the night, I would yearn for the love that is out-side morality, the fever that made death preferable to life for Barbara Stanwyck with her lip curling at Fred MacMurray, her stare as dirty and sinful as a whorehouse, and him ready to kill her husband to get her, willing for both of them to risk the elec-tric chair if he could have her just one time. The love-death floated out of the radio on Saturday afternoons, courtesy of the Texaco Company, and in its other forms rose up from the pages of my library books or emerged ten times my size on the screen of the Paramount Theater. I would picture myself on a cold slab in the Capulet mortuary, find my lover dead beside me and drive the dagger into my breast. On the deck of King Mark's boat, I drank the potion and lay in rapture, the Irish Sea waters washing over us, death the only possible punishment — not so much for what Tristan and Isolde were doing but for their terrible God-destroying attitudes, their lack of shame, their insistence that it was the potion that led them on rather than their own desires.

At some point, in mid-adolescence, I was brought briefly to my senses by *Life* magazine, and by my father. There she was in a photograph, grossly pregnant, Ingrid Bergman, whom I had last glimpsed in the chain mail of Jeanne d'Arc and earlier in a nun's habit, saintly tears glistening in her eyes, all innocence and virginity and virtue. Now, God spare us, she had run off with some Italian moviemaker named Roberto Rossellini and was expecting a baby by him. She had actually abandoned her dentist husband in California, and two children. (Their daughter was called Pia, which seemed an inexplicable crime in itself, as I imagined what I'd have gone through at school had that been my name.) When my father thrust the magazine with Ingrid's photo under my nose, his face was wrathful. "Can you beat this?" he asked. "What kind of woman would do a thing like this?"

"Why," I might have remarked, had I had the presence of mind, "almost any of the women I currently idolize, except for Jane Eyre, who would have obtained the marriage license first." The article said that Congress was passing some kind of law against Ingrid Bergman, revoking her passport, exiling her from American civilization to the ruinous Mediterranean embraces of the man my father called a "greasy Italian." I stared at her photograph, her huge belly, her averted face. Let him who is without sin among you cast the first stone, I thought, but I dared not utter the words. Was it not an adulterous woman of whom Jesus had been speaking, holding at bay the committee of the righteous who had come to stone poor Isolde, poor Guinevere? The world was populated with those eager to cast stones, especially at erring women. I tried to set my mental house to rights, lest I ever land among the candidates for stoning. I tried valiantly to position myself among the stoners, but they made me sick.

The house of overdecorated, tragic dreams I inhabited had a back door leading to reality, to plain ordinary life or some version of it. For one thing, there were boys. Love affairs, infidelities and small adulteries, acts that told me I need not always arrive at love's encounters armed with either a fatal potion and a symphony orchestra or matched luggage and a flawless manicure and a washer-dryer. Other girls necked in the back seat and nobody stoned them. Other girls did a lot more than just necking. My own encounters were nothing more than skin on skin. Sensations. Once or twice they proved joyous, overwhelming, or delicious. My first kiss occurred at a party, when a tall, bony boy I hardly knew enveloped me in the sort of swooning kiss that so enchanted me onscreen. On my few dates or other encounters, the fellows were sweaty or whiskery and I wished it were eleven-thirty so I could legitimately ask to go home. Sometimes the tongue thrust into my mouth was the metaphor, the objective correlative, for what I really wanted; sometimes it merely made me want to stop. Sometimes the boy was not the sort my parents wanted me to get mixed up with, such as Leonard Jones, who drank a lot of beer and skipped school and had been jailed once for stealing hubcaps. Nevertheless, how arousing his kisses, how sweet his hands, and what a comfort to be in his arms, two outcasts, necking and petting with no chance of commitment or of cursed, cursed love! O blessed activity with no consequence!

I learned to neck, go just so far and no further, firmly dislodge the hand that was moving in an interesting direction, moan a bit, wonder what this was all about, wish he had had a closer shave, wonder if Mother would notice the whisker-burn around my tender mouth, imagine what it might be like if his fingers pushed aside my panties, occasionally even permit him to do that, to explore, even permit myself some cautious, actually squeamish, exploration of him. As I grew into adulthood, the very word "virginity" began taking on fresh connotations — a joke and a burden. A few years down the road, society, or some segment of it, would conclude that a virgin bride had more to be ashamed of than the fully orgasmic one. Shame would always be part of the equation, however. There would never be a right way.

Sometimes my temporary lovers had already given jackets or rings to some other girl — cheating for real, just as I fantasized I had somebody to cheat on. Once in a while there was simply a sweet young man who wanted to be friends, even though I had the highest grade-point average in school. Even though I starred in English lit and Latin III, was editor of this or that publication, holder of appointive but not elective posts. With the razor of academic achievement I cut off my nose to spite my face. Be sure you aren't smarter than they are, be sure you don't crowd them, because if you crowd them, you'll sit by yourself Saturday night. Up against the choice that girls must make in adolescence, I took the wrong turn.

And in the upstairs of my mind were other forbidden and delightful rooms. French was not offered at our high school, but the guidance counselor Josie Dupont spoke it and treasured it. She offered to set up a class. She had copper hair, even thicker and fuzzier than mine, and jumpy blue eyes behind blocks of glass, so nearsighted she could scarcely tell one of us from another. But though those eyes seemed never to focus, she watched her flock like a shepherd — was as merciful and tender to the boy working in a gas station after hours and barely getting Ds as she was to the lost, aspiring, and unformed intellectual. Indeed, in the harsh environment of this public high school, she had appointed herself a physician empowered to seek cures for adolescent anger and grief. Five students, she deemed, would form an after-school French class. For three, including me, it would brighten up our college applications, but Miss Dupont also included two youngsters who did mediocre work, or worse, in every subject and needed some success, some astounding thing to tell their siblings. The principal of the school looked upon this project with suspicion and only reluctantly agreed to give us credit for the work. Josie Dupont was never compensated for her time.

Struggling with *avoir* and *être*, piecing together the customary French sentences about pencils on tables and the weather making hot or making cold, I could envision, over some far horizon, the domain of Frédéric and George, a domain where the music of the piano man was the brilliant accompaniment to life, a domain where a woman could wear boots and do as she pleased, where love was so heady and so passionate that dying for it was the least you could do. Like a pilgrim, I would go there. This suited me a lot better than the Romans who haunted my Latin classes, and I switched my historical allegiance to the Gauls. Those French, they knew how to love. What was even more seductive, they knew how to think.

After about a year of plodding through irregular verbs and making stupid errors (I would make them all my life; I still skid all over French syntax like a cat on ice, still find myself in midsentence desperately groping for "windowsill" or "stockbroker" or "can't hold a candle to"), I made an odd discovery. Josie Dupont had led us sufficiently along so that with a dictionary as our constant companion, we were able to tackle a real book, *Le Petit Prince*, Saint-Exupéry's coy tale. But one day, like Alice eating the cake, I somehow transformed myself into the right size. What was on the page began to make sense. For the second time, I learned to read.

Ah, French was freedom, this was the latchkey to some garden I earnestly wanted to explore, my escape from the dilemmas of life, a code that my parents and relations could never decipher. Here I might discover my inmost self, if ever I could manage to link those words together just the way they were supposed to go. How difficult it was, how impossible, how it brought tears to my eyes, unforgiving French rules that had to be done quite precisely, not in the homey, natural English but in their exasperating yet logical French way! You had to bow down to it, as you might to a religion. Here was a language to hide within, a sanctuary — and not another soul outside French class could know what I thought, if only I could learn to think in French. Rather than dreading the conjugations, I liked them. I yearned for France, adopted the American Standard Version of Paris, scribbling in a garret, watching the cancan at the Moulin Rouge, sitting in a café. But it was more than the canned dream, it was the words themselves. It hardly mattered what was on the page — the baobab trees of the little prince, or his spoiled-darling rose that he finds in the desert and cultivates. I read it as a sacred text, not for what it was but because I could triumphantly struggle through it.

"Tu es responsable de ce que tu as apprivoisé," Saint-Exupéry said about love. Responsible for what thou hast tamed, thou art! Another maxim! Through this ineffable, inexpressible door that the language had opened lay my escape route. This was how I should somehow get out of here. Passionate as I still felt about Joey Cash, hard as it was to admit that I could grow away from him, the thought finally arose that he was a dead end in the labyrinth.

Other passports, puzzling documents that I scarcely knew what to make of, fell into my hands during my high school years. Names, mostly, of writers. Gertrude Stein, Balzac (at least the stories that had given him such a wicked reputation), Freud, Karl Marx. I had already applied in vain to Cora Lena Brown for all these books. Cora Lena did find me a short article about Sand, where I learned that she was Aurore Dupin Dudevant — a mother of two who got rid of her husband, though never divorced. And she really had smoked cigars and dressed like a man, though the article downplayed this. She had written more books and plays than most people could even find time to read. And she really had been the lover of a lot of men, though

they downplayed this too, emphasizing her talents as a grandmother.

About this time, I should confess, I began to smoke. My darling George smoked, and, so far as I could see, the whole
French nation. The sort of woman I wished to be — Lauren
Bacall and Bette Davis in their trenchcoats, Barbara Stanwyck
in a negligee — smoked. Carmen worked in a cigarette factory.
Now that Ingrid Bergman no longer had to be a nun, she probably smoked. (Given the chance, Anna Karenina, Jane Eyre,
Isolde, and Juliet, I thought, probably would have smoked.) I
practiced regularly in a stall in the girls' toilet. I fainted twice
but was undeterred. I began carrying my own pack and
matches, then spent a week of lunch money on a lighter. When
a girlfriend scornfully pointed out that I was not inhaling, I
learned to inhale, savoring the stab of poison in both my lungs,
battling and overcoming the lightheadedness that threatened to
topple me once more.

My mother was as determined to keep me from smoking as I
was determined to smoke, so I turned into a secret agent from
that moment forward — hiding the Pall Mall packs, matches,
and supplies of chlorophyll gum, disposing of the ashes and
butts so that they could never be found, switching to Luckies
because that was my father's brand and I could pass the butts off
as his, performing quick mending jobs on the tiny charred holes
in my clothing, giving the habit up entirely for weeks at a time
because it was too much trouble, then starting again, arranging
to sleep over at girlfriends' houses merely so I could smoke. I
could have been recruited by the Communist party to steal
atomic secrets, so adept did I grow in the deceitful arts, so willing to tell calm, transparent lies to my mother when she detected the smell of tobacco on my breath or in my hair. I rather
hated the cigarettes but relished my own profound corruption.

When I had asked Cora Lena about Gertrude Stein and
Marx and Freud, she had seemed troubled. "Well now, we don't

have any of that. And we won't ever have any of it either, not even if the bond issue passes for the fine new building and we can buy some books finally. My detective stories are dog-eared and the covers fall off." The passing of the bond issue, as we both knew, might put Cora Lena out of a job, since she lacked the proper academic credentials to wrestle with the Dewey decimal system and win. Still, she wanted the new library to come into being.

"You don't need to read any Gertrude Stein. She doesn't make the least bit of sense anyhow. Karl Marx is a Communist. Young minds should not go near him, any more than you would go near somebody with tuberculosis and eat off their plate. I have no Communists in this library. And it's Froyd, not Frood."

"Froyd?"

"Froyd. What would you want with him?"

"I read in *Life* magazine that he knew how to interpret dreams. I want to understand my dreams." This was untrue. What I actually had read was that he not only deciphered dreams but thought everything in life was sex. He even thought little babies knew about sex, which was not so shocking, since I had certainly known about it at least since Gulliver and might have thought about it earlier. But he thought — this was the part that really was surprising — boys wanted to do it with their mothers and girls with their fathers. Preposterous, perverse, destructive, shocking, adorable notion! Freud also thought, if I read it aright, that women wished they had penises. My experience with penises had been pretty limited, but I certainly did not yearn to have this dangly, lumpy, hooded thing attached to my body, this unruly worm who at any moment might go hard as a bone and raise his blind head unbidden. Freckles, fuzzy hair, and monthly bleeding were bad enough without having a thing that poked through your clothing. I, for one, did not envy males their penises.

Who could this great philosopher be? Though *Life* had

implied that you could not call yourself an educated person if you had not read Freud, I could not find him in Cora Lena's library.

As my quest for Modern Thought went unsatisfied, so did my love for Joey. Dally in old Fords and Chevrolets though I might, dream of escape to other countries though I did, I had married myself to Joey, obedient to the savage ideal soaked up from printed pages and the silver screen and imbibed from the airwaves. If I could not have Joey as Jane had Mr. Rochester after the fire, I would have him only in my obstinate, implacable fantasies.

Just as implacably, he ignored me, fled from me, no doubt writhing in his own adolescent bed of hot coals, putting questions to himself that had nothing to do with me, embarrassed by my idiotic devotion, my obsession, and — if he understood it at all — frightened by it. By tenth grade he had become Joe Cash, grown to over six feet, looked almost virile, developed what we girls alluded to as "bedroom eyes," though his pictures in the yearbooks showed (and still show) a nondescript and pimply kid. Rumors flew, now and then, about his attachment to this or that girl. This would reduce me temporarily to desperation, would cause me to patrol my countenance for pimples and excavate them as viciously as I could, and finally, in one especially self-destructive fit, to take the scissors to my thick, unruly hair. In a rage one afternoon, using the hand mirror to inspect my work, I cut a path from ear to ear across the back of my head, hoping this would make the topmost layer lie smooth. There, *Seventeen*, God damn you. You said I must make the most of what I had, and I mowed a swath across the back of my head like a McCormick reaper.

"What on earth happened to you? Did you go assbackwards into the electric fan, ha-ha?" was the question I fielded during the year it took for the hole to fill in. The first question had come from my startled mother — "Honey, what on earth have you done to your head?" She was "just sick about it," as she was obliged to say a hundred times during the next few months, and I knew it made her wonder about the turmoil under the stubble, though she asked no leading questions, simply folded her lips into a tight line and no doubt cursed the day adolescence had been invented.

I spent many hours staring out into the hallway from my classrooms, waiting for a glimpse of Joey. Because he was in the band, his schedule was quite different from mine. We rarely shared a class. But I knew which staircase he was likely to be ascending or descending, and when. I threw myself in his pathway with the skill of a lobbyist. For the most part he was merciful, if not adoring. Once, in an unforgettable moment by his locker, we exchanged school pictures. I put "always" on mine, but he wrote "love." I looked up amazed, believing I had won the game or stood some chance of winning it, or that his colossal reserve had somehow begun to crack, and he smiled in what I saw as a suggestive manner. But later, when I showed the scrap to my best friend, she pulled out an identical one he had given her. Indeed, he had signed a dozen pictures "love" and given them out to a dozen girls. Still, there was that look in his eyes. Surely that had been for me alone. I forced my best friend to admit that Joey had bedroom eyes. She then went and told Joe that I said he had bedroom eyes, and reported back that he had laughed. I wadded his picture up and put it in the trash. Then I ironed it out, sorrowful to see that the cracks and wrinkles were irreparable. I carried it in my purse, as always, and continued to prop it against my table radio when I went to bed at night.

My girlfriends told me I was crazy, told me to grow up, that I was making a fool of myself and nobody else would ever ask me for a date until I swore off this babyish crush on Joe, asked me what I saw in this skinny, sissified boy who was hardly on anybody's dreamboat list. But I could not rid myself of this terrible love. It was beyond my control. At eighteen, facing graduation, I still loved Joey Cash. I had loved him with undiminished passion for six years, an eternity at that age, a feat of endurance I was seldom to match again.

And then, to my surprise, as if the story were at last to find its happy ending, he asked me to accompany him to the formal banquet that followed commencement. He waited so late to invite me that I knew I was not his first choice. Thus I hardly felt like the all-American girl. No "*Life* Goes to a Party" for me.

On graduation night I delivered the valedictory address, in which I enumerated and stressed, for an excruciating half-hour, leadership qualities. My voice tremulous, I called for independent thinking and citizens who stood up to lead. "We can each be leaders in our own walks of life, in our churches, in our businesses, in our homes, at school. We only need to think of ourselves as leaders." A stunning little piece of hypocrisy from one who, in her dreams at least, had plotted sedition, suicide, and orgasmic passion. In my heart I was terrified and miserable, afraid I was somehow embarrassing Joe Cash, who sat with the band and tootled out some version of "Pomp and Circumstance." The salutatorian spoke of followership, as she termed it, in which she stressed the importance of doing what you were told.

Then, having changed my cap and gown for a party dress, I attended the commencement banquet at a local hotel, with Joe as my date. I had borrowed one of my cousin's old formals, a yellow taffeta puffed-sleeve creation with ruffles at the bottom, edged in black velvet ribbon. I had painted my nails bright red. I tried to feel elated, but elation eluded me. He had sent me pink carnations, dreadful on yellow, but I wore them. By eleven we had heard all the speeches, swallowed all the roast turkey and green peas and chocolate cake, and drunk too much coffee. Joe clearly had no idea what to do next, no money to do it with, and no car to do it in. My girlfriend Nell had no date but did have the keys to her father's Packard. The three of us climbed into it and began aimlessly driving around. Glamorous parties were no doubt in progress here and there, but nobody had invited us.

We thought we might find some forbidden activity. Somebody staging a riot, or hosting a beer bust, ripping off his clothes and jumping into the fountain in the park. We did encounter a few other dead souls parked at the drive-in barbecue. We had chopped pork on a bun, with french fries. We smoked three packs of cigarettes. I lit Nell's cigarettes so she could keep her eyes on the road. Joe once took my hand, but I didn't feel like necking in front of Nell.

Nell gossiped about girls who'd slept with the whole football team. Sluts. I wondered how you went about being a slut and whether they weren't scared of getting pregnant. Joe said they did get pregnant. There was a man up on Mountain Street who did abortions, two hundred dollars, no painkiller. And some of the real docs in town did abortions, he said, with anesthetics, but you had to have connections and they charged a lot. I asked him how he knew. "Everybody knows," he said. Maybe this really was what love brought you — an abortion without anesthetic.

Nell told us about a flagrant example of brother-sister incest in our very own graduating class; at least, the boy was in our class. His sister was a junior. Yes, they did it all the time. Once the girl had even had to go to Mountain Street. I was startled, felt naive, had never imagined such things. Could such horrors belong in the castle of love I had built in my imagination? I grew melancholy, bored. Shrank back against the car seat. Took my hand out of Joe's. I was sleepy, wanted to go home.

The streets were deserted. We ran out of gossip, nearly out of gas, and we realized we'd sat at every stoplight in town, waiting for it to change. Our cigarettes tasted lousy. We dropped Joe off within a block of his house. Nell and I went home and drank a bottle of champagne in expensive crystal goblets at her mother's mahogany dining table, then staggered nauseously to bed and, thanks to our youthfully efficient livers, woke up at noon feeling refreshed. High school graduates. Was the Joe who'd shared this aimless evening really the man I'd loved for a third of my life?

Years later, when I encountered the obsessive lovers in French literature — Adolphe, Julien Sorel (both of them ruined by love, finally, utterly, and without redemption), and most of all, the surrealist poet Guillaume Apollinaire, I required no explanation of their folly. "La chanson du mal-aimé," about Apollinaire's furious, murderous love for a German governess who scorned and abandoned him, made perfect sense to me. I too was an ill-loved lover. I too could have written *la chanson du mal-aimé*.

I was in my thirties, a married woman, a professional woman, clearing out my mother's house after her funeral, before I managed to throw out the two "Love, Joey" cards and the dried gardenia from seventh grade. The wrinkles still marred the school photo, but the bedroom eyes shone through. I rescued the picture from the garbage can and ironed it carefully with my fingers. Like the chickenpox scar in the middle of my forehead, my love for Joey Cash, which had nothing to do with Joey Cash, had faded almost to invisibility but would never go away.

MAZURKA

Whence arises this preference for whatever thwarts passion, hinders the lovers' happiness, and parts and torments them? To reply that so courtly love required is only to reply superficially; for this still leaves it to be ascertained why love of this kind is preferred to the other, the love that gets fulfilled and satisfied . . . If we delve into the recesses of the myth, we see that this obstruction is what passion really wants — its true object.

— Denis de Rougemont, *Love in the Western World*

Confined to the back seat of the family Dodge, the blistering wind of late August whipping at the car windows as the red southern earth rolled past, I traveled 150 miles to the college chosen for me. Know the truth, and the truth shall make you free — that was the motto of the college I was bound for, and I was indeed destined to discover what this meant, in some sense, though hardly the one I imagined. I was the first person on either side of my family to go to college. For my parents, State College for Women had a number of advantages. It was only half a day's drive from home, and tuition was cheap. More important, it was uninfested by males. This might preserve me intact, they thought, imagining that their vigilance and high moral purpose rather than my bony frame and strange state of mind had kept me innocent through high school.

I had my five-piece set of graduation luggage, beige trimmed in brown. The catches snapped like mousetraps. One of the pieces was a hat case, a huge square box designed for traveling in staterooms. I actually had put a couple of hats in it (church, tea party, funeral; one had to be prepared). My train case was the kind movie stars clutched in *Life* photographs on the rear platform of the Twentieth Century Limited. It was loaded with Pond's cold cream, Jergens lotion, and a box of powder that had been specially concocted to meet my complexion needs by a lady in a pink smock, who had peered analytically at my freckles.

On the seat beside me, in brown paper, was a Bates bedspread, dark green and soil-resistant, with a corrugated finish suitable for boot camp. I also had a set of ruffled green-and-pink print curtains, four pink towels and washrags, and a pink shag scatter rug. I had corresponded all summer with my prospective roommate, Penelope Elliot from Vicksburg, Mississippi, and she had proposed this decorating scheme. Then we ordered the stuff from Sears so that it would be identical, from the same dye lot. The college urged girls from distant towns to collaborate this way. We were required to keep a tidy room. However, the college wanted each room to reflect the girls' personality.

Ah, "personality," that ball and chain, that iron cage, that thing you invented to compensate for a plain face. I was okay with green and pink, but did it express my personality? Fire and brimstone would have been more the ticket, for something was boiling in me that could not be disguised by face powder and Pond's cream ("She's engaged, she's lovely, she uses . . ."). My heart still ached when I thought of Joey Cash, who had gone to a university in the North. Without taking my address. But my wounds had scabbed over, leaving a hard place with raw flesh underneath. Sick with unrequited and now quite unspecific love, burdened with my own virginity, I was ready to look for my true mate. All unawares, I was also about to be stranded in the equivalent of the Gobi Desert so far as men were concerned.

As at most women's colleges of the era, *in loco parentis* was practiced like a sacrament. Housemothers, residential assistants, and special plainclothes informers from among our own ranks formed a vast surveillance system, with the dean of women as spymaster. The CIA could have gone there for pointers. It's some comfort to know, as I now do, that these soft-spoken and vigilant minions of the Moral Order were soon to be smacked over and annihilated — along with *in loco parentis,* premarital virginity, and ladylike manners — in the tidal wave of rebellion that would sweep through colleges a few years later. (Less a rebellion, perhaps, than a weariness on the part of the guardians of the Moral Order, who so eagerly retreated from their gun emplacements as dorms went coed and young women ceased to obey dress codes and other rules.)

But for now, decorum and pure thoughts, hats and white gloves, no blue jeans or shorts within the possibility of a male glance, were what this women's college was selling. No men were allowed in the dorm. Even a brother or father who'd merely come to tote your matched luggage to your room could enter the upper precincts only with a residential assistant at his elbow crying "Man on the floor!" Curfew on weeknights was eight o'clock for first-year students, and the housemother checked rooms at ten, making sure we were all in bed. Students were not permitted to drink. Other dangerous activities went nameless in the handbook, but if one can of beer could bring your stay in the academy to an end, we could all imagine what the college thought of sex.

"Hello, I'm Penny Elliot, Vicksbu'g, Miss'ippi." My roommate and her parents were waiting for us, Bates spread and scatter rug already unpacked, in room 301, Harlan Hall, in a setting unembellished by so much as a shade tree on the sun-drenched campus. Relocated to the state mental hospital or reformatory, Harlan would have been an architectural fit. Penny was tiny and brown-eyed, with exquisite long lashes perfectly mascaraed, as though she'd painted each one separately with her little Maybelline brush, the way Jack Frost painted the grass blades in winter. Her hair, in a Breck shampoo pageboy, glinted auburn. Like me, she was dressed in a circle skirt, white peasant blouse, and ballet shoes. Like me, she was flat-chested, though it was less obvious on a thorax as small as hers. Still, we had a bond.

"Let's go get our post office box, roomie, and let our mommies do the fixing up," she suggested immediately. "We want those good letters from home to start rolling in." So we headed for the student union building, leaving our mothers with dust cloth and broom while our fathers stood around uncomfortably talking cars and weather.

"I never wanted to come here," Penny confided in her molasses accent as soon as we were out the door. "I wanted Ole Miss. But Daddy doesn't like my boyfriend, Ralph. He works in a gas station at home. Daddy thought this would get me away from him. He thought he could lock me up with all these girls and keep me safe. A lot he knows. Ralph's going to hitchhike down here next weekend. You've got to help me out. They watch you like damn ol' dragons. They kicked a girl out last year for lighting a cigarette in the living room. They'd put you in the dungeon with snakes, I 'magine, if they caught you with your boyfriend. What do you think about putting pillows in my bed for room check? We'll pile the covers up real good, and you say I need my beauty sleep and tell the old hag not to bother me." She giggled and gripped my arm.

Here, touching my arm, was an unmarried woman my own age who had actually had sex. Who talked about it in a casual way, plotted to get more of it, feared neither syphilis nor gonorrhea nor the home for unwed mothers. A bad girl, almost as bad as the girl at home who did it with her brother. How, I wondered yet again, did you get to be a bad girl? Still, wasn't it sordid, this stealthy lover and his gas station, this scheme to deceive the college, this matter-of-fact way Penny walked across campus with me in spite of having experienced the sublime? I noticed that not once did she mention love. I felt stupid. How was I to tell her I had never had sex except in my imagination? That passion was what I sought, not sex? Or that I dreaded being punished as an accessory to her crime?

We signed up for our mailbox, and she was unsurprised to
find a letter waiting from poor obedient Ralph — "He better
write me, I told him to mail me one before I even left" — and
by the time we returned to the dorm room, our mothers had
hung the pink-and-green curtains, made up the beds with the
Bates spreads, and scattered the scatter rugs; Penny's was
green, against my pink, and so were her towels, so that things
didn't get mixed up in the wash. Then all six of us went out to
supper at a local barbecue joint called the Juicy Pig. They drove
their Buick, we our Dodge. Some of us ordered pork, others
beef, though you couldn't tell much difference, as the buns
were soaked with the same delicious dark sauce, and we all had
identical stacks of cole slaw and fried potatoes. The grownups
drank coffee, we students Cokes. Afterward, at the dorm door-
step, I said goodbye to my parents, who were to leave at dawn
the next morning. A vast regret seized me, a sense that I was
about to turn traitor to these kindly people holding back their
tears, was going to abandon them forever, and I could not keep
from sobbing in my mother's arms. But once they left me at the
dorm, the fit of homesickness vanished like a summer cold, and
I made straight for the library, since it was only seven o'clock.

Tucked into a side pocket of my zipper notebook was
the list of titles, laboriously noted, that I had taken in vain
to Cora Lena:

> George Sand, anything by or about
> Marx, *Communist Manifesto* and *Capital*
> Gertrude Stein, anything by or about
> Freud, *The Interpretation of Dreams*

I intended to look these up as soon as I got into the college
library — the first real library I would ever have seen, far sur-
passing (I hoped) the sparse, heroic collection of Cora Lena
Brown. The prospectus had described the thousands of volumes, the up-to-date card catalogue. Here, certainly, I would
find what I burned to read. When others were putting stockings

in the dressers and hanging up their formals and going from door to door introducing themselves to their neighbors, and Penny was polishing her toenails and rolling her hair on rags, I loped along in the dark on the tree-lined path toward the library, dappled by lamplight, a lost dog heading for home.

I bounded up the library steps into the dimly lighted interior and began to look around, first at the long lines of open shelves, then at the card catalogue, larger than any I had ever dreamed of. I had thirsted for Modern Thought, and here it all was. Seemingly uncensored and listed by author. Once you got the hang of the system, you could locate the volumes yourself, which often sat side by side with even juicier titles you had never dreamed of. That night I didn't get very far. There was a whole shelf of George Sand, and I took two volumes, both of which looked a bit like children's stories, though the French was impenetrable to my high school skills. Among none of her own writing could I locate the story of her love affair with Chopin. (Why wouldn't she have written about that, described his sweet boy kisses, the sound of his piano in the house, the look of him as he lay dying? But there was nothing.) I did discover, though, that Chopin was only one of apparently dozens of love affairs. Hooray for you, George! And, for a miracle, I found a fairly new biography: *Lélia,* the title of one of her books.

I did find some portraits of her: not what I imagined, not as beautiful as Merle Oberon. And yet beautiful in her unbeautiful way: a dark, fiery-looking young woman with stringy hair and a proper dress, looking as if she might say something seditious at any moment, a creature I could easily picture as Chopin's love; and an actual photograph in which she appeared as a plump old lady with spit curls who might have served as the dean of women here. I thrust it away from me, tried to forget it. She who had been bent backwards in Chopin's arms, lain in his bed, sat under his piano and listened to his preludes and polonaises as he composed them had ended up a granny. No, it could not be true. Time did not betray lovers in such a manner.

Still, even in her granny clothes, she had those dark eyes, brimming with . . . what? Merely energy, perhaps. Merely restlessness. Merely intelligence. Or the desire to throw herself off whatever emotional or moral precipices she could find in the vicinity.

Das Kapital turned out to be a discouraging volume for a student looking for quick answers, so I read *The Communist Manifesto* instead (only a few words) — Workers of the world, unite, you have nothing to lose but your chains. Yes! I thought, a worthy idea, and returned the book to the shelf. Once again, seeking the truth that was to make me free, I ransacked the card catalogue, but found no mention of Gertrude Stein. For Freud, Sigmund, there were several cards. Locating the shelf, I chose *The Interpretation of Dreams,* because the version I laid hands on happened to be skinny. Then, trotting once more along the dark path with its dim lamps, I returned to Harlan Hall, 301, and found Penny surrounded by five new friends, with wads of cotton between her precision-painted toes. She was in the middle of what became a famous Penny narrative, her own meditation on history and mythology. Her family belonged to the old, beleaguered white aristocracy of Vicksburg; Penny was fond of pretending that time had stopped for them in 1863, the year of the siege. She loved to tell how her great-great-granny had hidden the family silver in the well when the city had finally fallen to General Grant. The slaves, she said, never ran away. She felt it would be better if there still were slaves, and regarded it as a great pity the North had won.

I'd no intention of becoming a recluse. Rather, now that I'd escaped my hometown, I meant to remake my identity. Nobody here knew me. I needn't tell anyone about Joey Cash or say that I had graduated first in my class. I was ready for men. The next day I met someone who seemed to know a great many. Olivia Fitzmorris, who lived on the floor below me, was from Dallas and had a sheen of money and social position about her. At four, all Harlan freshmen had convened for orientation in the parlor — a vast and shabby space with Federal-style woodwork and tall windows and the dimensions of an airplane hangar. The room was marked out into three islands by thin oriental carpets, each with groups of scroll-backed sofas, wing chairs, and an assortment of serviceable tables — end, tea, and coffee. The queen of this realm was our housemother, Hilda Ochs — "oaks," she informed us — a stout woman of about forty with a chignon and plain black dresses and lace-up shoes, who was known behind her back, of course, as the Ox. She had come to the college twenty years before as a student and stayed on as freshman housemother in Harlan Hall, an elderly woman at twenty-one.

Today she made us welcome — "precious girls," she called us — reviewed the rules and regulations, and afterward one of the RAs led us in singing "Beautiful, Beautiful Brown Eyes," a tribute from us Oxen to our Ox — a Harlan tradition. Indeed, Miss Ochs did have lovely, luminous brown eyes, and tears came into them as the young voices promised never to love blue eyes no more, and she hid her face and the magnificent eyes and shook her head, peering through her fingers like the animated doll in a ballet.

When "Brown Eyes" died down, Olivia introduced herself to me. She spoke without a trace of the Deep South accent so many of us had — which was why, I suppose, I tagged her instantly as upper-class. Her almost round eyes were hazel; she had that engaging manner of looking straight into your eyes and inviting an equally penetrating glance in return. She asked right off if I'd share a blind date that evening with some boys from a nearby air base. It was a joke, she said. Her cousin in Dallas had dared her to do it and had made the arrangements. Flyboys might be amusing — "Up in the air, junior birdmen, up in the air upside down," she sang. I had never before heard anyone make fun of the air force. She asked me to her room, taught me the song. She had paid extra not to have a roommate

— "I'm double-majoring in English and piano," she explained, "and I need the privacy." She had pushed the two single beds together and covered them with a feathery comforter. She alluded to boyfriends at nearby colleges, and on her dresser was her high school sweetheart's picture, "Love always, Philip." "Cute boy," I commented, and she agreed. I noticed a phonograph and stacks of LPs as well as several volumes of poetry. Both closets bulged with pretty clothes, including a couple of net formals.

That evening, in a newly ironed print skirt, Peter Pan blouse, and cinch belt, I was frightened but full of hope. I had tried to flatten my fuzzy hair with water and bobby pins but had only made it fatter. Olivia's short dark hair was smooth and shining in the heat, her sundress black-and-white dotted swiss, so that she looked air-cooled. The young men arrived early in crumpled khaki trousers and voluminous short-sleeved shirts. The short one came from Idabel, Oklahoma. His irises were an extraordinary, pale, undernourished blue. Hookworm. Pellagra. The tall one, cursing the heat, maneuvered to get Olivia, and I followed with the Oklahoman, half a foot shorter. Dutifully, considerately, I tried to stoop.

The outing was strictly school-approved. Two hours at a Formica table in the student union. Dr. Peppers. Potato chips. Olivia and the Plainsman danced several times to the day's hit, "Unchained Melody," "Ooooo, my love, my darlin', I've hungered for your touch a long lonely time."

"That song don't make a lot of sense," my guy said. "Anyhow, I can't dance."

"Time goes by so slowly, and time can do so much," moaned the jukebox, but eventually the men ran out of dimes. So after a while Olivia and I bought doughnuts, which had been sitting on the soda fountain counter, possibly for years, under a plastic dome, and another four bottles of Dr. Pepper. Then, having eaten and drunk it all, the four of us walked back to the parlor of Harlan Hall. It was a half-hour before curfew, but the men said goodbye.

"God Almighty," I cried in despair. "Is this what people do for fun around here?" Olivia laughed.

Infatuated with Olivia, her phonograph records, and the dates she fixed me up with on weekends, I began spending all my free time in her room, trotting to her door at all hours, abandoning Penny to her manicures, her touch-ups, her radio programs, and the Vicksburg siege. Without my help, she found ways to have sex with Ralph without getting caught. Instead of hitchhiking, he had bought a car, so they had somewhere to lie down. She signed out as visiting a mythical aunt in the next town, running the very real risk, of course, that her parents would call and say, "What aunt?" or that Miss Ochs would test the fake telephone number in the sign-out book. I was now playing the role of little sister to Olivia. She had dates almost every weekend, phone calls, messages tacked to the bulletin board, invitations, and legitimate, honorable reasons to sign out in the housemother's book. Philip in the picture on her desk had gone off to Princeton, it turned out, but another high school beau of hers attended the nearby military school, our brother college. Sometimes he was able to arrange an escort for me, but nobody ever asked me for a second date.

One lonely Saturday afternoon, when many in the freshman dorm were going to a dance at a nearby college, I helped Olivia into a long-line corset-bra called a merry widow, a merciless contraption with rows of bone or plastic staves, to which she anchored the top of her blue net strapless formal. After waving goodbye to her and several other girls in pastel tulle with corsages pinned to their waists, I went to the dining hall alone and ate fried chicken and a canned pear congealed in lime Jell-O, then spent the evening reading the works of Keats. Olivia had just given me the Modern Library Keats and Shelley, a plump doorstopper set in tiny type, a true hungry-student volume. I was eighteen, slightly younger than Keats when he wrote his first poems. I had done nothing, I was nothing. I tried to decide if Keats might have loved me, given the opportunity. I couldn't decide whether I wanted to be Keats himself or his girlfriend. Then it struck me that I was a foot taller than he. "Here lies one whose name was writ in water." You aren't the only one, John. I thought of his hopeless love for Fanny Brawne. I ached throughout my entire body simply thinking of Fanny Brawne, her chilliness, his longing for her. How could she have been so distant! Hopeless little idiot! Oh, I wished it had been me John Keats wanted. Or that I had been John Keats wanting Fanny. Over and over I read:

> And when I feel, fair creature of an hour,
>   That I shall never look upon thee more,
> Never have relish in the faery power
>   Of unreflecting love! — then on the shore
> Of the wide world I stand alone, and think
> Till Love and Fame to nothingness do sink.

I laid my head on the open book and wept into the pages. In the luxury of health and youth I prayed for an early death, for anything that would temper the monotonous loneliness, the self-doubt that plagued my life. Oh, to be composing odes, falling in love, coughing blood, dying. Tuberculosis was a blessing! To be finished with it all in Rome, at twenty-five! O weep for Adonais, he is dead! I had meant to sit up for Olivia, like a faithful servant, and to hang the blue net formal on its hanger, but I went to my room instead and fell asleep after a long fit of weeping. Penny, I knew, was in the car with Ralph.

One drizzly Saturday afternoon a few weeks later, I had a date with Olivia's young man's roommate — a presentable youth, polished and desirable compared with the flyboys. I resolved that he would fall in love with me. I flirted, I clung. The four of us went to a football game in the Cotton Bowl in Dallas, then drove around drinking beer and eating hot dogs all evening — there was a washtub of bottled beer on ice in the car trunk. Occasionally we parked and necked, with the radio playing. As unfamiliar with alcohol as with flirting and clinging, I got dizzy drunk. The boy and the car and the world lurched like the carnival Tilt-a-Whirl and spun me upside down. Sure that I was about to be launched out the window, I clutched my date's arm and the car seat, then vomited. On the way home, he spilled a full can of beer on my skirt and into my shoes.

Saturday nights, Miss Ochs stood at the dorm door to greet returning inmates ("Papieren, fräulein?"). I smelled sour. My shoes were squishing with beer, and my skirt was wet. We were right up against curfew. Even Olivia thought we were goners. "Goddammit!" She grabbed me by the elbow. "Walk straight and smile." But though Miss Ochs turned her sniffer inquiringly in our direction as we fled past her and up the stairs, she did not detect the horrid stale smells, or hear the quite audible squishing of my shoes. My date never asked me out again. I didn't care, really. His kisses had been stiff, unyielding, undifferentiated. I was taken with a sudden rage that an evening out, which I had dreamed about for a week in advance, should consist of a sodden football game and a lot of beer and a boy who didn't know how to kiss. Not what I was looking for. What was I looking for?

As the weeks went on, Olivia's invitations from young men in the area seemed to dwindle, or at any rate she went out less, and one Saturday night we went to a movie. One fall night the C&D series (Concert and Drama, the college enrichment program, which was always carefully highbrow) offered *The Red Shoes*, Michael Powell's ballet film of 1948, concerning a prima ballerina who eventually kills herself, hounded by an impresario who won't allow her to dance if she insists on being married and a husband who won't allow her to be his wife if she insists on dancing. She had to choose between marriage and the bally, as they so beguilingly called it. Bal-*lay*, I called it, in approximately two and a half syllables, and equated it with a scratchy tutu and toe shoes. But here, with a capital A, was Art. Art all mixed up with Love. Women all mixed up with Art. Love all mixed up with Death.

The exquisite, talented Victoria Page — she who the wicked impresario says dances with "ecstasy" — falls for Julian, the handsome, red-lipped composer, so gifted, so bursting with talent as to have had his compositions plagiarized before even emerging from the conservatory. Ah, red lips indeed, the genders melded! There before my shocked eyes, and Olivia's, was Robert Helpmann of the Sadler's Wells donning a hairnet, and other male dancers in makeup and tights, all so joyous, caring for nothing but art. How could this be, men in hairnets and lipstick, a woman dancer who takes center stage, not swathed in white feathers like Ginger Rogers, bending and swaying to Fred Astaire? Victoria and Julian, or it might have been Victor and Juliet, or Romeo and Juliet, so alike they were. He was as feminine as she — a piano man dancing at the keyboard, pursing his lips, wrinkling his noble forehead, as she whirled on point. That was why, I supposed, they were able to achieve what I was searching for — and now all at once I could define it: the sublime moment.

The moment occurs during a carriage ride the lovers take through the lush countryside around Monte Carlo. The coachman dozes with the reins in his hands, like a figure in a fairy tale. Vicky sleeps on Julian's shoulder, as in a postcoital trance, though nothing so earthy as intercourse has been seen. Holding his love in his arms, Julian says, "When I am an old man, they will ask me what was the happiest moment of my life, and I shall answer without hesitation . . ." Exactly. I almost rose from my seat in the college auditorium. This was it, this was something I could live for. The thing that endures only in recollection, the work of art, Keats's Grecian urn, "Forever wilt thou love, and she be fair," the moment that tears one's heart with nostalgia and regret, but in advance of the event rather than afterward.

There was no possible ending to such a love but the lovely young body hurled under the oncoming train and crushed, the spotlight tracking her empty steps in that evening's performance of *The Red Shoes*. Ah, how satisfying. If women want to be artists, or even simply not to be worked and/or bored to death, it will tear the world apart. Who will love the men and children? Who will care for them? What will God say, that great, demanding, impatient impresario? He'll send a chopper to chop off your feet, or your hands, or your head, or your tongue. And you'll be glad he did it, you'll thank him, just the way the *Red Shoes* girl kissed the feet of the priest and tears of joy ran down her cheeks when they carried her into the church, because she too wanted to be a good girl, not an outlaw. Up until now I had wanted to die that way, to give up everything and greet Joey Cash at the door in my apron. But now anger rose. Goodbye to all that. Let somebody else cook and clean and die for them. I would be an outlaw.

Olivia and I were stricken with pleasure, as ecstatic as two little girls with a crush on a new movie star. We were convinced, at the same time, that nobody could have understood *The Red Shoes* as well as we. "It would be useless to try to speak to anyone else about this," we told each other. "No one could see this as we see it." If we had been ten years younger, we'd have played *Red Shoes* dress-up, drawn *Red Shoes* paper dolls. "Only we can know," we said to each other.

In this, as in other ways, did Olivia and I take possession of each other. Thus did we enter, step by step, the realm of the forbidden. We became inseparable, meeting for breakfast, lunch, and dinner, sitting at our own all too conspicuous table in the dining hall, reading our history assignment together in the library stacks, contriving to fill the whole day with each other until eight o'clock, when freshman girls were to be locked into Harlan Hall — virgins in a castle keep.

Evening was, of course, the best part of the day. We had our poets. Besides Keats, we read to each other from Shelley, By-

ron, Coleridge, Yeats. Wordsworth was something of a bore,
we felt, the undeniably major poet English profs liked because
you could list the ideas in his works. You couldn't just skip the
old bird. He'd written too much. We liked the wicked poets
best, the suicides, the ones with scandal clinging round their
laurels. Byron was handsome, however, and thus more readily a
guest at our mental soirees, and Coleridge had composed under
the influence. Had begun "Kubla Khan" while stoned and had
never been able to finish it, a gentleman from Porlock having
broken the trance with a knock at the door. Opium was legal in
Coleridge's day, and people got high whenever they chose,
bought it cheap at the apothecary. Took laudanum as if it were
a spring tonic. Often overdosed and died. Ah, for such privileges! We had no drugs, but we approved of "drinking the milk
of paradise," as Coleridge put it.

With her phonograph and stack of LPs, Olivia began to
teach me something about music. She possessed perfect pitch,
could sing the notes along with the most complex piece, could
identify modulations from one key to another, knew a hundred
technical terms, could tell one pianist from another just by listening, knew when a soprano lurched slightly off key. I had
heard nothing but the operas on radio Saturday afternoons, but
she acquainted me with thrilling things: Ravel and Debussy,
Rachmaninoff, a Prokofiev piano concerto featuring a handsome young newcomer, William Kapell. (His photograph was
on the jacket. He was just our type.) She had Tchaikovsky, two
Beethoven symphonies, a lot of Chopin, all the romantic reper-
tory that ravished the adolescent ear before rock and rap were
invented. These musical evenings were more satisfying than
standing in a drizzle at the football game with some ROTC guy,
more nourishing than hot dogs at the Union Building and flyboys dancing to the jukebox.

Soon we agreed that I should go to Olivia's room every day
after supper to read the poets and dispose of whatever other

homework was required, and then we would indulge ourselves with music. I would return briefly to my bed for room check at ten, then, after the lights were out, creep down the stairs and along the corridor toward her room, clinging to the wall. She would be waiting in the dark, with the little phonograph light aglow and the scratchy needle at the ready.

Olivia knew a great deal about Chopin: indeed, she could play all the preludes by heart. It was hard at first for me to switch from Cornel Wilde/Chopin in my mind. Olivia's Chopin was not some actor in a ruffled shirt but a true Genius. Olivia worshiped him for his music, and adored him for dying young.

"I am sure I knew him in another life," she said. "He is buried in a famous cemetery in Paris, Père Lachaise, it's called, and I think I am buried there too. Do you know what I mean? That self I was who knew him? I wonder who I was. Probably one of those awful little rich girls he had to give lessons to. I hope I wasn't too much trouble. I hope my papa paid him well. I want you to come with me one day. We'll go there together and walk among the graves, and you'll help me find out who I am. I'll be right there on one of the tombstones. We'll know when we see the name." And I would respond with a eulogy about Keats, and announce plans to visit the English cemetery in Rome and search for his grave. I loved the idea of my former self being buried there but didn't want to snitch the concept from my friend.

On the wall above her desk, we made a gallery of the beloved dead. I pinned up a portrait of Chopin next to a reproduction of Keats's deathbed portrait that I had clipped from a magazine, along with a picture of the plaster cast of Chopin's hands. Shelley and Byron were there. That fall — not to our displeasure — our adored pianist William Kapell died in a plane crash on his way to Australia, and we added his portrait, from his newspaper obituary, to our *musée des morts*.

Olivia had a recording of the mazurkas, small masterpieces that seemed at the time to contain all I knew of human emotion, the very map of love, the anatomy of the romantic heart. One of them I loved especially — op. 17, no. 4 — and we played it a thousand times. "Hear that descending fourth?" she asked, and I nodded, though I'd only the sketchiest idea what she meant. "That's you, that's your name, this mazurka is the music your very self could be set to. This is your mazurka, so haunting. You hear, it ends on that poignant little unresolved note. That's the way you are too. Always looking for something. But you don't know what." She took my hand and for the first time leaned toward me and kissed me on the mouth. I drew back uneasily. "I couldn't help it," she said. "I hope I haven't gone too far. I don't mean to frighten you. But you must know how I feel about you." Her eyes filled with tears. I couldn't reply. I was indeed frightened.

Another evening after we listened to the Prokofiev piano concerto and wept again for William Kapell, I went to the basement, as usual, and brought back two Cokes. "Don't be shocked, my dear," she said when I returned, and from under her bed she pulled a train case identical to my own and unlocked it. Hers was provisioned not with Jergens lotion but with vodka, which, as she explained, left no trace on the breath. Olivia poured part of each Coke down the sink and refilled the bottles with the vodka, plugging the top with her thumb and mixing expertly so it didn't foam over. "Now drink it slow. You don't know how to drink yet. You have to dole it out to yourself in little sips. Otherwise it makes you puke. I guess you know that. God, you embarrassed me the other night."

An hour or so and a couple of Cokes later, she put Ravel's "Bolero" on the phonograph, and as the music progressed, she taught me how to beat the complex rhythm on the wooden floor with my hands. Two doctored Cokes later, screaming with laughter, we cranked the volume up, reeled out into the corridor, and danced the bolero in our nighties, beating the rhythm on the walls and on people's closed doors. Heads bristling with bobby pins and curling rags peered out of every door, then an audience descended from the third floor and ascended from the first. Some of the girls joined the dance, capering in their chenille bathrobes; others looked on with amazement as we leapt and pounded.

Miss Ochs appeared, still dressed in her daytime black and predictably horrified. But she thought it was simply high-spirited girls a bit out of hand, and she sent us back to our rooms without discovering that the high priestesses of the rite were drunk. As I was climbing into my bed, still wobbly and intoxicated, Penny said, "You're stewed, aren't you? What's she got down there, Smirnov? Why didn't you ask me to the party? You two really keep to yourselves these days. Mighty stingy with your liquor, aren't you? Think you're so smart with Beethoven and I don't know what all."

Soon after that Olivia and I began to make love. I would never attempt to describe those acts, or even vouch for the physical delights of them (two young bodies and minds, two inexperienced women in an epoch when the names of female sexual parts could scarcely be uttered). We thought we had invented something, which I suppose was the main satisfaction of it. More like children than grownup lovers, we were extravagantly poetic in what we said during and afterward. Yet the recollection that arises after all these years is not joy but terror. I sensed danger, tried to imagine what the penalty might be. If the penalty for adultery was death by stoning, what might be the penalty for this? There could be no penalty, I told myself, because this was a passion of my own invention, unique and unexampled. I knew little of homosexuality. I had learned what Gertrude Stein had done to get herself banned from respectable libraries but thought queers were male, for the most part. A woman who wanted to love another woman must surely want to be a man. Must somehow be a failed man. Neither Olivia nor I wished to be a man, or resembled one in any respect, except in our ambitions. Indeed, she was bewilderingly heterosexual, quite at her best in a net formal and a merry widow, prancing off with a date. Even as we shut the light out and undressed, she was planning to attend several dances during Christmas season at home. Was saving her virginity for her husband. And up until now, she had said she intended to have a husband.

I told myself that Olivia and I touched each other asexually, the way my mother touched my aunt. Could this be so evil, I inquired of her, could it really ignite the rage of the dean of women? If we went arm in arm across the campus, didn't many other girls? Yes, it was thought feminine, sweet, cousinly, to walk with a friend in that way. Holding hands would have been thought odd, but not offensive. Even women, even faculty members, went arm in arm. And yet we stopped going arm in arm, out of fear. And to say that making love was merely the logical extension of going arm in arm, or of hugs and kisses, was sophistry, I knew. A love this consuming could not be legal. Regardless of my philosophizing, I had a hunch that the dean of women and Miss Ochs would be unlikely to sympathize.

When Olivia first pronounced the word "lesbian," I flinched as though from a scalpel. I pretended not to understand the term, and she explained it to me and read a few Sapphic fragments aloud. But it did not really calm me to learn that female-female love had such a long pedigree and even a body of verse to dignify it. I thought of my darling George, in trousers and riding boots on the streets of Paris, smoking a cigar, going by a man's name. It was clear, however, that she loved men — a vast number of them, in fact. Any male in Paris who'd ever penned a poem, novel, or piece of music. So many men that even if she had slept with a woman occasionally — and apparently she had — it would hardly have mattered.

Olivia began to point out pairs of female lovers in our midst. The love that dared not speak its name certainly kept its lips buttoned, at least on weekdays, but on Saturday nights it sang at the top of its voice. The tall muscular girls, the physical education majors with cropped hair, the fencers and hockey players, the swim team who went arm in arm down campus paths, also had weekend parties at the home of the chairman of the Physical Education Department, who, according to Olivia, was herself a lesbian. But it was a private club for PE majors and their dates only, and the English Department, alas, did not sanction such carryings-on or have anything comparable. Just as there was a way to get away with drinking and having sex with men — firmly forbidden — there was a way to be a lesbian. But you had to know how. You couldn't simply walk around *being* one.

English majors had afternoon teas and literary societies. In our classrooms, the bisexual urges of Byron and Shelley as well as Oscar Wilde's various activities went unmentioned. We read *The Ballad of Reading Gaol* without ever asking, or being told, why the poet had been sent to prison in the first place. In the midst of so many young women training for practical careers or planning to drop out and get married next June, we English majors were already a deviant minority, and could probably not have borne the weight of any more deviance. In this place, at this time, to be queer as well as literary and artsy and intellectual and on the dean's list and female was too volatile, too unstable, and too unthinkable a chemical mix. If this was love, I was beginning to think I should pass it up.

Nevertheless I went on, headlong, summoning up a Byronic contempt of what our classmates had begun to say of us. Olivia and I were enraptured with our music, which seemed our private preserve, and our dreams of walking among the graves of Chopin and Sand, Keats and Shelley. What did we care what Penny Elliot and an increasing number of other observers were saying about us? We relied upon the stupidity of the caretakers and watchdogs around us, and in any case were ambitious to do something so shocking that we should be forced into exile. I saw us as expatriates in Greenwich Village or, better still, Montmartre or Montparnasse. Mount of the Martyrs, Mount Parnassus. Indeed, I thought, we belonged in Paris.

But though our liaison was an *amour de tête* formed out of rebelliousness and the venerable old art-worshiping, philistine-shunning clichés that still perfumed collegiate air in the 1950s, part of what we felt was pure passion. As deep and as wracking an emotion as I have ever known. Not for the body so much as the mind. The physical part was immaterial compared with the rest of it. Olivia often said that she did not love women, could not imagine finding them attractive as a group, but she did love me. I said similar things, even proposing that we had invented a new twist on love. Tristan and Isolde, Romeo and Juliet, Julian and Vicky — except that we were women and thus more "forbidden" than they. Olivia was pleased with our creation. It underscored her superiority as an English/music double major, as a Dallas girl who was ready for anything, and as a sophisticate among the bumpkins.

Strange how all my prior training, including Sunday school, fed into this romance. If we loved each other, it was time to make a commitment. To say forever. Trained as I had been in the Baptist church, I defined "commitment" very seriously. You fell in love with Jesus, and you went down the aisle of the church in a blinding moment of commitment, made an unbreakable vow. You belonged to him forever. Once saved, forever saved. Onward, even if it meant to Gethsemane and the cross.

Thus I carefully reckoned the cost of what we were up to. The dean of women and Miss Ochs would undoubtedly discover us and throw us out of school. I would live as an outcast, a source of anguish to my parents. I'd be barred from my home, my church. I would never have children. I would never be able to make love with a man, never take the curlers out of my hair at four o'clock and cook supper in the waterless cookware, never take his khaki pants out of the dryer and smooth them out. I would never read stories to my children when they had measles, the way my mother had read to me. Ordinary love might be only a matter of cooking and cleaning and being steady, as my mother seemed to think, but as I saw it slip out of my grasp, to be replaced with a death-defying relationship, I sometimes wept at what I was doing. At last someone was in love with me, but I went from one migraine headache to another, couldn't swallow my breakfast, and was noticeably losing weight.

Sometime in early December, Olivia and I swore that we would spend our lives together. We sketched out several plans. Greenwich Village, where we'd easily find an apartment large enough to hold a grand piano for her and a writer's studio for me. Paris would come later, when one of us had become famous. (I figured, secretly, that it would be me.) *Tu es responsable de ce que tu as apprivoisé*, I told her, citing my old Saint-Exupéry maxim that you must perpetually love the creatures you have "tamed." Peace returned to my heart. I had given my word, I would stick to it. This was exactly what I had been searching for all my life — an abyss. If the dean of women stripped me of my grade points before the entire student body, all right. If Olivia and I had to do the double suicide one day, okay. If they came for us with chains and knives, wheels and racks, send them on. I was ready, eager to die. Off the balcony and under the onrushing locomotive. We had made our pact, we had drunk our potion.

At any rate, I had downed my half of it.

As the winter went on, our glittering future in Paris and New York receded and grew dim. I rose each morning in the chill of my room; instead of chattering with me about the injustice of eight o'clock classes, Penny remained silent as she unwound her hair before the mirror, donned her pink or her blue angora sweater set, and placed the chain with Ralph's high school ring, weighty as a rock, around her neck. Once dressed, I hurried to meet Olivia at the breakfast table. She and I never quarreled, never grew tired of each other's company or of our poetry and music, but our sense of triumphant superiority was fading. The friends we had scorned in our delirium and pride now scorned us.

In January, a freshman and a senior, both of them English majors like Olivia and me, fell foul of the law. They too met evenings in the library. They too kept to themselves. Though seniors were allowed in the freshman dining room, freshmen could not dine with seniors, so the senior girl came conspicuously to ours. People left them alone, made a show of not sitting at the table with them. I pitied them, suggested to Olivia that we try to join them, befriend them.

"How can we be such cowards?" I said bitterly one wet February evening as we returned from the library together in the dark. "They're being treated like dogs, shunned. They look so forlorn sitting over in that corner alone. We could at least sit at the table with them. All these proper little Christians go off to church every Sunday in their damn hats and gloves and then pass judgment on other people. Anyway," I added sardonically, "we deviants have got to stick together."

"Don't call us that. We aren't deviants. But I'm not sure we need to volunteer for rescue duty."

I reminded Olivia of what the dean of women preached in assemblies — our tradition of warmth and friendliness here, of affection and Christian kindness toward one another. "How can anybody condemn us just for being friendly?"

"Sure," Olivia said listlessly, "we can say hi. But I don't think it will do them or us any good."

And we hurried on, shivering, gloveless, too lightly dressed for the wintry rain. Then we saw them, the guilty pair, sitting in the dark on a bench beneath a cottonwood tree, just recognizable in the light from a streetlamp. I wondered if they had their arms around each other. They seemed to be clinging. Why did they sit here in the cold, rather than in a dormitory or the union or the library? They saw us too but said nothing. We stared at one another for a moment, and my good intentions froze.

A week later, like smoke curling into the night air, they vanished. The freshman girl had been in my "Survey of English Lit." class; without comment or explanation, the teacher posted a retyped version of the class roll with that one name omitted. Gossip flew. Their parents had been sent for; the girls had been forbidden to be alone in each other's presence; they had been put under the care of psychiatrists; their entire academic record, grade points and all, had been nullified and expunged — even the senior's, who would have graduated that spring. That week, on my way to the Harlan Hall laundry room in the basement, I noticed that the room where the freshman had so recently lived stood open, the fuzzy throw rugs gone, the curtains stripped from the rods, the brown metal dressers emptied. The tan linoleum floor gleamed like a hospital ward's, mopped and waxed. The word "fumigated" occurred to me. I heard that the freshman's roommate was the one who had come upon the lovers *in flagrante* in that very room. She was returning early and unannounced from an off-campus weekend. Distraught at the sight of two women beneath the bedspread, she had run screaming down the hall. The registered nurse at the infirmary had been obliged to administer a sedative to quiet the child, it was whispered. No sedatives, to be sure, were given the guilty parties.

Like thieves witnessing a hanging, Olivia and I resolved to be more careful, to return to the world of normalcy and girl talk and dormitory camaraderie. We curbed our deliberately snooty conversation about poetry and music. We attended the weekly English Department teas. I joined the literary society, and Olivia volunteered for the school orchestra. Our teachers, at least, were still kind to us. Once or twice, when Olivia got an invitation, we even went out on double dates. We went showily, letting our escorts wait in the living room for a while and then making sure the Ox saw us signing out. Surely, we thought, we had appeased the authorities.

One day in April, Olivia and I lay on a quilt in the secluded woods behind the row of freshman and sophomore dormitories. We had brought a picnic basket and a pile of books. We meant to pass the afternoon reading aloud and eating lunch. We'd skip the dining hall. We'd stay out here until dark. Our efforts at rehabilitation had mostly come to nothing — we lived as outcasts. If we sat down with other girls at a table in the dining room, they found reasons to get up and leave. Penny Elliot had begun speaking to me again as we dressed in the morning, but with a warmth I thought exaggerated. I suspected she would soon apply for permission to change roommates. When I was called before house council on this matter, I knew what I would say. Olivia and I both had our speeches ready — we were tender friends, we were being maligned, we were intellectuals hounded by the ignorant, we didn't know what we could possibly be accused of. We were shocked and hurt. I knew it was hopeless sophistry, even as I rehearsed it.

"Both nuns and mothers worship images." As I read the beloved words aloud, Olivia paused to suck some meaning from them, though neither of us really grasped Yeats's poem, no matter how often we read it. "I don't understand how the nuns got in here or what they have to do with it. My mother worships images, and it's never anything that a daughter wants to be," she said despairingly. "I try to want what my mother wants for me, and I never succeed. Do you know she has been planning my wedding since I was born? There's this dress my grandma wore. She says I must wear it."

"Never mind," I said impatiently. "Don't talk about her. Maybe next year we'll be far away from her. God, it's some advantage to be poor. No heirloom wedding gown in some box in the closet. My daddy said he hoped I would elope so he wouldn't have to pay for anything. Like he and Mama did. But we came here to forget our troubles. Go on." I was waiting for our favorite line: "O body swayed to music, O brightening glance, / How can we know the dancer from the dance?"

I didn't know what that meant either, and then I thought, how can you know the dancer from the dance? The artist from the art? The young woman declaring that she loves the man she's married to and the suicide under the train? Would I always be as I was today, glancing nervously over my shoulder lest some apparition of righteousness be emerging from the back door of Harlan Hall? I rolled over on the quilt. Even in the worst days of my Joey Cash obsession, I had not suffered like this. Oh, if only there had been a true love potion like the one Isolde had drunk, because then nobody could blame us. One of my father's supper-table maxims was that you make your bed and have to lie in it. And I had, I had. I was sleeping badly, having regular and severe migraines, no longer believed my own propaganda about the beauty of forbidden love. I did love Olivia. But our moments of joy, of hope, were often quenched by terror.

The penalties attached to illicit love now threatened to overwhelm me. The previous week I had broken down weeping in the midst of writing a French exam. The subject was *The Red and the Black*, whose hero, Julien Sorel, was about to be guillotined for acting out his passions. My teacher, suddenly merciful and concerned as I began to sob, had led me to her office, placed a box of tissues on my lap. Though it was strictly against the rules, she said she trusted me and she would allow me to return the next morning, when surely I would feel calmer, and then I could finish filling my blue book with my views on Stendhal. I was an A student and she certainly did not want me to fail my midterm. Or perhaps she had some inkling of what was upsetting me. She was elderly but did not look entirely innocent.

Olivia had finished Yeats. My turn to read. I leafed through Shelley. A fragment caught me:

Are thou pale for weariness
Of climbing heaven and gazing on the earth,
   Wandering companionless
Among the stars that have a different birth, —
And ever changing, like a joyless eye
That finds no object worth its constancy?

"Oh, it is too sad." I put my head down on the Modern Library Giant once more and wet it with my tears. These days it hardly had time to dry between anointings.

"Why are you crying?" Olivia was annoyed.

"God, why not? Why aren't you crying too? I'm certain Penny has turned us in. Don't you know what will happen? They'll call my parents, your parents. They'll throw us out of here. What will we do? I don't know where we'd get the money to go to New York, do you?"

"Oh, ye of little faith. We'll get it somehow. I don't care if we get kicked out of this ratty place. I don't need this place. There is no object in this place worthy of our constancy. Stop giving in to them. You're a crybaby."

I sat up, tried to pin my mind on the beauties of nature. The southern spring begins in February, with crocuses and forsythia, azaleas in March, and in April camellias, crepe myrtle, and roses, flashy and perfumed as streetwalkers. Apple and redbud trees in full bloom crowded the walkways; elms and oaks were in full leaf, and the grass was deep. Around our quilt wildflowers grew. A setting of pure pleasure. In the distance, right on time, the westbound freight hooted in the wind, lifting my heart, as it always had. Out, cried the locomotive. You can get out, move on down the line. I struggled to be comforted by the train whistle, the warm blowziness of spring, the birdsong, all the signs and symbols of ordinary life from which I now felt perpetually barred. The thought of cookies and sandwiches in the picnic basket made me ill. The blood vessel in my left temple began to swell and pound, and I had forgotten to take my aspirin. My mother would die if they told her! My father would never speak to me again. I put my book aside and fell to sobbing once more, and though we had sworn never to touch each other in public, I threw myself into Olivia's arms. "This will never be over. It's like being a Communist or a Jew in Germany. There's no place we can go. I bet it's like this in Greenwich Village, even. Probably the same in Paris. Why does everybody hate this sort of love so much?"

I never figured out where she came from, or how much she had heard me say, or how she managed to walk all the way from the dormitory on such silent feet. We did not even hear the customary swish of her stout, stockinged legs as they brushed together under her tight black skirt. I later wondered if she had descended from a tree, or had flown through the air. But I shall always remember looking up from Olivia's arms and into the Ox's famous brown eyes, smooth gleaming opals. She was standing directly behind us. I leapt out of Olivia's arms; we stood up, moved apart. We should never have jumped. After all, it is not against the law for one college girl to weep in the arms of another on the April grass. But it made no difference, really.

"Gather your possessions, and follow me to my office." Miss Ochs herself lay hold of the picnic basket and put my damp, beloved Keats/Shelley under her arm. She wished to speak to us about extremely serious matters; she had only herself to blame for letting things run on so long when she ought to have acted weeks ago. After she had finished with us, we were to proceed to the dean of women's office for even more serious deliberations. "She will be waiting for you when I have finished. And you can get that look off your face, miss. You know what I am referring to. Pray spare me any self-justifying backtalk. We'll be telephoning your parents sometime this evening. Girls of your type are not welcome at this college."

Thus, like many another pair of illicit lovers here and elsewhere, then and in the past, we were unmasked, exposed. We would be led to understand the wages of sin. As a well-brought-up Christian and opera lover, I was hardly surprised. It took several deliberating sessions to settle matters. We tried to deny the nocturnal visits I made to Olivia's room, but it was useless. Penny Elliot had kept a very precise little notebook of my activities. She had even listened at Olivia's door. They had everything but a wiretap. I considered telling Miss Ochs about Penny and Ralph and the condoms she kept in her dresser drawer. But there would have been no profit in it. At one point I grew so hysterical with grief and fright that I too had to be taken to the infirmary and sedated. But we avoided being expelled. Partly because one couple had been exposed so recently — after all, the dean of women did not wish to be seen as coping with an epidemic of intramural romances — and partly because our academic records were good, we were allowed to continue to the end of the term. We were never to be seen in each other's company again. I must never go into Olivia's room. We must never sit at the same table in the dining hall or the library. And yes, our parents would be informed.

Our downfall left me in a turmoil of illness and sorrow. Penny Elliot moved to a room down the hall, and I was left alone. The news traveled quickly round the school. Only a few brave souls dared say hello to me when I crossed the campus going to and from class. I tried to keep working, but had not yet learned that anguish could sometimes be tempered with hard labor. I stopped visiting the dining room and lived on Coke and potato chips and an occasional candy bar, the only food I could swallow. I lived chiefly in my room, alone. If I caught a glimpse of Olivia in the hallway or on a campus path, I took care not to make eye contact, though I often was overcome with fits of weeping afterward. We began to write letters, two or three a day, which we slipped under each other's doors late at night or mailed from the downtown post office. Lest the college postmaster be part of the dean of women's secret service, as was probably the case, we typed the envelopes and furnished them with fake return addresses. Olivia's parents came to fetch her almost every weekend now; she returned by bus on Monday mornings.

My parents turned out to be much less horrified by the news of my shameful proclivities than I had expected. They believed me, or chose to believe me, when I claimed innocence and sobbed out my story of unjust accusations and barbarous, medieval treatment. This all took place by telephone, luckily for me. They had bravely scoffed at the notion that they should come for a conference immediately. "Intense, silly girlish friendship, and they turn it into a crime," said my father. "They find two children in each other's arms on an old quilt and make a federal case of it. Meddlesome old biddies with nothing better on their minds." Nevertheless, he thought this was a very serious charge, and while he intended to send an indignant letter of protest to the dean of women, he wanted me to tell him the truth of the matter. He encouraged me to hold my head high. I continued to deny everything. Ah, I thought, when he responded sympathetically, it's only a short jump to Manhattan. My parents feel sorry for me. They'll let me go. There must be some way to get Olivia to come with me. I'll get a job, I'll work to support us both while I go to school.

Olivia's parents, however, were enraged, and took the line that I was a seducer and a pervert. They said Olivia must come home that summer, possibly to undergo psychoanalysis, which they could well afford. But when they got wind of the New York plan, they threatened to wise my parents up and to ask the dean of women to expel me summarily. In desperation, toward the end of the school year, I wrote to them. The letter, which they kept in a bank safe deposit box for many years in case it came in handy, was only recently returned to me, after so many years that if I had not exactly forgotten writing it, I had forgotten what it said. Since it could perhaps serve as a model for all such pleading, none of which ever has the least effect, I reproduce it here.

> Dear Mr. and Mrs. Fitzmorris:
>
> I know the feelings of disgust and hostility that you have for me, and you know I bear no love for you. But you have much to be said on your side. I am not asking you for approval, help, or acceptance. I only ask you to read what I have to say.
>
> I love Olivia very much. She loves me. I know you dislike hearing this. Call us crazy or reckless, but we are not deformed. The relationship we have is pure and beautiful. I cannot be ashamed of it. We know what we face better than you think. We have suffered terribly already. We are prepared to suffer still more.
>
> I know that you plan to talk to my parents. I hope you won't. They don't believe what the dean of women says, which shows their faith in me.
>
> There will come a day when there is nothing you can do to keep Olivia and me apart. You cannot keep us from loving each other, even if you separate us until we are old.
>
> We need your understanding. We have a plan for our lives, and I beg you to hear it.

They never answered but at least took no action against me. School was about to end, and what Olivia and I assured each other was a temporary separation was about to begin. The evening before we were to leave, breaking the rule of silence the dean of women had imposed upon us, Olivia and I met in the woods in back of Harlan Hall, where we'd been apprehended such a brief time before. I found her under the trees, in the twilight. She looked upset, and when I moved to take her hand, she pulled away.

"I have something sad to tell you. It will kill you, but I don't know what else to do. I am not cut out for this life," she said, or words to that effect. "This has all been a mistake. A dream. I can't fight my parents anymore. I hate them and always will. But if I promise never to see you again, they will send me out of state next year. Someplace where nobody can have heard of all this. Somewhere with a good music program. Not this stupid place."

"What about New York?" I began, unable to absorb what she had said. "What about our apartment, our jobs . . . You had thought of Juilliard . . . You said you were writing them."

"You really don't understand," she explained. "I applied to Oberlin last winter. I never told you. It's a fine music school, you know. I have been accepted. My mother is already shopping for my winter things. Gets cold up there in Ohio."

I hardly recall my reply, which in any case would have been the standard reply in such circumstances. I do recall her warning me never to write to her again. The letter I had written to her parents was completely incriminating, she reminded me; if I tried to make contact with her, her parents would send a copy of that letter to my parents. Or to my boss, if I ever got a job. Or to anyplace where it could do me harm.

"They are crazy, vindictive people," Olivia said. "I know you must almost choke just to think of them. But understand — they are my parents, and I have to depend on them. In some way they are no crazier than you are, with your talk of absolutes. Anyway, I'm not dropping out of school to go starve in some garret."

Thus did Isolde tell Tristan she was bored and to shove off and leave her to be queen of Cornwall. Thus Romeo, instead of plunging the dagger in his heart, sighed with relief and backed out of the Capulet tomb, wondering what his old girlfriends were up to. Vicky told Julian that she had a job with a ballet company, and if he didn't like it, he could file for divorce.

I reeled at first as if hit by an automobile, my body whirling high in the air with every bone dislocated. It was a full-strength dose of love's anguish, of betrayal and guilt. On the way home, in the back seat of my parents' Dodge, I could not speak. At home, the pain was physical, producing stomach cramps and migraines. I wept at all hours of the night. I was anorectic, and acquired a hollow-eyed, tubercular, skeletal aspect over the summer, lost ten or fifteen pounds. I never smiled. Unacquainted with any tenets of psychiatry and unwilling to believe this was anything but another difficult late-teenage phase, my mother sighed over me, urged me to blow my nose and straighten up my face. Gingerly she and my father probed for the true cause of my anguish, but always retreated when I stubbornly refused to talk. Mostly my mother offered me milkshakes (two raw eggs and lots of sugar), which I sometimes drank. She insisted that I take a job for the summer. I would need the money, and she thought the distraction would be good for me. So I stood behind the counter at a hardware store eight hours a day, which indeed was good for me. My parents refrained from ridiculing my tearful requests to be allowed to depart for Paris alone, or for New York. But in the end my father insisted I stay where I was rather than transfer. "Show them what you're made of," he advised. "Don't run away."

Sometime in July my appetite returned. I began sampling and then actually eating the bacon and eggs my mother set in front of me each morning and the ice cream scooped onto her delicious apple pies. My clothes still hung on me, and my relatives told me I was too skinny to attract a man, but I slept long hours and was once more able to read. That had somehow been the worst of it, the way words melted together on the page, the letters upside down and senseless. Now I could once more withstand the terrible melancholy of reading the Romantic poets. I had sworn never to listen to Chopin again, but one day that summer I did.

I even managed to go to bed with a man and acquaint myself, for the very first time, with the pleasures of heterosexual sex, and somewhat to my astonishment, they proved intensely pleasurable. The man who demonstrated this to me was almost the ideal initiator for a person of my temperament and experience. The son of the man who owned the hardware store I worked in, he was twenty years my senior, a veteran of World War II, divorced. He too knew what it was like to be unable to sleep or eat because of a losing hand at love's poker table. He worked in the hardware store too, being at the moment out of a job, out of ideas for what to do next. He made time to talk with me, since we were seldom very busy. One evening after work he invited me home for lemonade and a sandwich. I walked with him to the small apartment where he lived, and in a fit of trust, at his tiny kitchen table, confessed to him what I could never have said to my father: not only that I had a broken heart but exactly who had broken it and under what circumstances. I expected him to show me immediately to the door, but he hardly blinked.

"Ah, yes," he said. "I can understand that. I know you expect me to be shocked, but I've seen men who loved men and women who loved women. I love women well enough that I've always wondered why they didn't just fall in love with one another. What would be so odd about that? After all, they are invariably so much nicer to look at than us men." He kissed me gently, and in the conversation that followed he went on to state that the dean of women and Miss Ochs and Olivia's parents were the true perverts in the situation, or maybe just idiots. It was unfair and barbarous to deal with a daughter in this manner, or students whose welfare you were charged with. Furthermore, if I'd like to try making love with a man, just to see what it was like, he'd be glad to show me how. I was under no obligation to return for seconds, he assured me. He did not expect me to become his girlfriend. Nor was he trying to reform me. I was too young and inexperienced to need reforming, he thought, and in any case, I had the right to do as I chose. If I wanted to love women all my life, that was okay with him. He was all for it. But unless I had an absolute aversion to the idea, maybe I should try it with a man. He just didn't want me to go on thinking, as I appeared to think, that no one, male or female, would ever desire me again. He thought my head was too full of guilt, and he wanted to show me that sex actually could be quite comforting. It didn't have to leave you broken in half. They didn't always send a lynching party. Furthermore, he assured me, he possessed the means to make sure I did not become pregnant. He did not want me running any risks on his behalf.

I shall always remember him gratefully, tenderly. I suppose I have sought him — his forgiving qualities, his adoration, his skill in evoking my responses, his naive belief in the beneficence and indeed innocence of sexual love, its comforting and reassuring aspects, its potential for joy — in every man since. He was only an episode, but an episode of sanity, an interlude of affection, in my trajectory toward the perfect passion, the love that I intended to craft for myself. His experiment quieted me, satisfied me, gave me something positive to remember, though I had no intention of pausing to become his true love or of allowing him to become mine. He was an old man, I thought, almost contemptuously, not realizing that his age gave him the qualities as a lover that I liked. He may have suffered over me when I returned to school: the letters that he wrote that year spoke of longing, of love that asked nothing in return. But I eventually discarded him with the casual, self-serving cruelty of one who was only beginning to invent her life. Though the dramas I had written for myself and Olivia never materialized, except the bitter sample of the love-death she concocted for me, I did finish my college education without further scandal. Soon afterward I won a scholarship for study abroad and got my chance at Paris.

8

TO THE FOUNTAIN

A la claire fontaine
M'en allant promener
J'ai trouvé l'eau si belle
Que je m'y suis baignée.

Il y a longtemps que je t'aime,
jamais je ne t'oublierais.

~

Chancing to pass a fountain
as I went on my way,
I bathed in its pure water,
Clear as a summer day.

I've always loved you, dearest,
Never could I forget.

— *old French song*

A scholarship student with one warm coat and two pairs of sensible shoes, I traveled to France by boat, in 1957, dreading and yearning to reach my destination. The problem was that I must now express my wishes and needs in French, an act fraught with risk outside the safety of the classroom. As a student, I'd seldom spoken French or been asked to read it aloud. The texts had lain voicelessly on the page like hieroglyphs on a stone tablet. Now I had to use the language that had served as my private code, my doorway to secret passageways of love and rebellion, my bulwark against banalities uttered in English. As was plain to all the world, French was the language of love — not because one uttered sweet nothings in French but because, as I could already see, it functioned like a sculptor's tool in describing states of loving. Yet in my mouth, so far, this great instrument was dull and mostly nonfunctional.

I couldn't manage more than a choked *"Vraiment?"* to the kindly steward in the tourist-class dining room who assured me, in his native tongue, that I might indeed eat *la croûte* of the Camembert, though not of other cheeses. I got the drift but could not reply or even sample the cheese — with or without its rind — because my mouth was glued shut with terror. What if he didn't understand me? What if I should seem a fool? My tongue went into spasm trying to leap from verb to direct object, or attempting to select the right gender. *Un verre* or *une?*

Apart from conducting its business in French, tourist class on the French Line was unimaginably luxurious, at least to me. My cabin was on level C, barely above the water line. Yet a smiling cabin steward in a white jacket answered my every question, and assured me that *"les jeunes filles charmantes, comme vous êtes, mademoiselle,"* could take advantage of the first-class swimming pool without anyone in the least objecting. (Unaware that ships could have swimming pools, I had not packed a bathing suit.) Each afternoon as I swung my legs onto my deck chair, the deck steward advanced to tuck a blanket round my feet. A chime sounded at appointed hours, announcing ample lunches and five-course dinners. With wine. And no bill to pay at the end, and then the chime called us to a film or other form of entertainment for which one need never purchase a ticket. There were no lessons to learn, no dishes to wash. I was an all-too-easy mark for the notion of pleasure, leisure, comfort. Ah, if only I had a lover! Ah, but in just a few days I would disembark in a country where everybody spoke in syllabic tangles and no chime rang for meals!

Like housework after the honeymoon, reality commenced in the confusion of the pier at Le Havre, the chill aboard the boat-train into which I was shunted like baggage, unsure whether I was headed for Paris or elsewhere. Grim little towns rolled past the window — this was Normandy? This shabby industrial landscape was France? — and then, as I struggled out of the Gare du Nord with my suitcases, mist turned to rain. My next stop, after a couple of hours wandering around the *métro* — I got lost in the world's most logical subway system — was the Fondation des Etats-Unis at the Cité Universitaire, in the southeast quadrant of Paris, a dormitory where I would stay for two weeks of orientation. The desk clerk handed me a letter from my parents, dated the day of my departure. In the dim light, I slit open the flaps of the aerogram, somehow not destroying the flimsy paper. One sentence leapt out: "Your daddy will be thinking of you out on that big ocean." And from Mother: "I sure hope, honey, you haven't come down with the flu." Thank God they were four thousand miles away! My quarters were a monastic cell with bed. No shag rugs and matching curtains, no housemother checking rooms, and no hot water in the showers. A bare room, a crust of bread: these were what I wanted.

Though I planned to enroll at the University of Paris, as my grant-in-aid required me to do, I had come to France, of course, to find love. Maybe I could acquire loose morals here, and learn to be happy with them. I'd heard that French women were easy (a myth, I soon found out) and that French men were utterly casual about adultery (another myth). But I did not quest for casual love but for the sort that Frédéric and George had known. Or perhaps they hadn't known it. Still, because of what I heard in his music, I was not ready to admit that George Sand had merely acted as his mama. Or that while the two of them sojourned in Majorca, he had been coughing too hard to make love. Or that after they had lived together for years and quarreled daily, she had grown to hate him so much that she hadn't even rushed to his deathbed or bothered to visit his grave.

I had come, at least on paper, on a halfway legitimate pretext — to study Stendhal, who had fled his native Grenoble, who hated his provincial origins. I was filled with the sort of pas-

sionate ambition that Stendhal's hero Julien Sorel had died for
— I would be better than my times, better than my origins,
than myself.

I wanted nothing further to do with Gertrude Stein's brand
of love, though I was glad enough that lesbians and pederasts
could exist in Paris. But where were they? You didn't see them
on the streets, or at the University of Paris. Indeed, French
women, casually observed, were the most intensely and sub-
missively feminine I had ever seen, outdistancing American
women and certainly me in their passion for dress, nylon stockings, and makeup, their obsession with womanliness. I'd had
vague visions of female French intellectuals wreathed in cigarette smoke and all done up in black. But such details as my
short hair and flat shoes and black stockings, rather than tag-
ging me as an intellectual, marked me instantly as non-French
and unfeminine. How lovely they were on the streets, those
French women, even the students in their cheap coats and shoes
and sheer nylons. My sense of being up against some superior
sort of femininity filled me with determination to do the most
womanly thing I could think of — go to bed with an attractive
man, a Frenchman, I hoped. Besides making love, he and I
would speak French. I would grow fluent in all things. When in
due course he introduced me to Maman, she would mistake me
for a French girl. She would be *enchantée*.

Then too, now that I was twenty-one, I had heard sophisticated people talk about the free, wild, proletarian love pro-
claimed by Henry Miller and D. H. Lawrence, love with "fuck"
and "cunt" and "cock" attached to it — words I dared not even
whisper. Writers who used such language had been banned by
court order in my native land. The French found our legalistic
prudery silly, as well they might. Though I feared and dreaded
any activity that could be called fucking, I was deeply curious
about that kind of love, the kind that didn't really count as love
— accompanied by grunts, bathed in sweat, bestial, naked.

As always, some other kind of love drew me, one that had

nothing to do with physicality, the love implicit for me in French syntax, in the language itself, in the way French writers took over your mind like aliens from outer space and thought your thoughts for you, radical thoughts about sex, about freedom, about truth and justice, thoughts you could never have fabricated yourself. And yet, thirsting for all this otherness, I almost instantly took up with two fellow lonely Americans, Bill James (dark, compact, his gravitational center close to the ground) and Henry Robinson (tall, red-haired, and as knobby and angular as a grasshopper). Both were letting their beards grow. The three of us met at orientation, conducted in one of the amphitheaters of the Sorbonne, where they rescued me from drowning.

I had expected the Sorbonne to be something grand and colonnaded, with a portico, on the order of the average American university, but once I managed to find it, it looked puzzlingly like a church, and then off to the side of the church was simply a door, like any other, in the gray-brown city walls, and the door led into a cobblestone courtyard, as if it were a secret, ecclesiastical place rather than a great public university. I could see that the paving stones had been polished by the boots of thousands, perhaps millions of students. Joachim du Bellay and a dozen others from my literature books — Pascal, Claudel, Sartre, Simone de Beauvoir. Had Abelard and Heloise passed this way before they cut off his testicles? (Oh, poor souls! How I did pity them! The price of love was always too damned high. Or was it?) My Stendhal had not passed this door, I supposed, and neither had George Sand, but Proust? I'd no idea, but French culture rose in all its glory as I crossed the pavement and threatened to engulf me like a whale seining a bit of algae into its gullet. Terrified, almost weeping, I stumbled into the wrong classroom, a vast, barnlike chamber with graduated rows of seats and a faded mural behind the professorial podium. It was called the Salle Descartes, crushing in its antiquity and dignity. Realizing quickly that I was in the wrong place, I fled, climbing over knees and feet to the accompaniment of snickers and an annoyed comment from the lectern that I did not quite catch.

By the time I found the right *salle,* I had missed most of orientation, including instructions on how to get a card for the student restaurant and how to locate permanent lodgings. I fell into despair. What should I do? Nobody here or anywhere else could understand anything I said. Strangers arrogantly answered my French with English. I wanted to go home. As these thoughts passed through my head, Bill and Henry materialized on either side of me, stubbly and unshaven. They explained that you needed to register at the police station, you needed a photo to get your student card, that the government restaurant for students was the best cheap place to eat, that there were a few hotels in the Latin Quarter where one could live, bedbugless, for about a dollar and a half a day.

They helped me locate a hotel room, on rue Casimir Delavigne, in the heart of the Quartier Latin, where they also lived. A day or two later, they helped transport my luggage by *métro* from the cell temporarily assigned me at the Cité Universitaire. Now I had a home, a permanent address in the Latin Quarter, even a phone number, though people hardly made transatlantic phone calls except in case of death. My room was five flights up, another cell with a single bed and a sink, a chest of drawers but no closet, and the toilet down a long hallway illuminated by a light that shut itself off after thirty seconds (you had to run). But my window was an enormous casement facing south, and light occasionally poured through the ragged lace curtain.

I promised myself to quit clinging to Bill and Henry as soon as I was better integrated into French student life, but for now we met each afternoon in a café on the boulevard St.-Michel, not far from the Sorbonne. Bill James, an intellectual who had sprung up, like an orchid amid cornstalks, on the Great Plains, had a face as square as the map of Nebraska, gray eyes, heavy glasses, flat black hair, and an unalterable pallor. His hands shook slightly, as if he expected at any moment to be dragged away by the police. Henry Robinson, of Chicago, had brown eyes and seemed never to find room anywhere for his long arms and legs. But he was kindhearted, and already smoked French cigarettes and called for *un demi* when he wanted a beer. (I had switched to Gauloises too; *américaines* cost double. And blond tobacco had some unspecified moral taint that I wanted to avoid.) Both Bill and Henry had come to Paris on scholarship, as I had. Bill had already been admitted to the Ph.D. program at Princeton for the next year. Henry planned to enter corporate life — maybe work for a firm that did business in France, an ambition that I privately thought sordid.

And yet his mouth was delectable with the auburn thatch around it, like that of a youthful Norseman about to cross the Channel and subdue the Anglo-Saxons. He thirsted for high culture, as did I. (In his pocket he carried a list of Paris museums. He planned to visit every one.) And he had a streak of gaiety — in spite of some underlying timidity, some absolute refusal to connect. A man in hiding. Though I did not think of it, he was in some way the reincarnation of Joey Cash — delicate but unexceptional, the sort of man I could take home to my mother and father with a happy heart. They would like him. Yes, they would. Robinson was the right sort of name. I could see him shaking hands with my father. He was hardly the man I'd dreamed of. But I mustn't rule him out.

I thought that surely, with an address in the student quarter, I would become more Parisian. But a month went by and I was still a ghost, my comings and goings unremarked by anyone at the Sorbonne except Bill and Henry. The professors whose lectures I attended lacked any intention, or possibility, of learning my name, since they never took attendance or looked up from their lecture notes. If you wished to learn anything, it was up to you. Though I was surrounded by thin, ill-clad, handsome

Frenchmen in my class on Stendhal, hardly a one ever noticed me or even exchanged *bonjour*. Like the prof, they were blind to me. Was I here at all?

"You been to class?" Bill would ask when at two in the afternoon I would arrive at our table. Palms upward, eyes rolling, I would do my French shrug. *"Eh b'en, mon vieux, penses-tu!"* He would laugh, tucking his thoroughly read copy of *Le Monde* under his stack of books. He not only attended lectures but read one or two books a day, so something new was always on the table — Abbé Prévost, Laclos, Huysmans, Zola, Gérard de Nerval. His intention was to read the entire *Comédie humaine*, and he was ten novels into it. The only Balzac I had read, besides the *Contes drolatiques* (in cleaned-up English) of my childhood, was *Le père Goriot*, and I hadn't much liked it.

Bill also knew all about Stendhal, astonishing things I had never dreamed of. "He was a fat bald little man who fell in love with lots of women, but they never loved him. It was always from a distance. Also he wore a corset. You should read his essay on love. Yes, you should definitely read it. He talks about something called crystallization — that's when you fall so much in love you think the person you love is perfect. It's like salt crystallizing on a tree branch abandoned in a salt mine. That's passion when it is perfected. You don't need any response. What you have is this crystallization. It's in your own head, which is why you don't need any response." His anxious eyes would grow cheery as he explained the Stendhalian philosophy of eros. He would smile, wave his cigarette in the air. The waiter would arrive about then with my breakfast — bread, a *café crème*, and a pot of jam.

"Naturally," I retorted, "a Frenchman would think of passion as something crystallizing on a branch in a salt mine. How could you have love without a response?"

"Well, it happens all the time. You should read what he says. Also, there are better novels than *The Red and the Black*. Better novelists than Stendhal. You could read Flaubert. Emma Bovary is more interesting than Julien, more heroic. Heroism isn't just assaulting the world the way Julien did. Emma was married to an unbearable man, and she took lovers. A married woman who takes lovers may be the ultimate revolutionary. The only problem is that adultery for women is so often fatal."

How would he know? I would sip my coffee, think of ordering a cognac for my Gauloises Bleues cough later on in the afternoon. The rain, never letting up all winter, would course down the plate-glass window, sealing us off from the foot traffic and dripping umbrellas on the sidewalk, the gray tin *deux-chevaux* and scooters clashing on the boulevard, polluting the air with lead. And then Henry would arrive, his raincoat and his red hair dripping, and call for a coffee, and amid cigarette fumes and the scent of damp hair and wet shoe leather, the three of us would pass the afternoon. We'd read Bill's copy of *Le Monde* and use his Swiss Army knife to slit the pages of our newly purchased NRF and Classiques Garnier editions. Bill advised us to save our money for just one or two of the fine leather-bound Pléiades texts, whose silky pages did not need to be cut apart, treasures we could carry home and keep forever. We checked *Le Figaro* for the plays and movies we could barely afford to see, and I took to buying *Le Canard enchaîné*, because Bill actually appeared to understand the jokes and political satire and would sometimes decipher them.

Surely there were no more devoted slaves of France than we, Christians come at last to Bethlehem, praying only to be accepted into some inner circle of our imaginings — Bill as a brilliant young American scholar among his French professors, Henry by some beautiful French girl, and me by nearly anybody as long as he was French. As the weeks went on, the countenances of my companions grew hairier. Though penis envy was not among my emotional disabilities, I did envy my friends their beards. How convenient to be able to grow one's own disguise. But rather than conferring Gallic cachet, the facial hair only emphasized what their wearers wished to disguise: Bill's gray eyes grew more vulnerable above his bushy jaw, while Henry's whiskers, now thick, ceased lending him a Viking aspect and instead gave him the solemn, seedy look of a tintype Civil War general.

As soon as I was settled on rue Casimir Delavigne, I set about an errand that had been uppermost in my mind from the moment I set sail from New York Harbor. I purchased a work "not to be introduced into the British Empire or the United States," according to the subscript on the title page, *Lady Chatterley's Lover.* Wrapped in the bedclothes against the subfreezing temperature of my room, warming first my right, then my left hand beneath my buttocks, trying not to smoke because then both hands had to be uncovered and thus both would turn blue instead of only one, I read this book as thirstily as I had gone through Freud a few years earlier, or the biography of George Sand. This was different from anything I had ever known. All my ideas about love had been wrong, wrong, wrong. I had been in Clifford Chatterley's camp. A prude. But where I wanted to be was out in the woods like Constance Chatterley and her gamekeeper-lover, Oliver Mellors. I saw that it was wrong to fear becoming pregnant or being ejected from school or shocking your parents. To make it into Mellors's cabin, you needed to turn your back on the unnatural, industrial world, the sort of world that America unfortunately represented, which was crushing the life out of us all. You had to get over your class prejudices (or at least admit how decadent the upper crust had become) and most of all consider the rewards of physical love rather than the penalties. Panting, and deeply regretting my errors, I read and reread:

> He too had bared the front part of his body and she felt his
> naked flesh against her as he came in to her. For a moment he

was still inside her, turgid there and quivering. Then as he began to move, in the sudden helpless orgasm, there awoke in her new strange thrills rippling inside her. Rippling, rippling, rippling, like a flapping overlapping of soft flames, soft as feathers, running to points of brilliance, exquisite, exquisite and melting her all molten inside. It was like bells rippling up and up to a culmination. She lay unconscious of the wild little cries she uttered at the last.

Nothing in my limited experience had ever approached that — no soft flames, no flapping, and no feathers inside or out. My one experience with a man had been sweet, even memorable. But his patience, not my passion, had carried us through. As for Olivia, what we had thought of at the time as highly original, daring lovemaking had simply been the deep affection of two timid adolescents, an episode I wanted to forget. Here in the city of Gide, far from small-minded America, D. H. Lawrence made me ashamed of what I had done. What, I wondered, would Oliver Mellors have said about lesbians? Well, no one need ever know. (After all, that's what it meant to study abroad. You fabricated a new identity.) What would Mellors have said about Stendhal's kind of love, which took place at a distance, entirely in the mind, and grew ever more piercing precisely because it did not result in couplings and inner thrills?

In spite of my evening with the gentle lover who had relieved me of my virginity, I did not feel relieved of it. Was there such a thing as ineffaceable virginity? He had been adoring, had most considerately insisted on a condom, but he had not turned me completely molten inside. No bells had rippled up. I had not been overwhelmed at the sight of his body — a little embarrassed, actually, ignorant of what I had to do. I lost heart at times, secretly wished to stop, was tight and unyielding even after I sincerely wished to yield, though I did eventually experience pleasure and what I imagined was an orgasm only now I wasn't sure, it was surely because he was so romantically thrilled with me. My youth must have captivated him, for it certainly could not have been my talent as a lover.

I adored the way Lawrence/Mellors talked of cocks, gave his penis a name. I loved the way Connie decked it with flowers, worshiped it. Nevertheless, out of this reddish pink organ, decked in posies and nicknamed John Thomas, came the seed that turned you into a mother. Lady Chatterley didn't mind that — why should she? She had no money problems and no anxious mama and papa in the background. I minded.

I gave some thought to Lawrence's idea that if you hadn't had a proper orgasm, it gave you a raw look, the way *Seventeen* used to say that not eating a proper diet dulled your hair. Thinking about this, I got up one evening, crossed the room wrapped in the bedclothes, and inspected myself in the tiny yellowed mirror above my sink. I had a very raw look, exacerbated by French stinginess when it came to central heating, and I wanted to rid myself of rawness. I thought of Henry Robinson. At least I saw him frequently. I didn't have to go out and find him. I was afraid to wait much longer. How many more years could elapse before I achieved the sort of physical passion that ought to accompany the obsessive attachments I had already mastered? What if I withered up, and my rawness turned to wrinkles? Henry at least was available.

Bill James, for all the isolation of his spirit, required our company. He preferred the two of us, apparently, but either of us would do. Though Henry occasionally failed to show up for dinner at the student restaurant, Bill would always be there, valiantly holding a place for me in the crushing, contentious line of ravenous young people, ignoring the catcalls as he tucked me in front of him and put a tray into my hands. Then there I would be, picking at my plate of soggy pasta in the company of the wrong man. Rather than maneuvering for an afternoon or evening alone with me, Henry was increasingly opting out of the trio entirely. He had work to do, he said. He actually meant to write a paper about the Marshall plan and France. I suspected that his work also involved ingratiating himself with some pretty French girl.

But in the thin and unwonted sunshine of an occasional December afternoon, Henry and I would abandon Bill to his books and his *café filtre* and walk from bridge to bridge along the Seine, as Americans have always done, crisscrossing the river, admiring the statuary, believing against all evidence that these lovely old precincts express the essence of French life, failing to notice the snarled traffic and the dog leavings underfoot, not imagining what life might be like for Parisians outside the *beaux quartiers*. For us, the ancient palaces of Paris rising on either side of the river, this perfect cityscape crafted by French hands, was more beautiful than the Grand Canyon or the Rocky Mountains.

As Henry and I walked the streets of the Ile St.-Louis, the Ile de la Cité, where Paris was invented, the moated islands where the city was founded — Lutetia, where the first French dug in against the barbarians — I talked incessantly, hoping to explain the ideas that flitted through my head. Hoping that Henry would see what I saw, that he would love me for my words. I was moved to tears at the sight of houses built while North America was a wilderness, of streets that had wobbled their narrow cobblestone way under the shoe soles of generations when my natal village had been a forest. I wanted to touch this seductive grit, imagining that it contained the lint from Rabelais's cloak, the dust from Molière's shoes, the deposit of filth from George Sand's carriage wheels, the ashes of her cigar, endearing, beguiling dirt. I would lurk around doorways in the rue de Seine and on the quai St.-Michel, where I knew George had lived after escaping her husband and her house in the country, where she had begun to write and become the most sought-after woman in Paris. I half expected her to appear and speak to me. Guidebook in hand, I rode the *métro* to Montmartre and tracked down the square d'Orléans, far up a sheer hillside, where she had lived when Chopin was her lover. I had to restrain myself from kissing the threshold where their feet must surely have trod. I stood gazing at the shuttered casements that had no doubt hidden their embraces, half expecting the lamps to be lighted at dusk and the lovers to appear. Henry indulged me in these archaeological expeditions, toiling upward with me out of Montmartre *métro* stations deep as mines, the two of us breathless as pilgrims after the thousands of steps, obliged to sit down before proceeding. But sometimes he said, "You're crazy, Bébé," using a nickname he'd recently picked for me.

One evening, as the mist rose from the Seine, we saw a man and woman kissing on the quai, lip to lip, body to body, the way lovers did in those black-and-white French photographs on posters, Brassaï, Doisneau, those great penetrating Gallic eyes, skillfully capturing those lovers, who were so artless, so heedless of the camera lens! And in the background, in my head, perpetually wheezing onward, an accordion and the voice of Georges Brassens or Yves Montand, their *r*'s rolling off their tongues in the southern way, extolling the simple men and women who kissed on the public benches. *Ah, très sympa'!* Yes, this was the way it was in Paris, thought I meltingly, ever unmindful that I was responding to propaganda rather than life. Why was love so simple, so easy for the French, I wondered, and so difficult for me? Why could I not just go to bed with this man and not worry about anything? Be a total, natural woman.

"There they are, *les amants de Paris*," I told Henry, pointing. "We should get Edith Piaf to come and serenade them." He replied that it was a prostitute and her mark and told me not to get too dewy-eyed about it. We walked on to the right bank and then, as night fell, returned to the Latin Quarter through the Ile St.-Louis, crossing the pont Louis Philippe (citizen king, Revolution of 1848, I informed Henry somewhat bitterly, not caring if he thought I was playing Miss A-Student or not). Perhaps because we were arm in arm, or because we were shivering in the chill, or perhaps because he could not keep from granting me my dearest wish, Henry kissed me, first gently and then like a lover, his mouth sweet and wet, his beard silky. I responded eagerly, trembling inside my raincoat and layers of woolens, overwhelmed with sexual need. I would have lain down on the bridge for him. I could have made love standing up. I was dizzy with love or what I took to be love. This time I would not be afraid, I would helplessly surrender. I would not count up to see whether it was the fertile time of the month or ask him if he had a rubber. Paris, D. H. Lawrence, and my own hormones said I must have Henry.

But he disentangled himself from my arms, avoiding my eyes. "I probably shouldn't have done that," he muttered. Stunned, I could not find the words to point out that I too had kissed; it had not been his mistake entirely.

"Don't set too much store by what I did. Don't think about it too much. I like you a lot, *chérie*. But I'm not ready for anything major. You know, you're just so intense." He was annoyed. I did not take his arm again. Intense, dammit. Yes, I was intense. Was intensity a disadvantage? Fog was settling on the river now, and we were too late to eat dinner at the student restaurant. I could ill afford a sandwich and a beer. We hurried on through the mist, one hunger suddenly more urgent than the other, and neither to be satisfied that evening.

By January I had not gotten Henry or anyone else into my bed. Only once daily, around noon, did the proprietor of my hotel send up any heat, and I had taken to sleeping in long underwear, a nightcap, wool socks, and gloves. Though the management of my hotel forbade any sort of electrical appliance, I harbored a tiny electric coil that hooked over the edge of a cup and was capable of heating enough water to make instant coffee and to defrost my toothbrush, which tended to freeze overnight. Shortly after my arrival, the desk clerk had actually searched my room and had confiscated my travel iron, which he triumphantly flourished in my face as I passed the desk that evening. *"C'est défendu, vous le savez bien,"* he spouted, while I tried to find the words for "illegal search and seizure." He then began muttering about the cost of electricity and the profligacy of Americans, who did not know the value of money, lived only to waste resources, ought to return to their own country, and so on. Luckily for me, he had overlooked my little electric coil.

As the months went on, becoming French seemed less and less a possibility. I had a few French acquaintances by now, but the wall was impenetrable. My presence in France, according to the grantors of my stipend, was meant to foster international understanding; they should have sent me to some other country. Where was the kind family I had imagined would befriend me? The delightful young man who would help me improve my French? The union between me and France was never going to be celebrated.

I had discovered a phenomenon I could not have imagined — French contempt for Americans. They were not eager to welcome us. We were "Amerloques," racist, commercial, spoiled, materialistic, uncultured, and ultimately a threat to European civilization. Being female did not excuse one from the general category. Indeed, being a female student, with pretensions to the intellectual life, only made things worse. Once, looking at the movie listings, I was briefly cheered to see that a film called *La belle américaine* had opened; then I learned that the beautiful American in question was an imported car.

The news from home that year was that an army stood guard at Central High School in Little Rock, Arkansas, in order to keep white people — my people — from attacking a few black youngsters, whom the soldiers had to escort into school. One morning, in a preamble to his lecture, my Stendhal professor alluded to this, spoke his mind about American racism. I shrank inside my coat, stared at the floor. I wanted a chance to explain that I was no part of what was happening in Little Rock, that I hated it as much as he did. After that, I was unable to hear anything he said about Stendhal. I still yearned to conform to French ideals, to let them know I too haughtily disapproved of my country. I counted myself an existentialist. I could speak knowledgeably of anomie, *la nausée, engagement*. I shifted easily from phrase to slogan. "Man is condemned to be free," Sartre had written, a statement that seemed as apt to me as "Workers of the world, unite" had a few years earlier. I intended to read Sartre's *L'être et le néant* and had already got through the first few pages. Albert Camus loomed as the new conscience of France: I was halfway through *La peste*. America, my professor had said, was an arrogant colonial power with no conscience. But I believed I had one.

At the same time, *Paix en Algérie* was scrawled on every wall. Dien Bien Phu had fallen four years earlier, in 1954, and the French had abandoned Vietnam to the United States and its growing handful of "advisers," though few people knew it yet. The final French colonial war was under way just across the Mediterranean. Young men were being drafted, trained, packed off to kill rebellious Muslims. French Resistance heroes who had fought the Gestapo fifteen years earlier were now using Gestapo methods to torture Algerians. In one of my occasional, painful conversations with French students, a fellow I'd only just met flung Arkansas at me, and I instantly flung Algeria back at him. This proved to be a mistake. Not only had I made a grotesque grammatical error, so that I was obliged to repeat what I had said and finally to lapse into English, but then he questioned me intently about Julius and Ethel Rosenberg, falsely accused of treason by the American right wing, tried and sentenced unfairly, he said, officially murdered as Soviet spies — yes, murdered. Plus they were Jewish. Why had I not renounced my citizenship the day they were executed? He would have done so. Through some feat of logic I could not follow, he and his friends were not personally responsible for Algeria but I was personally responsible for the Rosenbergs. I hadn't been old enough to vote when the Rosenbergs were electrocuted. I believed with all my heart that American schools ought to be integrated and that racial discrimination should end right now. I thought executing the Rosenbergs had been an unpardonable crime. I believed with Camus that capital punishment itself was a crime. This got me nowhere with the French.

And now, to my displeasure, Henry had begun keeping company with thin, dark Marta from Frankfurt, who looked more Spanish than German and began accompanying Henry to the café every afternoon. She spoke correct, beautiful, slightly accented French, far superior to mine, and had a great deal to say about sewing. She made all her own dresses, had brought her own sewing machine to Paris. Sometimes she sat doing some needlework — a hem, a row of buttons. Henry would smile protectively at her gleaming black head, bent over thimble and needle. I could sew, myself, but I had not come to Paris to practice domestic arts. Henry stopped meeting Bill and me for dinner. I wondered where he and Marta were having their supper. Maybe she cooked for him, little hausfrau!

But sometimes Marta failed to appear, and our trio would once more share a baguette and cheese and join the rowdy line for cheap student tickets at the Comédie-Française, scrambling up the narrow stairs, grabbing the best seats we could find in *paradis*, just like the music students at the beginning of *The Red Shoes*, noisy, ragged, caring only for Art. (The plans I had made long before with Olivia would emerge like the after-effects of pneumonia, but I would carefully repress them.) Though the Comédie was staid and threadbare in those years, I loved it, for the classic French theater came far more easily to my ears than the French of films or the street. Under Bill's guidance, I soon became obsessed with Racine — the purity of his tragedy, the keen suffering of his heroes and heroines, the certainty of death.

Phaedra in particular drew me, the mythic princess from Crete, daughter of Minos and Pasiphaë (she who invented a machine that enabled her to have intercourse with a bull). Married to Theseus, a strapping army man, a certified Athenian hero who had slain the Minotaur, the very George Patton of his day, Phaedra falls in love with Hippolytus, her own step-son, Theseus's offspring by an Amazon queen he had loved and left. Phaedra's love is more damnable by far than the love of Isolde and Tristan or Juliet and Romeo. At least none of my earlier role models had committed incest. Not that Phaedra ever gets within kissing distance of Hippolytus — no. She simply throws herself feet first into that emotional gristmill I fancied I understood myself. Then she swallows poison. Ah, poison! Thou shalt not commit adultery, thou shalt not lust even in thy heart.

But after these excursions, Henry often made some joking remark about not having understood a word and then returned to Marta. I was left to drink medicinal tea with Bill, as January drizzled toward February and Bill expounded on such subjects as the imitation of reality in Western lit. or made up such maxims as "The only poets we really love are those who have confronted the anguish we ourselves know." Facing him glumly across the table, half asleep, I tried to calculate what anguish he might mean. What was that peculiar pain in his eyes, and why did he seem never to touch another human, not even to shake hands, and why did he never respond to my sometimes idly seductive remarks and movements?

One evening I decided to let him in on one of my small fantasies — a ritual I had devised on certain evenings alone. Crossing from the left bank to the Ile de la Cité, I would come to a certain four-story house where every night the topmost windows were brilliantly lit. Standing below it, I could see only the ceiling and a pair of sconces against the far wall, but I was certain that a fire crackled in the grate, a bottle of red wine was on the table, bread in a basket, and maybe a roast chicken on a platter. (Chronically hungry, I usually allowed myself a plate of cheese and assorted pastries too.) It would be mine one day. Seated on the hearth rug was a man — still faceless in my fantasy, still formless. I would pace the street, alone, staring up at the light.

I took Bill's arm, guided him to the very street, afraid that the apartment on the top floor would be dark tonight, and without the lights glowing up there, it wasn't much of a fantasy. But everything was just as I wished it.

"There," I said. "That's my future address. I wouldn't tell this to anybody but you. I'm going to live in that house one day with my lover and be a writer."

Bill laughed. "A nice fantasy. A very nice dream indeed. I'd like to come and visit you there. The two of you, of course. But is it the dream of a writer? Why must you always have the lover in the picture? Writing seems to me to be a lonely business. Maybe it wouldn't be lonely for you."

My French gradually improved, becoming almost fluent, though still marred by error and my ineradicable American accent, and as if that marked the crumbling of some barrier for me, I had less trouble finding male companions, though French ones remained beyond my grasp. Sometimes a man called Richard Van showed up at the café. He told me right off that a story of his had appeared in the *Paris Review*. He mused from time to time about existential aspects of fly-fishing, and in the spring he intended to be at Pamplona for the running of the bulls. He expounded on the prerogatives of the artist. A man had to be self-centered in order to create art. Love could not interfere. I was impressed. But then one afternoon as we strolled along the riverbank, he began teasing me about Bill James.

"Why do you hang around with that guy so much? How do you stand him? The guy's null and void, got no fire, doesn't know what pain is, wouldn't bleed if he was cut."

"He damn well would bleed. He damn well does know what pain is. He knows better than you," I retorted, surprised at my own rage and not at all sure what I meant.

"Gee, I'm sorry. Is the guy balling you?"

"He is not balling me. Is that all there is in the world? Is that the only reason I could like a guy?" I abandoned Richard at the next corner.

I began playing bridge with other foreigners on Saturday nights. I'd always thought I had some talent for the game; I soon became the partner of Johann, from Cologne, a blond giant who briefed me on French bridge vocabulary and explained his bidding system. Toward two o'clock one morning, after he had drunk a great many beers and I'd bid and made a small slam, cleverly endplaying our opponents, Johann walked me back to my hotel. Leaning heavily on my shoulder, he kissed me beerily, murmured in my ear. I was glad to be in someone's arms, particularly a man not toting an American passport. But he cornered me at the entrance to my hotel and got his hands inside my coat. Planting his mouth on mine, he told me he was coming up to my room, that he wanted to give me something I'd like.

"No, thanks. You can't come up. I'm not allowed to have anybody in my room. It is strictly forbidden." I tried in vain to twist out of his grasp.

"I'm coming upstairs with you. If you scream, I'll say you're a whore. They'll evict you." He bit my neck, twisted my arm behind me. At this hour of the morning, I was obliged to ring a bell to be admitted. I hoped the night clerk would emerge to scold me, as he occasionally did, but the buzzer merely sounded and the lock clicked. Johann pushed me through the door. "Walk toward the stairs." He stayed close behind me, pinning my hands behind my back in his paw, pushing me roughly upward. On the first landing he paused to kiss me and to fumble at the buttons on my coat, pull up my sweater. I squirmed and cursed him — *salaud, con,* bastard, let me go — but he shoved me on up the staircase. Love with grunts and sweat, love unveiled and bestial — apparently I was at last destined to know it. On the fourth landing I screeched, involuntarily, and as he grabbed for me I managed to shove him backwards, then started up the stairs two at a bound. I heard a muffled thunking sound and saw that Johann had lost his balance and fallen half a flight. I heard exclamations in German. I turned my key in the lock and slammed the door.

For a couple of days afterward I hid out with Bill James, wearing a turtleneck to hide the bruises on my neck. "Are you okay? You don't seem okay," Bill remarked from time to time, inspecting me anxiously, suggesting that I have yet another tisane and maybe a brandy. I answered sourly and refused to tell him anything. One afternoon he put a book into my hands. "You must read this. It's by Laclos, a novel. Eighteenth century. *Les liaisons dangereuses*. It's written in the form of letters. Laclos never wrote anything else. But then, if a person can write this, why should he write anything else?"

"Why should I read it?"

"You need to. It is a wonderful book. And you need to read something like this. You have too much romantic stuff in your head, that's what's making you unhappy. *Liaisons dangereuses* is about the abuse of power. *Le seigneur méchant-homme*. The big powerful male who does evil as his birthright. The *seigneur* in this book is called Valmont. His lady friend is pretty bad too. Together they almost destroy the world. All for the pleasures of destroying it."

"My God, do I have to read it? Umpteen million letters?"

"Yes. You need to know that love is politics. Love is not romance. Love is war. Sex is a weapon people use to get what they want. Love is not soft and cuddly. More often than not, it's selfish and mean."

Eventually spring came, and the weather grew warm enough that I could sleep in the soft batiste nightgown my mother had sent me as an Easter gift. I discarded my woolly socks and long underwear, opened the hotel room window at night. An occasional May wind lifted the tattered curtain and brought in the agreeable racket of the street. In the café now, Henry was talking about the summer, Bill was booking passage home. Henry had borrowed money from his mother and planned to spend six more months in Europe. If only I could stay in Paris another year! But I could not extend my scholarship. Finding a job was impossible as well as illegal. I had to begin cutting my ties, bidding goodbye to the Paris of my mind. The thing I supposed I had come for had utterly eluded me. Like Casanova, however, I had begun to see that the quest might be more satisfying, more entertaining, than its fulfillment.

Curiously, Henry turned attentive to me once again in spring. Marta had disappeared — whether she had taken her sewing machine and returned to Germany or found another boyfriend, Henry did not specify. Like me, he had renounced all hope of finding a French lover. Dipping into his summer travel allowance, he took Bill and me to dinner at modest restaurants, ordering a carafe of wine, insisting that we have dessert. Leaving Bill behind some days, we resumed our long walks, spent Sundays together. We kissed, held hands, touched. I deliberately restrained my intensity, became casual, feigned a lack of interest. I toyed once again with the notion of introducing Henry to my mother, my father — so different from the notion of having a love affair with him. I tried Henry on mentally as if he were a garment in a shop. Would he do? Yes, maybe he would do.

I finally booked my passage for early June, which was as long as I could imagine my funds lasting. Henry was heading for Madrid the last week in May, and dipping into his mother's loan again, he invited me to dinner at one of the most expensive restaurants in Paris on the eve of his departure. Neither of us had ever tasted four-star French cuisine, which he explained was just as much a part of French culture as any statue in the Louvre and any old play in five acts and rhymed iambic sexameter. I had a dress, left over from a college party, that I could imagine wearing for such an occasion. With the few francs remaining from my stipend I bought sling-back pumps and sheer stockings and visited a *coiffeur*. Ushered to our seats in the famous restaurant Henry had chosen, we ordered a gluttonous dinner — fois gras, snails, rack of lamb, wine, a salad, and an orange soufflé for dessert. With coffee we had a couple of cognacs, inhaled our Gauloises, and felt heavy and ill. Out on the street, I said, "If a meal like this is the truest form of French culture, the way you say, I think I'll stick with *Phèdre*. At least Racine doesn't make you so dizzy."

"Oh, my love," I recall him saying then, pausing and waving his arms dramatically as in la Comédie-Française. "Will you come home with me this last night? What if we never see each other again? Wouldn't it be a shame to waste this opportunity?"

"Henry, I thought you'd never ask me."

Thus, at least through the years I have been able to recollect one Parisian night and two inexperienced lovers — for it seemed to me that Henry was a virgin and I was still almost one, though of course virginity does not go by "almost." I did not ask him, of course, and he did not confess — a man of twenty-two and a virgin? Were such things possible? But this was the late 1950s, and Henry was a shy American who'd gone to Sunday school since babyhood and (it now appeared to me) was more terrified of his sexuality than I was of mine. Curious, that a man should have such fears! In the morning, as we lay in each other's arms, I asked him to postpone his trip until after my sailing, but his plans were made — somebody with a car would be meeting him in Madrid, he explained. He could not tarry. I wept a great deal at the train station, and we kissed goodbye lingeringly, like the lovers on the quai. I wished nothing more than to be like them, a young girl kissing her lover, melting with love, a poster on sale at the *bouquiniste's* in silvery black-and-white. Oh, but in those posters love never hurt, love was as gentle and natural as the mist from the eternal river. No one wept, snarled, threw someone out of the house in the middle of the night, lied, used sex as a weapon. Even prostitutes were happy and well-adjusted in the made-for-export version of love that the French were so skillful at devising. And that Americans like me were so eager to imbibe, like Beaujolais nouveau.

That afternoon I sat dejected, tearful, reading Guillaume Apollinaire, mad poet, who appeared before my eyes like an image on the silver screen. Here in my book was his photograph: he'd been shot in battle and his head was swathed in a white bandage. His head ached, no doubt, as mine ached. He wandered the streets of Paris, singing the song of the *mal-aimé*, the badly loved, the man who had never been loved properly, the man crazed by the sun in the day, the fog in the night, without enough sense just to go ahead and die. So he claimed, stumbling.

> June's sun a burning harp
> Scorches my aching fingers
> Dejected, melodiously mad,
> I wander through my beautiful Paris
> Without heart enough even to die here.

But as the day wore on and my tears dried up, it occurred to me that whatever actually had remained of my virginity was finally gone. I was stoking my own grief, I finally admitted. I took out my portable typewriter and began an account of my night with Henry Robinson, an account that grew more elaborate as I rewrote it, laced with erotic detail. I have preserved those sheafs of paper, so thin that the typewriter keys tore holes in them. I find as I refer to an early version of the story that I thought he looked a bit silly wearing only his socks, with all that gangly frame high above the argyles, but soon I began taking matters *au sérieux* and crossed that out. (Constance either did not glimpse Oliver Mellors wearing only his socks or did not think he looked silly. Or maybe gamekeepers don't wear socks.) My first coupling with Henry, I stated, was "clean, passionate, and artless," whatever that may have meant — no doubt that youth and determination had somehow overcome initial fright.

I recounted, cryptically — and I've no notion what I could have been alluding to — that we both "lost control." Did we make love five times? Six? Did we weep with joy? Achieve perfect mutual orgasms? The quality of the prose-poems on those fragile leaves of onionskin, filled with many energetic xxxxxings, would indicate that we did, though I profoundly doubt it. Did I make him happy? Did he make me happy? Why did he leave me? Why had he waited so long to make love to me?

The narrative has long ago eclipsed the experience, so that I can no longer say what occurred. Art, as art is determined to do, once more obliterated life. I do vividly recall, though I failed to make a note of it, some uneasy sessions with the calendar in the two weeks after he boarded the train. For Henry had not been as zealous to protect me as my first lover had been, and I was left to count anxiously backward and forward and watch for portents like a priest of the Maya. Luck was with me, however: the blood flowed. I awoke in a puddle of it one sultry morning. I recollect a slight pang of disappointment that the drama was finished. And from that moment, Henry Robinson turned into a shadow, the handwriting on a thirty-five-year series of sporadic announcements, greeting cards, and brief letters. One of these communiqués, arriving at my address in New York City two years after I had left France, announced his marriage to Alissa. She was not the French woman he had hoped to find in Paris but an American from Macon, Georgia. He encountered her in the Prado in Madrid, scarcely a week after he left me weeping at the Gare Montparnasse.

Before he sailed for home, Bill James also bade me goodbye with food and drink. His grandmother had sent him a check to tide him over until he got back to Nebraska, and he used part of the money to buy a bottle of gin. "I'm sick of wine," he said, "and even sicker of this piss the French call beer. Let's have something real to drink." That evening in his hotel room — to which he had brought a supply of ice, two proper martini glasses obtained from God knows where, and a pitcher — we drank gin and vermouth until we had to get out for a sobering breath of air. Then we walked the streets giggling and tipsy, finally collapsing together on chairs in the Jardin des Tuileries, after hours, too late for the war-wounded guardian of park benches to approach us and extract payment for the seat. Bill put his arms around me, probably to keep me from falling off my chair. Idly, bibulously, I wondered if I couldn't pull that trick Humphrey Bogart and Jimmy Stewart always used on secretaries: I'd pull his horn-rimmed glasses off his nose and say, "How handsome you are! I never noticed you before, baby. Where have you been all my life?" Or words to that effect. But though we managed a drunken hug or two, I could not take hold of the glasses. I wondered if Bill would ask me to come to his hotel.

An hour later, sobering up over steak and *frites,* I studied him once more. He had by now resumed his customary lecture on literary criticism, warming to the subject of Serious Discourse and how it had taken many centuries for ordinary people like ourselves to be selected as subjects of Serious Discourse rather than being portrayed as buffoons and fools, or not mentioned at all, except as parlormaids and spear carriers. "You had to be a count to count, ha-ha!" I ventured, hoping to derail him, but he steamed on. There was a great work of literary criticism I must read, something about the imitation of reality in Western literature, of which he just happened to have a copy . . . His face was alight, as always when he thought of Stendhal's corset, Emma Bovary's arsenic, or almost any other imitation of reality in Western literature.

I had once suspected Bill of loving me secretly, and had dreaded having to turn him away. Now I saw that I should never have to turn him away, that he was determined to live out his passions on paper. His god had endowed him with the gift, or the curse, of celibacy. He would be a monk for literature, of the written word. It occurred to me that Bill James was in some

manner my ideal match, the sort of man who obviously had no
intention of touching me but who, if he ever loved at all, would
love with a destructive, consuming, literary love of the sort I
craved.

"Thanks, my friend," I said as he left me at the entrance to
my hotel.

"For what? Oh, the gin. My grandmother bought that."

The words almost took shape: Thank you for teaching me
the little I have learned this year. Thank you for telling me to
read that epistolary novel about the vile aristocrats who destroyed the world using love as their weapon, and for telling me
what Stendhal thought of passion: that it crystallizes like a
chemical, a thing unto itself, a thing in the mind of the man or
woman who feels it but not always perceived, let alone shared,
by the object of the passion. For saying that an adulterous
woman is perhaps the greatest heroine of all, arsenic or no arsenic (an assertion that I would one day have cause to reflect
upon once more). Thank you for showing me, though I was in-
credulous about it, that sex takes place in the brain, not the
body. But I could not tell him that I had become his disciple, or
that I loved him dearly, almost as much as I loved France, almost as much as I loved Paris — whatever he might be or
France or Paris might be, and all this seemed indeterminate and
in flux and beyond my ability to decipher — so I merely kissed
him on each cheek, the French way, and said goodbye.

9

SCHOOL FOR
LOVERS

In my mid-twenties in New York City, when John F. Kennedy was president of the United States, I worked at a magazine checking facts in manuscripts by writers of repute — a beginner's task, at a beginner's salary. Yet each day, like a diplomat on some important mission, I mounted the broad marble stairs of the New York Public Library, a Renaissance palace crumbling into shabbiness, seated myself at an enormous table in the third-floor reading room, vast and vaulted as heaven itself, and searched the pages of scores and then hundreds of volumes. Unaware that a young female fact-checker such as myself would one day be bending over his typescript, the author might state that Thomas Jefferson wrote the Constitution, but was that so? (No.) Or that witches were persecuted chiefly in the Middle Ages, but were they? (No, later, when people certainly ought to have known better.) Or that the battle of Gettysburg was fought in 1863 (yes). My companions at the reading room table were sometimes seeking the answers to crossword puzzles, or simply trying to keep warm. I became a nodding acquaintance of one dark-haired man who wore the same shabby gray tweed suit and muffler the year around. His black eyes shone like mirrors; he would stare appraisingly at my piles of books, though he never spoke to me. When he went to the men's room or the card catalogue, I would cautiously inspect his piles of books: philosophy, the occult.

Once I overheard a reference librarian ask him what he was looking for, and he replied, "The truth."

My task too was to determine what the truth was, as well as how things ought to be spelled. With a red dot above each fact and my source notes in the margin, my say-so would be final. Though I later had better-paying jobs, I may never have possessed more power. My mandate was clear — truth existed, and I had been commissioned to find it. My opinions, if any, would be heard. My boss would stand up for my opinions against those of Oxford and Cambridge dons, against emeritus professors at Harvard, if I could demonstrate that I'd found the truth.

Yet my own heart's mandate was far from clear. I did not notice (and would not have minded) that the company I worked for was run on the model of an overseas colony — the people producing, reproducing, or storing raw materials (researchers, secretaries) were women. It would have been unthinkable for a young man to begin his career on the reception desk or as a secretary. Men began in the mailroom or as editorial assistants, posts from which it was possible to rise. But unheard-of events had begun to take place, as though some glacier were melting. Though half a dozen different personnel directors had told me I ought to learn to type and take dictation, I refused. "I don't want a job where my typing speed matters," said I. "I don't want to take dictation." And indeed, at the magazine I now worked for, two or three women (ten or fifteen years older than I) got paid for what they knew, not how fast they typed. And they never "took" letters. One of these women, sunny, energetic, and beautiful, was also the mother of three children, who occasionally visited her in the office, following her up and down the corridors like a line of ducklings. I watched the four of them incredulously, jealously, hardly aware of what I was witnessing. How reckless she was, I thought, to show herself the mother of three and still expect to be taken seriously by men.

Nevertheless, no woman had yet risen beyond a certain level. Mostly, the writers, editors, promoters, marketers, and executives, who turned the raw material into a product and sold it, were men. Intelligent, witty, handsome, well-mannered men, out of Princeton and Harvard, Yale and Brown. Married. I was overjoyed to climb the stairs of the New York Public Library on errands they had devised for me.

My paycheck was reliable, though small. I could afford one pair of shoes, and often sat in a little booth that hid my stockinged feet while the shoemaker patched up my presentable, working-girl black pumps. My winter coat, the one I had worn in Paris, was ratty now, but I learned to slip quickly out of it upon entering a room; anyway, it was an emblem of youth, superior to mink and sable. Since I did without my evening meal, dental care, and home furnishings, I could afford haircuts, an occasional new dress, and tickets to the theater or ballet or whatever else tempted me in the banquet of high culture in New York. Though ten pounds underweight, I wore a girdle with supporters to hold my stockings up. (On the beach or the roof, I tanned my legs in June in order to go without stockings in July and August, but I always wore the girdle.) Nevertheless, I had a sense of overwhelming modernity, of being a pioneer, of having surpassed my mother's generation by leagues and light-years. If women needed any additional rights, I'd have been hard-pressed to enumerate them. Many years before, a lot of funny old birds called suffragettes had won us the right to vote. It embarrassed me to think of it, those high-bosomed ladies marching and making nuisances of themselves. We voted; we held property in our own names. What more did we now require?

Plenty, and part of it was sexual. There was talk of a pill that absolutely protected a woman from pregnancy, no fuss, no muss, but it was still being tested (on a group of Puerto Rican woman, I had read), so I went to get my diaphragm. "Why are you here?" the gynecologist inquired curtly as I entered his consulting room. "If you were my daughter," he said after I explained, "I would turn you over my knee and spank you."

"I'm not your daughter. I want a diaphragm, and if you won't give me one, I'll find somebody who will." How many single women all over America were saying as much to their gynecologists at that moment? The doctor relented, and sternly instructed me never to skip the spermicide and to be sure I didn't puncture the latex with a fingernail. Now that I had this springy coil in my hand, and the tube of jelly, it seemed a very frail shield against the catastrophe of pregnancy and a possible visit to some kitchen table up three flights in a New Jersey tenement. My roommate said that many men frowned on contraception as unaesthetic and unsporting — against the natural order, really. It was still illegal in Connecticut. Well, they'd all have to get used to it. I'd already heard two horrifying stories from women who had gone blindfolded in the back of a car to meet some sadist with a scraping tool but no anesthetic, and I wanted none of it.

My quest for absolutes in adolescence and my early twenties, the union of artistic souls, the love-death, D. H. Lawrence's promotion pieces for the female orgasm and the sublimity of the male member, now took on a silly aura in my mind: outgrown clothing to be packed up and donated to the Salvation Army. The idea of a destructive passion that defied the grave now struck me as neurotic. Jane Eyre, according to some critic I'd just encountered, was a flawed and unnatural female who could mate only after her man was maimed and blinded, thus removing the phallic threat. Yes, that was it, I concluded after rereading the book. I veered back toward normalcy, harkened to Freud, who seemed to find all women's behavior neurotic. Most of my friends, men as well as women, were undergoing analysis or psychotherapy. I couldn't afford a shrink of my own, but psychiatry came in free samples, like the cocktail-party sandwiches and peanuts of which I often made my dinner. Everybody had neuroses and lengthy opinions about their own and others' neuroses. We believed, profoundly and uncritically, that talking frankly enough and long enough would cure anything.

I had looked upon my early sexual adventures, limited as they had been, as small acts of defiance, at least in part — for they were more than that. Love and desire, a yearning for permanence, had played a role in all of them. All had had some element of risk, of the forbidden, even the hopeless, all contrary to the pro-virginity, pro-marriage teachings of my youth. But virginity in a woman over twenty had now become a sign of maladjustment, even mental illness, to be shed as soon as possible. Love wanted to be casual now, in the same category with good nutrition, vitamins, minerals, regular baths. But what was the use of sexual passion if it was merely healthful?

If, like George Sand, a woman took time to squabble, to overturn the rules, to stalk around in trousers smoking a cigar, to go lubriciously from bed to bed, to finance her mode of living with the most copious outpouring of work ever to come from a female hand, and then to confound her enemies by turning into a model grandmama and the literary companion of distinguished men who called her "master," that may have been admirable in France in the nineteenth century but would not have been in the United States in the 1960s. George Sand would have been a misfit in the ecology of my office, a misfit in New York. This "revolution" pretended to create radicals but ended only with new versions of conformity, tighter than my girdle.

With a girlfriend from Vermont named Carol Perkins, I lived in a tiny third-floor apartment in a Federal-style townhouse on West Fifteenth Street, decent, working-class Chelsea. We had a kitchen-in-the-wall, a pleasant living room, two tiny bedrooms, a bathroom that was crowded if you hung up a towel. I craved but could not afford a Village address — a low number on Charles or Bank or Jane. But Chelsea was okay, and Carol and I wore the same size everything, so one closet and one clothing budget supplied us both. We were looking for husbands, though Carol was much surer of her mission than I. We were also in love with the president.

Having grown up under Franklin Roosevelt and Harry Truman and turned into first-time voters under Eisenhower, we now had a president who wasn't our father. Even Nixon supporters our age were deeply under John F. Kennedy's spell. As a candidate, he had actually shaken my hand, looked into my eyes, and breathed "Thank you" when I was addressing envelopes one evening at Democratic headquarters in the Biltmore Hotel. On our kitchen wall was an autographed photo of Kennedy on his sailboat, in khaki pants and a sports shirt, his legs parted — all the seductive verve of a pinup boy, a male version of Rita Hayworth kneeling in her lace nightie.

Carol and I relished the rumors about his love affairs. Ah, *droit du seigneur,* and welcome to it. He had more power than anyone in the world — the "Leader of the Alliance," the London *Economist* termed him, as if he had been Churchill. Jackie Kennedy was the other half — the teased coiffures, pillbox hats, hard-sided handbags, stiff little tailored suits and dresses, her bony knees and aristocratic long feet. But her childish, socialite's voice, her propriety, her highly visible good taste, her upper-class perfection, somehow diminished me. Here was the ultimate counterrevolutionary, an utter conformist and rich to boot, yet with regiments of swooning would-be Jackies, poor girls like me, at her feet. Jack was politics and war, she was motherhood and interior design. Nevertheless, I began backcombing my hair to straighten it and wearing four-square little frocks. At least her bosom was as insignificant as mine. As a female ideal, she was not as toxic as Betty Grable or Marilyn Monroe, yet somehow more treacherous because of her education, her intelligence, her status as wife to the Leader of the Alliance. Was this the only acceptable package for female brains?

Though out of reach, men were everywhere up and down Fifth and Madison avenues, rushing across the streets in the summer swelter, their jackets hooked over one shoulder by a finger. As I waited for the walk light, young men climbed out of taxis, paid their fare through the open window, went into Brooks Brothers, which was right around the corner from my office. I would watch them vanish inside the store and marvel at their good looks, their slim figures. Could all of them be spoken for? Surely not. Did I want one of these desirable creatures for my own? I could not be sure.

My heart brimming with hope, my shoes and fingernails polished, clutching a clutch bag with a lipstick and a few dollars, I attended cocktail parties, ducking past the doorman, up the elevator into some apartment packed with young bodies crushing toward a bar. Sometimes I hardly knew the host, usually stood speechless even if introduced to half a dozen men. Sometimes I drank too much and afterward walked dizzily to the subway — would the man who had taken my phone number really call me? Sometimes I went home in a taxi, kissing some man I'd met. Would he really invite me to dinner and a play the next weekend? Take me to meet his family? No, for such men vanished like dreams interrupted by an alarm clock. Carol, in contrast, had a knack for bringing people home — men, women, in matched or unmatched sets. She always forgot her keys and had to ring the doorbell at three A.M. I would put on my bathrobe and make coffee, wondering if one of the men would fall for me. Gradually, out of this floating world, a few molecules coalesced.

In and out our door, at our kitchen table, seated on the pair of living room couches (made from lumberyard doors, screw-on legs, and foam-rubber mattresses) came an assortment of men, Christian and Jewish and atheist, black and white, heterosexual and homosexual. Among them were a stockbroker named Joe (short, plump, a devotee of good wine and food); twin brother lawyers, Jamie and Hal (they hated each other and never appeared at the same time), a black physician studying to be a psychoanalyst, a successful writer (that is, a short story of his had appeared two years before in *The New Yorker,* though all subsequent ones had been rejected and he seemed to live on the suppers we provided), an actor who made his living in radio commercials, an advertising space salesman, a magazine editor, a composer scraping by as temporary office help.

In addition, there was a handsome, muscular giant from Alabama, Albert by name, always willing to build you a bookshelf or scavenge you a sofa from street discards and carry it up the stairs single-handedly. His sexual inclinations went in all directions, as did his ambitions. He showed up regularly at theater auditions, wrote a novel in longhand that filled a suitcase and composed plays besides, and was periodically reduced to repentance and cold sweat by a compelling vocation for the ministry — Baptist. He worked, when he worked, as an office temp, a lumberjack among the file cabinets and typewriters. Sporadically, he would propose marriage to me, painting our lives together in some tiny clapboard church in Alabama, with me refraining from all sinful activity such as drinking and swearing and him thumping the Bible on Sundays and caring for his flock, safe from all his tormenting fiends of desire. He could kiss most romantically. There were days when I was in love with him, in spite of knowing that he sometimes cruised in drag.

Two others from this floating world stood out. Allen Gillian, a sporadically employed newspaper reporter with a secondhand silver sports car, usually arrived with bags of groceries or took us both out for Chinese food — or else arrived hungry, looking for a meal. I thought he was in love with Carol, and he maneuvered time alone with her when he could. Gil drifted from job to job, waiting by his mailbox for the check from some freelance project, hoping it would arrive before the eviction notice. He did without new clothes and haircuts to keep his car running. Sometimes the three of us went for long drives in the sports car, Carol and Gil in the front, me hunkering long-leggedly in the space behind the bucket seats. Sometimes Gil and I went alone — for Carol was cool to him, and he was desperately in need of a listener, thirsty for companionship like no other man I knew. He had dreams about his future, visions of himself in positions of power, visions of himself accepting the Pulitzer — entirely seductive visions, for me at least, not because I imagined he'd ever win a Pulitzer but because he wanted to. I was a drifter and dreamer too, and I liked both Gil and the car.

Saturday mornings we'd stop at a little store on the Upper West Side and invest five dollars in cigarettes, apples, cookies, and a few other provisions; we lunched or dined at roadside stands on the Connecticut shore or in Rhode Island, wherever we happened to be. He would fold down the rag top of his car, more like a motorized sardine can than an automobile; it shot from a standing start to eighty miles per hour in one fierce surge. The dashboard, he was pleased to say, boasted no cigarette lighter or any other convenience beyond a knob for the heater, and I ignited our cigarettes by crouching down to the floorboards with a book of matches. Our hair whipping in the wind, we doted on the glances of solid citizens high above us in sedans.

Past midnight, on the return voyage, we often stopped at an enormous, rickety amusement park, the Palisades, across the Hudson in New Jersey. In the wilting heat of July or August, grimy as urchins, we would climb into the little motorized tub that putted through the funhouse on a stream of dirty water. Tattered ghosts popped out of hidden closets, green monsters emerged in our wake — that was the "fun" of the funhouse. Then we'd ride the sagging roller coaster until our money ran out. At two or three o'clock, with the gas tank empty, we'd coast into a parking spot near his apartment. On one such occasion, I spent the night with him. He was an intelligent, enthusiastic, playful lover, and we were content enough with each other, buddies and good fellows, though he did tend toward fits of melancholy and would be unable to communicate for hours at a time. I tried to be good to him, to tolerate his depressions as one might tolerate the tears of an unhappy child. I never thought of Gil as a future husband.

"He's in love with you," I told Carol, who knew I'd slept with Gil. "We have a good time together, but it's you he wants. He likes your wit."

"Yes, no doubt. But I have to do better than an unemployed newspaperman fixated on his car." I was beginning to think Carol was too hardhearted for her own good. Gil's old clothes, his disordered life, his very ineligibility as a spouse, were for me a relief from three-piece suits at cocktail parties and the unattainable gods at the office.

The other man that caught my interest, among all those drifting in and out of our apartment, was Antonio Piazza, six and a half feet tall, former altar boy of Our Lady of Pompeii Church at Bleecker Street and Sixth Avenue and now an acolyte priest scheduled for ordination within a few months, the only native-born New Yorker I knew in my world of immigrants from the South and Midwest. His mother, her head covered with a scarf, sat with other Italian matriarchs on the benches in Father Demo Square, a fast-vanishing enclave of Calabrians opposite Our Lady of Pompeii, the old Greenwich Village where everybody along Bleecker Street spoke Italian. Like Gil, Antonio usually arrived at our apartment with bags of groceries in either arm, plus spiky loaves of bread he'd bought at Zito's bakery. He never drank our gin or beer without replacing it. He cooked sausages, spaghetti, his mother's recipe for tomato sauce. Along with the groceries and bread he carried his guitar, and after supper sang Petrarch's love sonnets in the original to music of his own composition, translating for me occasionally.

I loved these performances — his bony, expert fingers on the guitar, his prominent Adam's apple pumping, the brown eyes, the smile that broke open over a mouthful of crooked teeth. How could he tether himself to the church, adhere to pa-

pal doctrine on sexuality or marriage or God? We often argued heatedly about God after he finished singing, sometimes far into the night, far past the hour when a young priest ought to have been drinking beer with a woman. I waved Sartre, Camus, Flaubert at him. He countered with Pascal, Jacques Maritain, Saint Thomas Aquinas, brought me books to read, queried me on what I had learned from them, teased me, pushed me into philosophical tight places, exasperated me, attempted to convert me on purely intellectual grounds, refused to concede even a single point. He even told me he prayed for me nightly, for my salvation. But he laughed as he said it, and as I assured him that his prayers were wasted on me.

"He's in love with you," Carol said. Perhaps he was, for of all the men who came to West Fifteenth Street, I loved Antonio best, adhering in secret to my adolescent philosophy: any obstacle between myself and a potential lover became a powerful source of attraction. I dreamed of detaching Antonio from his vows, of endangering his immortal soul, of saying to the pope himself, "You see, my kind of love is stronger." I rehearsed taking him home to my parents after he'd renounced his vocation for me, a dark-eyed, dark-skinned musician of the same ethnic persuasion as the man who'd lured Ingrid Bergman out of the paths of righteousness. Oh, for someone to defy propriety and God with me, not just somebody looking for a wife.

Summer weekends, the editorial assistants and gal Fridays of Manhattan went to the beach. Fire Island, a sandbar thirty-two miles long and less than half a mile wide, parallel to Long Island's south shore, was the scene a hundred years ago of spectacular bonfires that illuminated the Great South Bay. Standing on the ferry deck on Friday nights, with the engine rattling and the wind whipping, I looked eagerly ahead of me, hoping the fires would be burning still. In the part of the island where I went that summer, huge groups shared ramshackle, airless cottages, furnished with wicker and a couple of coal-oil lamps, with insufficient numbers of beds or mattresses. Some tenants in our cottage were full shares, entitled to come every weekend; others, like me, paid only half, came every other weekend, and were last in line for a bed. Rumors flew about "orgies" in some distant cottage, but in our house food was the central issue — its cost, quality, and supply, as well as whose turn it was to wash dishes. The steaks were always gristly, and no matter how many packages of cookies were in the pantry Friday night, they were all gone by Saturday. Nevertheless, we all sprinted courageously into the surf and daubed our agonizing sunburns with smelly salves that did more harm than good.

My friend Joe, the stockbroker, who had organized the cottage, had seen to it that there was a balance of genders. Besides dinner, the point was matchmaking, if not necessarily love. I was immediately attracted to Simon, tall and blond but balding, a Californian, a full share, of course, forty-five years old. Too old, way too old. Yet as the sun set and the wind grew chill on the ferry crossing, Simon offered me his jacket, then carried my overnight bag down the gangway. He insisted on hefting the grocery box into our little red wagon and pulling it along the boardwalk. These were the courtly good manners my mother had always said a man should have, though she hardly pictured a grown man pulling a little red wagon. Simon was an engineer, and I perceived that his job was substantial. He never waited desperately at his mailbox for a check to arrive, nor, unlike most of the men I knew, did he lull himself to sleep with promises that the big break, the book contract, the job at the hot ad agency would materialize next week. He was an established man. No woman who married him would need to worry about the rent money.

Yet Simon was a bachelor. Watching him swimming out to sea and playing volleyball on the beach, I could see that he was also an athlete. There was only one troubling thing about him. Like Antonio Piazza, he was pious. Not an aspiring priest, but Sunday mornings, when everybody else on Fire Island was sleeping, Simon walked ten miles down the beach to the nearest mass. His two older sisters, he told me, were both nuns. One of them a mother superior. His parents had wanted him to become a priest or even a monk. But he had never felt the call and had majored in mathematics instead. I wondered if I could make him fall in love with me. Marry me. There was an Episcopal church at the corner of Tenth Street and Fifth Avenue that I'd picked as the ideal setting for a wedding, should I ever get married. Here was a serious candidate. How difficult could it be to get Simon from early mass to the Church of the Ascension? It was distressing, that two of the men who interested me were Catholics who would have to be persuaded to abandon their faith.

Simon began meeting me for the train ride to Patchogue, Long Island, and the ferry trip. One Friday, having made the very last boat, we arrived to find our cottage inexplicably empty. Having quickly put on our bathing suits — in separate rooms, of course — we ran barefoot together over the boardwalk, down the steep wooden steps to the ocean. The water was warm, and fingers of surf uncurled up the sand in the moonlight.

"Somebody should be playing the ukulele," I said, trying to blunt the edge of scenic rapture. Simon took my hand and we waded into the Atlantic. Soon we opened our lips in long, salty kisses, lay down in the surf, explored the skin under the bathing suits. Foreplay, nothing more. I wondered whether he had noticed the bony, wiry structure in the top of my suit. Nipples must not show. We lay in the surf together until past midnight, until the advancing tide drove us further up the beach and home.

"You're beautiful," he said. "And you have some quality I can't define. Something like sexiness, but it isn't that." I had always hearkened to any man who told me of my beauty, aware as I was of not being beautiful, of conforming to no known canon of female gorgeousness. The man who alluded to my beauty must be either a flatterer or speaking of an inner beauty. And for Simon to spot inner beauty — and I could see that he meant his compliment — as well as something sexy that was at the same time more demure than sexiness, was a good sign.

Saturday evening, Simon accompanied me to the "sixish," a cocktail party that began at seven, not six, every week. By some means resembling pheromones, a cottage would be chosen and a procession would form, a hundred or more men and women, in shorts, tight pants, long sarongs and halters, everybody carrying bottles of gin or vodka, quinine water, packages of plastic glasses, packing themselves in, hanging off the porch, climbing onto the roof. Nobody was turned away, and a house had actually collapsed under the weight the previous summer. If you wanted a drink you had to get it from the gin-bottle carrier in your party, and another one of us would be appointed runner, to fetch ice from home. I had always found the sixish terrifying and often bolted after fifteen minutes, offering time and again to fetch the ice for my group. This fearful round of sizing up and being sized up made me yearn for my mother's epoch, when suitors came and sat in the porch swing. Tonight, however, I had Simon by my side, and peculiarly enough, I attracted another man. I have always remembered his name as Fred C. Dobbs, the paranoid gold miner Humphrey Bogart played in *Treasure of the Sierra Madre*, though in fact his name was probably Bill or Herbert. Fred C. Dobbs was the name he gave me later that same evening. At the sixish, though, Fred C. Dobbs and I chatted briefly, and he invited me to drop by his house after dinner. It was a fine house, he assured me, not like most of these beachside shanties with forty people in them. He had only four housemates, and a stereo that worked off a generator and some great LPs.

"Oh, I don't know. I have a date," I told him. Nevertheless, he took a scrap of paper and began writing something on it, but then Simon turned around.

"Let's get out of here, I hate this thing."

I felt a hand clutching mine and realized that Fred C. Dobbs was transferring his scrap of paper from his palm to mine. "Second walk back from ocean side, fourth house down on the right, hidden by bushes," I read, sheltering behind Simon's back as he forced a path for me through the throng. I thought of throwing the scrap to the floor but put it into my pants pocket instead. If all went well, I'd never need it, not tonight or ever.

We went down the long wooden staircase to the beach, abandoning our sandals at the foot of the steps, not caring if we never found them again. The waves broke all along the strip of pearl-gray sand, and the moon was rising — round and full tonight, Oh, wanderer, that finds no object worthy of its constancy! The wind smelled of the weedy green ropes cast up on the sand, dried the sweat on our faces and arms, sent us skimming along the beach like seabirds. Simon laid his arm around my shoulders. We wanted only to put plenty of distance between ourselves and the squalid cottage to which we eventually must return, the supper rituals, somebody mixing the fifth round of gin and tonics — the formless, shapeless evening that set in about ten. Well, let them chew on their gristly T-bones and wonder what had become of us.

Finally, when the village lights looked like dots on the horizon, we lay down behind a swell of white sand dotted with scrubby beach plums. We kissed. We kissed again. We clasped. Time passed. Nothing seemed to be happening, and in so splendid a setting, I was at first content to wait. The sand raked my sunburned arms, but I could bear it. Simon was perfect — all the strength and muscularity and health of my long-ago fantasies. Gulliver. The gamekeeper. Not an adolescent or a shy, tortured youth. A grown man. At last he seemed ready for what I so yearned to give. The T-shirt I was wearing came easily over my head, the bra unsnapped. He bent over me, shivering in the wind. Relaxing into passive pleasure, I realized that something was wrong. He began to clutch me desperately, as if only cracking my ribs would ease his passion. Groaning, tormented, he suddenly rolled away from me, onto his back, and I rolled toward him, fumbling with his clothes. Ah, yes, yes he will, yes! But he was paralyzed, catatonic, and held on to me like a prizefighter in a clinch. I efficiently took off my slacks and unbuckled his belt. He seemed to return to consciousness then, and responded to me, undressed, finished undressing me. Suddenly glistening in the moonbeams appeared John Thomas, as Oliver Mellors had called his own, this one somewhat gritty, but I welcomed it. Then he got that deathly look again. Eyes closed, face contorted. He twisted suddenly away from me, burying his penis in the sand and his face in his arms. To my horror, he began to sob aloud. "I can't," he wept. "It isn't right. I just can't. Please forgive me."

Where was the sonnet or ballad about a man with the body of a movie star who breaks down in sobs and swears he cannot do it? Women had behaved this way since the beginning of time, I supposed. But a man? How curious were the ways of Eros! Or perhaps this was the work of some other god. As if I were behind the wheel of an out-of-control car, I braked and swerved and tried desperately to get back on the road. I assured him he need not worry about getting me pregnant, but this only provoked more sobs. If a man rejected a woman, I thought, turning creative, he probably was yearning for a man. That he might be yearning for celibacy never occurred to me. I tried to take him in my arms, calm him, comfort him. But having set out to delight him, to free him from his neuroses or religion or prudery in the same way that Mellors had freed Lady Chatterley from her frigidity, I seemed to have broken his heart.

I sat for some time on my haunches behind the dune, wearing only my panties. What was Simon's problem? What was mine? I was young, as beautiful as ever I would be, filled with desire. Yet this man lay beside me with his beautiful, masculine buttocks and back upturned to the dark blue sky. He was almost old enough to be my father but seemed to be a virgin. He needed a psychiatrist, some other woman, a male lover, a monastery. He needed a handkerchief.

He sat up presently and fumbled for his clothes. I stood up when he did, somehow unashamed of being naked and out on the beach. But I found my clothes and dressed. He too began collecting himself, apologized for having brought me down behind the dunes and then behaving in such a manner. I tried to be a game girl, a decent girl. I turned back his apologies, assured him that he was lovable, offered him friendship, introductions to psychiatrists or other women. My humiliation was nothing compared with his. "You should let me be your friend," I said, or words to that effect, eager to sell him on the benefits of the talking cure. "Maybe I could help you."

He tried setting his face like a high magistrate pronouncing sentence, but his eyes flashed pure anguish. This splendid aggregate of brain and bone and muscle could swim five miles, carry fifty-pound packages, outrun anybody, but had apparently never performed the most natural of all possible acts. Or at least I had assumed it was natural for men, up to now. It had been natural enough for Oliver Mellors, but not for Henry Robinson, as I vaguely recalled in spite of my poetic memoirs about his abilities as a lover. Not a simple matter, or perhaps not even doable, for Bill James. Antonio Piazzo would go to hell if he did it. It was simple for Allen Gillian but not with the woman he really wanted. It had never been simple for me. Ah, this game of love had many byways.

"Don't worry, Simon. It was just a mistake. Nothing to be ashamed of. Everybody has problems. Me more than most. You're a good guy. But it's time for dinner." The effects of the gin had worn off, and I wanted food. At the foot of the stairs that had led us to the beach I found my sandals, and I went back to the cottage. My housemates were giggly drunk and had eaten all the potato chips and clam dip, but the steaks were just coming out of the broiler. I ate mine hurriedly. There was always Fred C. Dobbs.

Second walk back from the ocean side, fourth house on the right. Fred was waiting for me, right on the porch of his cottage, behind the thicket of beach plums, all alone. "I guess he thinks I'm easy," I said to myself, hoping that I could be easy. I could hear warning voices in the background. Not good to seek solace from a stranger. Maybe he was a sadist. Maybe he would tie me up and torture me. But maybe Fred would turn out to be a shy young man who had spotted me as a fellow literary soul. We could talk about Keats, Yeats, Stendhal, Tolstoy. What if Fred turned out to be an implacable virgin like Simon? I had been ready for commitment behind the dune. I no longer had any idea what I was ready for. Here was a man, however, who at least did not need saving, or not that I could see.

He seemed pleased enough to see me, and I quickly realized no one else was in the house. I turned down his offer of a drink, pleading the heat. I could just see his face by the light of the kerosene lamp inside. He did somehow look like Humphrey Bogart, a thin face, the shadow of a beard. I sat down in the wicker chair opposite him and breathed deeply. He proposed we go to the rooftop, where it was a lot cooler, he said, and where his stereo was set up. On the way through the kitchen to the staircase, we each took a cold bottle of ginger ale from the gas-powered refrigerator. I asked where his housemates had gone, and he said he neither knew nor cared. It was his night to have the house; they took turns. I instantly became the child who had accompanied Joey Cash to her first party. Only two hours earlier I had been determined to have ecstatic sex and possibly extract a marital commitment from a man with the emotional superstructure of a Carthusian monk. Now I wanted enlightened conversation, sweet kisses, and gentle playfulness from an apparently cynical, inarticulate young man who had invited me here for sex.

Billie Holiday sang scratchily out from his phonograph, and after drinking our ginger ale and hearing a couple of records, and after a few preliminary kisses, he persuaded me to lie down with him on the rather skimpy rag rug. Up to that point we had cuddled on a dangerously creaking wicker settee. My desire to cut and run almost got the better of me, but he got out of his clothes, or most of them, and somehow got me out of most of mine. I wanted to want to respond to him. I didn't wish to be a nonresponder, to lose heart, to need coaching. But the rag rug was not large enough to shield me from the rooftop, and I had to interrupt our attempts at lovemaking to search — unsuccessfully — for splinters in my legs. The sky was wide open above us, and Percy Bysshe Shelley's moon stared down, a joyless eye finding no object worthy of its constancy.

Though this man was businesslike and insistent, I have no recollection of being forced. I wanted to be a woman of daring, a member of the new generation. I wanted sex to be easy, healthy, natural, casual, without problems or guilt. I also yearned to shake the feeling of failure Simon had left me with, to erase the glimpse into the abyss of fear and disinclination that he had given me on the beach. For of course when a man cannot perform, a woman instantly assumes it's her own body that's malfunctioning, her own approach that's wrong. But suddenly I was in Simon's position: my body refused to obey the commands of my mind. Where was the passion that was supposed to overpower me? Where was my desire for this? Sex could be pleasant, dangerous, destructive, painful, blissful, but until now it had never crossed my mind that it might be boring and stupid. In annoyance and desperation and shame, I pushed my partner away. He sighed deeply, cursed lightly. Rolled over on his back. I sat upright.

"Fred C. Dobbs," he said. "You remember the line?"

I said I remembered it and obligingly identified the film, the director, and the actor. He expressed his admiration of my cinematic knowledge. Few of us remembered directors' names in those days. I asked him what Fred C. Dobbs had to do with anything. "You remind me of him. 'Nobody tells Fred C. Dobbs what to do.' Remember that line? That's you, I guess." I was deeply hurt, but he might have said, or done, worse. For the second time that evening I got up and dressed, abandoning my would-be lover, but thank God, this one did not weep.

When I got to my front door, slumbering bodies were everywhere. My suitcase was unretrievable, unless I woke up the four women sleeping in the female bedroom. I located my sleeping bag and spread it on the porch, grateful that the night was fair. The splinters in my leg had begun to fester. My sleeping bag was gritty with sand, lacerating my sunburned back and arms. I awoke every hour or so on the penitential boards, and at some point Simon tiptoed past me, weaving on his feet, drunk. I lay awake while the sun rose, its rays persistent on my face. I slept once more, then woke to the nauseating smell of bacon frying, the sound of voices in the kitchen. It was eleven o'clock. I went inside to the shower, where I stood for ten minutes, quite against house rules, deliberately using up all the hot water. My housemates lingered over a mess of toast and jelly, bacon and stuccoish scrambled eggs. They were reading the Sunday *New York Times* and discussing the various orgies that had taken place the previous night in some ever-to-be-unspecified locale. They related that a young woman had sprayed herself all over with aerosol dessert topping, which her companions, male and female, had licked off in the most lascivious manner. I said I didn't believe it. Somebody else observed that she might at least have used real whipped cream, because aerosol was tacky. And thus another Sunday began on Fire Island. They began anointing their skins with baby oil, in preparation for roasting on the beach. Someone mentioned that Simon had arisen at eight and walked to mass.

10

OFFICER AND
LAUGHING GIRL

The men I worked for talked books and music and pictures as naturally, as knowingly, as other men talked
sports. Graceful, honorable men they were too, faithful
husbands with almost no exceptions. Long ago one of them had
left his wife for his secretary, but only after due process (a stay
in Nevada and alimony for the first) and a proper small wedding for the second. Another of the bosses, a famous writer,
was famous for preying on receptionists. But we editorial assistants considered ourselves a new breed; our B.A. degrees,
we vaguely felt, shielded us from the perils and temptations
of office love. Anyway, sleeping with your boss was disgusting
as well as dangerous. We would discuss such matters at the
Schrafft's across from the office — a chain of restaurants (long
since defunct) specializing in dainty portions brought to the
table by young women in the frilly black-and-white uniforms of
parlormaids, a charade lost on me since I had never seen a parlormaid except in movies.

Over miniature tunafish sandwiches on white toast and little caramel-nut sundaes, we chattered about Ingrid, our receptionist, who had a heavy Swedish accent and big breasts and
was sleeping with top management. Sweden was at this time a
major exporter of soft-porn films (much in demand among
New York intellectuals), and we were therefore not surprised
that Ingrid casually displayed snapshots of herself and her
lover, nude. He had commissioned the photos himself, from a

photographer whose name was well known in the magazine business. We dimly perceived that Ingrid had been set up for a fall, like a prostitute by the vice squad, but not one of us could break through our wall of disapproval to warn her. Better to ignore it.

What I wanted, however, was a mentor. Female intelligence, ordinarily as valuable as buckteeth, now seemed a useful commodity. I tried to think of witty remarks, read difficult books, went to plays, operas, and ballets not simply because I enjoyed them but to be able to talk about them.

I had apprenticed only a short time as a fact-checker and researcher when I was sent to work for Peter Klein, who was writing an article about the Netherlands in the seventeenth century, the "Golden Age of the Dutch Republic," as it was to be called. Peter was dark and green-eyed, slender but solid, the man we all wanted to work for, a standout among his colleagues, who tended to be stuffy in spite of their high gloss. Also he was Jewish, another somewhat unusual attribute in this Anglo-Saxon place, which I found exotic and enticing. He came from a poor family in the Bronx — had gone to City College instead of Yale or Harvard. He transgressed pleasantly against the unspoken class rules in other ways. For one thing, he refused to be called "mister." And when the Schrafft's coffee wagon appeared — two huge coffee urns and stacks of cheese danish on a metal pushcart, maneuvered on and off the elevator by a struggling young woman inevitably wearing parlormaid frills — Peter stood in line with the rank and file rather than sending a secretary to buy his breakfast, as management did.

There was the fascinating matter of his war record — he'd been a flier in World War II, or at least had served as a navigator or bombardier in raids over Germany — and had a war injury, a charming, nondisabling kind of disability like Gary Cooper's perpetual shoulder wounds. Peter was almost deaf in his right ear, and you had to speak to his left side, or if you happened to be sitting on his right, he would tilt his head beguilingly toward you. How this had come about nobody knew, though mythology quickly turned him into a war hero. One researcher told me it was from being beaten at Gestapo headquarters in Paris after having been captured as a spy. This turned out to be preposterous. He'd been deafened by the noise of the B-17 he flew in.

When I reported to his office, he took a sheaf of pictures and magazine clippings from a folder and spread them on his desk: sailing ships in full rig, shimmering watery landscapes, richly homey interiors. "This is a wonderful project, and we'll have fun with it. Beautiful stuff. Here they were, these Dutch, in their waterlogged little mudflats, due to be inundated every day, and they built cities and imported goods in sailing ships that they sent all over the world. Have a look at these paintings." He opened a book and shoved it toward me, then put his hands behind his head and leaned backwards in his chair, displaying an expanse of chest sheathed in blue chambray and bisected by a rep stripe tie.

In the 1600s, I quickly read, the Dutch Republic had freed itself of Spanish rule and the Catholic Church. Protestant, and amazingly tolerant for the time, these flying Dutchmen were merchant-adventurers and businessmen — not the stodgy mannequins of my sixth-grade geography book (tulips, wooden shoes, windmills) but masters of the world's luxury trade. Turning the pages of Peter's beautiful new book, I inspected the splendid, rosy fruits of Dutch enterprise. "Civilization" was a word that came easily to us then, a thrilling word, not yet dismembered and exposed as a vile disguise of capitalism, an excuse for exploiting the poor of the earth. An intelligent person might still speak of civilization in polite gatherings without a small disclaiming gesture, the quick citation with the index and middle fingers of both hands and a click of the tongue, or the politically sensitive wince of irony and contempt.

"Imagine a country that could produce Rembrandt, Frans Hals, and Vermeer practically at the same moment." Of the three, I had heard only of Rembrandt and could scarcely name one of his works. "The Night Watch" floated into my mind from the pages of some long-ago issue of *Life*. But what else had he painted? Peter galloped onward, opening books and jotting down queries, as deeply engaged as if Dutch caravels still rode at anchor in New York Harbor. No one since Bill James had talked to me with such absorption about the past. And whereas Bill James had swum through history gasping toward a lifeline to keep from drowning, Peter Klein skimmed the top of the waves like some Dutch merchant ship outrunning a Spanish galleon.

In four days, rather than the six Peter had allotted for the work, I took him his manuscript red-dotted in every line and comma, plus an industrious stack of research filled with publishable goodies — a long citation from some English ambassador claiming that the Dutch "furnish infinite luxury which they never practice and traffic in pleasure which they never taste." A people, the ambassador said, who impersonated lovers but were never at heart in love. "Delightful" — Peter laughed — "and Lord save us all from such a fate."

At five-thirty, when senior staff members donned their overcoats and gray fedoras and ran toward Grand Central Station, Peter usually opened a quart of scotch and served generous shots of it to us city folks. This was another kind of class marker: certain masthead positions required a man to live in Cos Cob or Greenwich or Westport and have a wife who did not work. But Peter lived in town, in a rent-controlled apartment in a comfortable building on lower Fifth Avenue, and Hannah Klein was a curator at the Museum of Modern Art, ten blocks away from our office. Other executive wives never appeared in the office, but Hannah often came to our after-hours parties — beautiful Hannah, almost forty, with large brown eyes, heart-shaped face, and heavy dark hair pinned to the back of her head with a barrette. Like Jackie Kennedy, she wore Chanel suits, expensive department store copies rather than the real thing, and silk blouses with a strand of pearls, a tiny gold chain holding the jacket together — in a protocol as rigid as the maids' uniforms at Schrafft's. Not one of us, and certainly not Hannah Klein, knew that Mme. Chanel, now designing suits worn by millions of American women, had been a Nazi or at least had lived with one at the Ritz Hotel during World War II.

Besides Hannah, ten other women and men would perch on Peter's desk or lean against the door, our whisky in thin paper cups from the water cooler. We argued about the cold war and how Jackie Kennedy had redecorated the White House and whether she was an admirable woman or as silly and feathery as she sounded, and about atomic weapons and whether it was better to be red or dead — for we all expected to be vaporized by missiles from the USSR some afternoon. Red, I thought, though I hoped to remain a democrat.

Careless as we were of our own good luck in being young and having decent jobs in this particular time and place, attentive as we were to our own heartaches and neuroses, we were buoyed up by a dozen remote circumstances or personalities that nevertheless were quite real to us: our handsome president, our own glamorous Mayor Lindsay, the steady rise of the stock market (though none of us were investors), and even the fortunes of the New York Jets and Joe Namath, a deity along with Lindsay and Kennedy — not that any of us cared about pro football, but Namath was a good-looking guy who *won*. We gloried in the New York City Ballet, the New York Philharmonic, the Metropolitan Opera, everything that was the best of the best, as if we had created it. Our optimism was also firmly founded in "the movement," that is, the civil rights movement, which we all supported in one way or another, because we believed in the possibility of justice, especially justice painlessly achieved through legislation enforced in somebody else's part of the country.

Peter sometimes spoke anxiously, angrily, about American activities in a place called Vietnam — Indochina, a quagmire bequeathed us by the French, their most cunning cultural legacy, their deadly revenge against our arrogance, a swamp of injustice beyond our imaginings, a trap for the well-equipped and overendowed. But Peter was the only one who mentioned the unpleasant aspects of American politics. Most of us preferred to discuss the arts, and whether Bobby and Jack Kennedy were humping Marilyn Monroe. We assumed so. Why should they not?

About eight o'clock, the Kleins would take a taxi downtown and I would go woozily into the subway alone. I was convinced, in spite of all evidence to the contrary, that Peter did not love his wife. I detected an edginess between them, a distance. Occasionally the after-hours gatherings included only Peter and me — no scotch, only stacks of books and papers. He too had studied in Paris, a dozen years before I had, spoke better French than I did, knew the same streets I knew, had sat for hours in a café on the boulevard St.-Germain, where he had actually had a conversation one day with Jean-Paul Sartre. But he had not utterly succumbed to the French. Contrary to myth, he pointed out, few Frenchmen had served in the Resistance. The majority had acquiesced or willingly collaborated with the Nazis, had independently persecuted and murdered French Jews. They hardly waited for the invitation. I would beg him to write an article about this, or suggest other ideas for books and essays he could write, mostly culled from my student conversations with Bill James. With Peter, I never had to grope for something to say.

Like me, Peter had fled to the city from the provinces — on the Manhattan-bound IRT train from the Bronx, in one sense as distant from midtown Manhattan as the small town I came from. His grandparents had immigrated from Russia to the tenements of the Lower East Side. Moving to the Bronx had been a sign of success for them, like buying a house in the suburbs. In summers, Peter and his three brothers had worked in his uncle's clothing factory downtown. Thus Peter was a blend of gorgeous mythologies in my mind. The bright kid who slept on a narrow bed in the hallway of his parents' overpopulated apartment, who kept his books and stacks of compositions in a desk behind the door, who pushed racks of dresses along Seventh Avenue, melded with the energetic, polished man who nowadays spoke standard English and lunched regularly at the Harvard Club. But under his good manners and elegant tastes I saw a runaway, like myself, a commoner disguised as a prince.

Hannah began inviting me to her dinner parties on Saturday nights. At the Klein apartment people had habits that amazed me, such as specifying the brand of scotch or gin they liked, and Peter always had the right thing. Bacon-wrapped, cheesy appetizers were the style then, but Hannah set out cherry tomatoes and raw carrots, and green beans in some kind of dill sauce. I once bit into a rotten tomato, but swallowed it without even making a face. At nine o'clock she and Peter would serve lobster Newburg or lamb chops with roasted potatoes, tiny French ones, and a salad as a separate course. The wine was always French, and dessert was chocolate mousse in thin stemmed glasses, followed by French coffee and brandy in the living room. All of this the two of them concocted and cleaned up after without ever mentioning the time and trouble it took.

I tried to imagine myself at home in such a setting, the apartment with its subtle Chinese carpets and chintz sofas, its bowlegged little antique end tables, its wing chairs, the perpetually fresh flowers. How different from my parents' living room with the scratchy maroon couch and matching rug, the upholstered platform rocker, the furniture-store picture on the wall, and, atop a ruffled doily on the coffee table, my mother's dime-store china swan, with its serpentine neck, its gold beak, its wings raised over the cavern of its hollowed-out body, where we stored stray straight pins and the odd penny or nickel that turned up in vacuuming. Hannah would never have tolerated a china swan or a ruffled doily, and yet her parlor had the propriety of, the same need for controlled display as, my mother's. On my way down the hall to the bathroom, I peered into the shadows of the wood-paneled master bedroom with its four-poster bed. I imagined Peter and Hannah slumbering back to back, not touching, individually wrapped in their pajamas.

One morning at the office, as Peter and I began work on his forthcoming article about Vermeer, he remarked on how much he loved this particular painter, possibly the best painter, the most purely visual painter, who ever lived.

I told him I had never actually seen a Vermeer, and he replied that it would not do, merely looking at the Vermeers in books, when the real thing was there for the viewing. Actually, he continued, the Frick Collection had three Vermeers, two fairly minor but one very, very good. Could I be ready to go in fifteen minutes? Art history, yes. I did very much yearn to see a real Vermeer, but even more to leave this office in the company of Peter Klein. I was once more cultivating the art of the crush, determined to have what I could certainly not possess.

The taxi had no air-conditioning, and the temperature was close to ninety. As often in the 1960s, the city sky hung low and yellow on the spires of midtown, and the air stank of some chemical fire in the smokestacks of New Jersey. Grit floated through the open windows and settled palpably on our foreheads. Traffic was jammed. I had made a point of sitting on his good-ear side, so we could talk more easily, but it was too hot to talk. Peter offered me his handkerchief to mop my face and neck. In this epoch young women wore French perfume, purchased for them by friends going through airport duty-free shops, and I had a very stylish new scent called Diorissimo, a lemony, green scent that diffused into my own nostrils as I sweated, and I firmly hoped that Peter could smell it too. But if he did, he said nothing. He was just beginning to have the look of a middle-aged man, the solid look that comes from regular doses of whisky and lobster Newburg. I thought of Hannah at her desk not many blocks away. A ray of sunlight broke through the overhead muck as the traffic cleared and we shot northward from Fifty-ninth Street. He was thinking of picture research, no doubt — of his mission to educate me, to turn me into an editor like himself. But as was my habit, I succumbed to fantasy. I had no idea my lust for him would surface with such force on the way to an art museum on a ninety-degree day.

Henry Clay Frick, Peter told me as we entered the mansion-museum, was a millionaire steel baron and a mean old bastard who shot down the strikers. (Workers of the world, unite, you have nothing to lose but your lives!) However, he had spent a lot of money on art, and the Internal Revenue Service had almost succeeded in democratizing the Frick mansion. Now anybody could walk right in the house and see the paintings, for free. We passed through the glass-domed peristyle, with its small fountain and shallow pool, on which lotuses drifted. Relieved to have somehow blundered out of the hot, polluted August air into a secret place, a Persian garden, we sat down on a stone bench to cool off. The only sound was clean water, splashing discreetly.

The Vermeer he had in mind was small and modest-looking, even in its heavy frame: *Officer and Laughing Girl*. An open casement window with leaded glass, and a bold, radiant young woman at a table in a tavern (perhaps), her head in a white kerchief, a wineglass glistening between her fingers. The phosphorescent light pours through the window in the tavern room, transfiguring the woman's face as though she distills her smile from it. Her bodice clamps her like a suit of armor, pushing her breasts upward, but the curve is modestly covered with white linen. And to the left a man, his back to Vermeer's camera — an officer in red, with a huge, velvety, floppy hat, gallant as the hero of some Hollywood costume film. Above them hangs an enormous, detailed, and accurate map of the Netherlands, covering half the background of the painting. Why was it there? Was this young woman thinking of unbuckling the officer's sword, running her fingers upward under the ruffles of his coat sleeve, taking off his plumed hat and kissing him, as I now yearned to kiss Peter? Did seventeenth-century Dutch girls think such thoughts? It seemed to me that the man was only part of the young woman's dreams, not a real officer at all.

Then, because there was no reason to hurry back to the office, this being a legitimate research errand, we spent a while going from room to room, taking in the rest of the Frick Collection. The steely old steel baron apparently preferred his art proper and chaste — not one nude, only one bare breast in the whole museum. I was nevertheless overwhelmed with the eroticism of it all — Whistler's society matrons in their gauzy pinks and mauves; beautiful Emma Hamilton, a London prostitute who married an ambassador and became the mistress of Lord Nelson (Peter helpfully explained); a young Renaissance prince, the very portrait of arrogance and privilege, his sword hilt protruding from the skirt of his doublet like an erect penis. I moved quickly onward, fearful that Peter might read my thoughts.

We made other art-historical trips, which I imagined as trysts, though they were perfectly businesslike. At our office nobody thought it odd for an editor and editorial assistant to wander through museums together, to visit libraries, to search the city for interesting material. The journalism of high culture was having its moment just then, and we were hunting for story ideas. It was part of our job to go to exhibitions and lectures. As we walked the halls of the Metropolitan Museum and the Cloisters, Peter hardly touched me, except rarely to take my hand, help me with a jacket, or share the menu with me in some luncheonette. Yet sexuality loomed up everywhere for me, even in Romanesque madonnas holding the infant Jesus, even in Roman sarcophagi and giant Buddhas ritually displaying their graceful, slim fingers, palm outward, the index finger upward, in a gesture I tried unsuccessfully to mimic. Peter had a favorite Titian — a two-hundred-pound Venus, languorous and only half satisfied, occupying a place of pride in the Metropolitan. Smiling, she holds out her arms to her retreating Mars as he exits with his broad sword and a knowing glance, off to the wars, off to tend the affairs of men. Ah, to feel the way this Venus looked! Postcoitum, rosy as a peach. "It's hubby off to catch the 7:37," Peter joked. A Titian with Peter seemed superior to gritty misadventures on Fire Island or fishing for men at cocktail parties. I loved the chasm separating Mars and Venus, yearned to be the ample lady on the satin-draped couch murmuring adieu to her departing warrior. If I could not wrest Antonio Piazza from the arms of God, perhaps I could separate Peter Klein from Hannah.

In other ways as well, Peter became my tutor. He and Hannah had no children; I was the only daughter of a doting father. Though I had vociferously refused to enroll at the Katharine Gibbs Secretarial School or study speed writing, I knew very well how to take dictation, to play the role of docile pupil taking copious notes as the master spoke. It was more than simply a minor erotic game — it was an opening. Writing for publication was a man's job then, sacramental and priestly, for which women were permitted only to supply the raw materials, but Peter nevertheless began teaching me his craft. To write anything, as opposed to simply typing it, was a privilege. For a few hours each morning I sat composing little paragraphs, brief biographical notes, letters to outside authors, picture captions, story outlines. I learned the trick of shaping an idea and writing a lead. I deciphered specifications from the art director as to the size and shape of copy blocks. Making every possible beginner's error, I slaved over unnecessary changes, threw out my good lines, and fell for fancy phrases that I dragged through draft after draft like dead bodies.

Peter combed through everything I put on his desk, identified promising bits and showed me how to build on them, slashed out whole paragraphs, and taught me how to pack a line with information.

"What exactly do you have in mind here?" he would say in frank exasperation. "I don't get it. You're trying to tell too much. Don't try to show off your research. Pick one thing and tell it well. Make it fit. For Christ's sake, it has to square. Five lines by forty-five characters, that's all you've got. Don't worry about poetic diction — the line has to fill." And again, even less gently, "Use your head. Rewrite this, and stop getting tears in your eyes. I won't bite you, but the copy chief certainly will."

Eventually, when he thought I'd done my job, he would correct a word or two and smile, then pass these efforts on up the editorial ladder, with my initials in the upper right-hand corner to indicate that the work was mine. Thus, because it was so perceived, it increasingly *became* mine. Writing might be a men's club, but maybe I could struggle up from picture captions to entire articles.

Fridays, Peter often stayed at home and wrote at the desk in his bedroom, telephoning me for help, directing me to dispatch books and papers by messenger when necessary. I hated these work-at-home Fridays, for his office door would be closed, his office empty. Nobody to talk to but the other editorial assistants. I might find myself doing errands for somebody else. Then one Friday morning he called with a long list of questions. Could I collect certain clip files from the office, do some research at the library, go to the nearest bookshop and buy three volumes reviewed in last Sunday's paper, and then send everything to his apartment without delay? Hannah was out of town: her father had had a stroke, and she had flown to Chicago that morning. He was in a jam, he said, up against his deadline, and if his father-in-law got worse, he too would have to fly to Chicago.

It was late afternoon before I found all the material he wanted. I thought of Peter alone. What could he have meant by telling me that Hannah was out of town? Perhaps merely that Hannah was out of town, that he might have to leave too. That he felt harried. Or was it some sort of invitation? I wrapped up the books and clip files, as well as a long memo I had just finished, placed them in two separate manila envelopes, which I taped securely together for the trip downtown. I typed out a label. It took three tries to get it right, since I still wasn't much of a typist and my mind was not on the keyboard. Instead of calling the messenger service, I took a taxi to the Klein address on lower Fifth Avenue and asked the doorman to announce me. What if Peter shouted through the intercom that I was to leave the things downstairs?

"Send her up," I heard him say.

He wore old trousers with his shirttail out, old loafers with no socks. I had never seen him without a tie and jacket. "How nice of you to bring all this yourself. You needn't have come all this way in the heat. But now that you're here, could you go over this stuff with me? Point me in the right direction? That would help a lot."

I had never been in the Klein apartment in the daytime. The September sun blazed through the west windows, turning the Chinese carpet slightly garish. The yellow freesia and blue cornflowers on the coffee table had wilted. Peter poured two drinks, and like dinner guests we sat down on the couch. One sip of the whisky he handed me got me instantly drunk. He spread the contents of my package on the coffee table, skimming the indexes of the new books. For my part, using the vocabulary and syntax of *True Romance*, ransacking old films and novels as if they were a prop room, I composed a love scene in my head, thinking how beautiful his broad chest was, how I would lie against it, how passionately he would kiss me, how he would carry me off to bed. The only sound was the clack of ice cubes in my glass. Though I tried always to sit on his left side, by his good ear, I was sitting on his right. He apparently did not hear me whisper that I loved him. Nevertheless, I maneuvered to kiss his cheek and then, as he somewhat hesitantly responded, his lips. The anticipated blinding flash did not, alas, occur. He moved out of my arms, stood up. Sat down again. Scratched his head. I was crushed, abandoned on an ice floe of doubt.

"I should have told you to leave that research packet with the doorman."

"I love you, Peter."

"No, you don't love me, you can't. I have a wife. I'm your boss, at least for the moment. This is not right."

"I love you anyway." I was determined to win this skirmish. I had feared he might pat me on the head and send me to the elevator. He was attracted to me, or he wouldn't have given me a drink, wouldn't have kissed me back. Wouldn't have let me in at all. I took his hand, drew him close to me, insisted that he kiss me, and he did. And then I myself grew afraid.

With a sudden access of wisdom, I realized that what I was contemplating would be *adultery,* a word I had not yet applied to myself — a word I had so far associated with Emma Bovary and Rodolphe, but this afternoon the marital ties belonged to the man. "You frighten me. This is wrong. I am crazy," said Emma, the eternal cry of the heroine about to give in. What if Hannah found out? What if I really fell for him? What, God forbid, if he spread it around the office? As headstrong as Emma had been that terrible afternoon when her lover kissed her out under the trees and she set her feet on the pathway to destruction, I heard my mother's voice crying "Stop!" but I had no intention of stopping. Nor, I realized with an ambivalent delight, did he.

He asked if I had a diaphragm. Yes, of course, it was my badge of rebellion, of modernity, and a wonder I didn't just wear it on my lapel. He was relieved. Otherwise, he said, if I hadn't had one, he would have sent me home in a taxi that very instant, because there had to be some limit to the chances we took with each other's lives.

I shut the bathroom door, grasped the coil between my left thumb and index finger, unscrewed the cap from the tube with my teeth, and applied the jelly. But it sprang from my fingers as if from a slingshot, depositing its dollop of spermicide on the bathroom floor. I wiped it up, started over, tried to steady my hands, and finally felt it slide into place, safe, tight. Mustn't remove it for twenty-four hours. Not wishing to go into the marital four-poster I had glimpsed from the hallway at several dinner parties, I had asked Peter to put a comforter on the floor for us. I found him taking a quilt and two pillows out of the perfectly organized linen closet; the pillows were goose down, the pillowslips appliquéd. Ah, the *things* — the expensive pretty things with their correct labels, the things of married life. This was what married life was about — appliquéd pillowslips, orderly linen closets, parlors with china swans and vases of flowers, and we were mocking order. With the quilt and a thick comforter he made a bed on the living room floor, and we undressed and lay down together. I could taste the scotch in his mouth.

Mountains of papyrus, paper, and ink, not to mention electrical power, have been spent in the description of this simple act, which cannot vary too much from one epoch to the next: scribes have scriven, presses have rolled, poetic flights have filled a million youthful notebooks, everything from the unlaced bodices and insistent mouths I panted over as a teenager to the casual, monosyllabic brutality of pornography, in the struggle to manufacture sentences out of flesh against flesh, mouths and tongues, vulvas and vaginas moistening, penises rising, secret places visited and touched and kissed, the urgency, the delight. *"Elle s'abandonna,"* said Flaubert after Emma slipped out of her hoop skirt and gave herself — in the phrase beloved of a thousand novelists.

I too abandoned myself, recreated myself as Peter's equal rather than his acolyte, since love can equalize as easily as subjugate, can momentarily, at least, erase inequities of power or age. I liked the idea that the pathway to this illicit, makeshift bed had been strewn with art masterpieces and uplifting conversation. I was determined to be joyous, not to get tears in my eyes, not to let my mother's disapproving voice overwhelm me. We had seduced each other by looking at paintings. Why should love itself not be a work of art?

Because I live not in the event but in the reconstruction of it, because I favor memory over sensation, I can hardly recall how I felt as I left the Kleins' apartment the next morning. I believe I must have wept. I believe he must have too. In any case, he was filled with remorse — not so much for Hannah or himself as for me. He told me that he would never allow this to happen again and cautioned me to tell no one. "Not even your room-mate — nobody must know. Having you as my girlfriend might advance my status at the shop, but believe me, it won't advance yours," he warned. "Maybe in some twenty-first-cen-tury utopia editors and assistants, old men and young women, even old women and young men, will be able to have love af-fairs with no destructive consequences, but this is now." He told me, I remember, that he loved me in spite of what he had said earlier. That I must find someone else and above all keep writing. I must have been shaken and suffering. Surely it was beyond me (it has always been beyond me) to emerge serene and indifferent from a lover's bed. Henry Robinson generated his sheaf of overwritten, tear-stained airmail paper. I have only a recollection of Peter Klein, fabricated and refabricated, rewo-ven like a tapestry: a long-skirted and bejeweled medieval woman with a unicorn at her side; the girl at a tavern table, her face glowing in the peerless Dutch light.

During the next week, as I bought subway tokens, read the *New York Times,* washed out my stockings in the bathroom sink, I would assure myself, "I have a lover, I have a lover," though I had no lover. I had had a lover, and he had fled. Yet I felt elevated to a brilliant peak of sentiment; ordinary life lay below me, like a river in a valley, while I levitated crazily above. Icarus with his wings glued to his shoulders, rising recklessly toward the sun. I managed to face Peter calmly during the weeks that followed. He maintained the same proper, professional distance as always, and we visited no more museums together.

Because of his high commendation of my work, however, the head of research gave me a more responsible job. I was no longer Peter's trainee, his girl researcher. He was given a new researcher to train. And though the move had nothing to do with me — or at least I assumed so — he gave two months' notice. At the end of the year he would take a job at another magazine, a higher post, a better salary.

And another change of staff occurred that fall. Ingrid, the receptionist, finally showed her pack of nude photos to the wrong person — a new employee, it was said, who was so shocked and disgusted that she reported the matter to the personnel director, saying she'd rather resign than work in a place that tolerated such behavior. The personnel director fired Ingrid that afternoon, with no severance pay and no recommendation, as housemaids used to be dismissed when caught in the bed of the master's son. Yet Ingrid had conducted her adventures in adultery openly, with a kind of naive or possibly cynical pride, whereas I had contrived a one-nighter and kept it secret.

In November a disaster struck down our optimism, bit the first small, bloody hunk out of the flank of American hubris, and made us think twice about our pleasant, breezy belief in liberty and justice and fine art for all. I happened to be standing in line in the bank early one afternoon when a shout went up from somewhere that President Kennedy had been assassinated. In the erupting confusion around the tellers' windows, I heard somebody say that several others had been killed, including Jackie Kennedy and a score of spectators. Someone wondered aloud if it was the beginning of World War III. "They must have opened fire on that car with a machine gun," the teller said, weeping. I too began sobbing. I'd been wondering what kind of sandwich to buy for lunch and whether to eat it at my desk or in a coffee shop. Now I was weeping aloud in public for a man whose immortality I had taken for granted.

At my office, people had resurrected portable radios from bottom drawers. Yes, the president was dead, his skull sundered by bullets, his brains and blood splattered on Jackie's pink Chanel suit with its navy blue trim. No, she wasn't dead. Nobody else was dead. Lyndon Johnson was being sworn in, and the plane with the coffin was on its way to Washington. Passing Peter's door, I saw that he had buried his face in his arms. I sat down briefly and put my hand on his shoulder, the first time I had touched him in all those weeks. We spoke of what was gone — an era assassinated as much as a man, a brief interlude in American life when it had seemed legitimate to read French authors and discuss them publicly, to go to museums and vote to spend money on the arts, an era of delicious, fatuous optimism shaped by the belief that enough good will on the part of people like ourselves could repair anything, that bombs would never fall on us because we were too intelligent and energetic, that life on earth would continue on its upward course until every human being had grown to feel the way we did. John F. Kennedy was dead, and Peter and I were too. The golden age of the Dutch Republic was over. By four o'clock no one was left in the office but us. Peter and I went down in the elevator together and said goodbye.

In the winter after Kennedy's assassination and Peter's departure, the thought of him, of his gentleness and intensity as a lover and his admiration for me, brought me pleasure and eased my loneliness. It also gave me the courage, as well as the desire, to be solitary. Lone women were unwelcome in public in those days; in expensive restaurants, for example, a woman at a table by herself was deemed too forlorn, unchic, a damper on legitimate gaiety and sociability. Expensive restaurants were not among my hangouts, of course. But even bartenders in the Village assumed that an unescorted woman was a whore. Movie ushers gave you funny looks if you came in alone. Nevertheless, I took to wandering around the city by myself some Saturdays and Sundays.

It was painful at first to retrace the steps I had taken with Peter, but I went back to the Frick Collection one spring afternoon for another look at the Vermeer. The portraits of the young Renaissance aristocrat and of Whistler's women, so erotic when illuminated by my own eroticism, simply mere society portraits now, the sort of thing you'd expect an American millionaire to collect. But the Vermeer was as luminous, as transcendent as ever. Light radiated from the beautiful young woman's face. Forever wilt thou love and she be fair! Perhaps, as I had imagined, the officer at the table with his velvet coat and plumed hat was only a dream, a creature of the woman's imagining. Was this the way of love — the light emanating from the woman's face, the man's a blank, his back forever to the camera, his glance turned privately toward his one eternal observer? Or perhaps the light was merely oil on canvas, a luminous phenomenon not visible to the heart at all.

11

READER,
I MARRIED HIM

> We declare and affirm, by the tenor of these presents,
> that love cannot extend its rights over two married per-
> sons. For indeed lovers grant one another all things mu-
> tually and freely, without being impelled by any motive
> of necessity, whereas husband and wife are held by their
> duty to submit their wills to each other and to refuse each
> other nothing.
>
> May this judgment, which we have delivered with ex-
> treme caution, and after consulting with a great number
> of other ladies, be for you a constant and unassailable
> truth.
>
> — *Verdict rendered in 1174 by ladies at the court of*
> *the countess of Champagne, in northeastern France,*
> *to settle an argument over love vs. marriage*

Because of Fire Island, because of Peter, even because the national romance with John F. Kennedy, at least as a living man, was over, I got serious. My desire for marriage became a disease, causing symptoms such as headaches and insomnia. I yearned to be a married woman with rights and privileges, such as choosing the decorating scheme, decreeing that the sofa should be floral or striped, demanding and giving fidelity. Women must marry; otherwise they would be *un*married, a condition society scorned. A man should cleave to his wife and a wife to her husband, Jesus had said. And what God has joined together, let no man put asunder. But why were novels always about something else, the preliminaries?

"Happy love," I read one afternoon in the work of a great French savant, "has no history — in European literature." But ah, the millions of edifying stories that ended at the justice of the peace or the church-house door!

Why did the Bible itself so often describe everything but wedded bliss: patriarchs lusting after servant girls, David and Bathsheba — David and Jonathan, for that matter — the sensual poetry of the Song of Songs, the refusal of Jesus to marry, and Saint Paul telling us all in one breath that "a wife hath not power of her own body but the husband" and that it was better to remain single if possible, because marriage was only marginally better than burning? But we had now abolished burning. Contraception, penicillin, and jobs for women had deconstructed marriage, as well as virginity, sin, and hell. I was as capable of earning a living as most of the men I knew. Why marry? There could be only one reason: children. Truly the last motive to survive the onslaught.

I reasoned alone, wakeful at night, frightened to share my thoughts even with Carol, because they seemed so perverse. The feminist movement had not yet articulated itself, and I was incapable, all alone, of devising theories, lacked the words to proclaim blisteringly, as feminist thinkers soon would, that marriage was no different from chattel slavery in structure and intent. "The peculiar institution," as rich white southerners used to call slavery, the brick with which the grand mansion of state, church, and politics had been built. I pitied the husbands equally with the wives, men forced to labor for all eternity, never to look at another woman, at least in theory, bound by honor to turn away all petitioners. Searching Bartlett's *Familiar Quotations* under "marriage," I found the following references in the index:

> a noose
> a necessary evil
> and hanging go by destiny

is a desperate thing
a field of battle
has many pains
O curse of marriage

as well as this definition of marriage by Ambrose Bierce: "a community consisting of a master, a mistress, and two slaves, making in all, two."

Who needed Betty Friedan and Kate Millett?

Yet the necessity to marry, to live a legitimate life, swung shut on me like a jailhouse door. Like a heretic tortured sufficiently in the dungeons of the grand inquisitor, I converted, and sincerely craved the thing I had dreaded. It was, after all, the road to respectability, to tax deductions and medical insurance, to being taken seriously in butcher shops, to never having to attend another party as a single woman, not having to shop around.

My hope of creating a perfect love affair, a love worth dying for, vanished. Instead of childish things, I wanted children. I wanted my parents to stop worrying about me. I wanted never again to wake up on Saturday morning with no idea how to spend the day — for marriage gives you tasks. The home economist in my soul took over, that person from my past who wore a clean apron and steamed vegetables so as to preserve the vitamins, that person whose deepest desire was to possess the very best household machinery and to go for a shampoo and set once a week. But I remembered what George Sand had written: "In marriage women are ill used. They are forced to live a life of imbecility, and are blamed for doing so. If ignorant, they are despised, if learned mocked. In love they are reduced to the status of courtesans. As wives they are treated more as servants than as companions. Men do not love them: they make use of them, they exploit them, and expect, in that way, to make them subject to the law of fidelity." Could any of that be so?

I would be not Carmen but Michaela, not Lauren Bacall in a

trenchcoat but June Allyson. I would be Jane Eyre, the good wedded Jane Eyre, Mrs. Rochester, looking to the household, laying the baby in her husband's arms. Yet poor Bertha Rochester roamed through my dreams with a torch. Was her madness not a logical outcome of marriage? And Mr. Rochester blinded and broken? Bertha, stop howling. Would I too one day retire to the attic and comb my hair with my fingernails?

One by one, my friends were getting married. Love was always the first cause cited. Yet it seemed a matter of timing — not that they were overpowered by love and certainly not by lust, since we all assumed that postponing sex was not only unnecessary but neurotic, a decision that would land you in group therapy twice a week. They married because they had the chance, because their mothers expected them to, because of being on the wrong side of twenty-five or even thirty, because once married they could afford a car or a larger apartment. Could throw out the orange crates and foam-rubber couches and buy real furniture. Discard the chipped coffee cups and buy new. Getting married was about acquiring and hoarding a large supply of sexy underclothes and a white nylon nightie with matching peignoir for the honeymoon ("pen-*war*," I rehearsed Carol, who was shopping for one). Once engaged, you could pick out a silver pattern (Melrose, Chantilly, Grand Baroque) and some English china. Did we want the floral, or gold-rimmed? Then you could serve dinner on large plates with a separate fork for the salad and yet another for dessert. You would labor to make the entrées and salads and desserts that would in turn make the plates and covered vegetable dishes and dessert forks a necessity.

I had already bought a certain number of wedding presents: cake servers and tablespoons, as well as a covered vegetable dish or two in Spode or Lenox, tightly wrapped in white paper and satin ribbons. Hope chests: not for nothing were hope chests invented, and I knew from my research work on Peter Klein's behalf that the hope chest was a major art form, its carved panels prized since the early Renaissance. I thought of my mother's cedar chest, filled with coverlets that she had pieced out of dress scraps and quilted with her own hands. Yes, every woman must have a hope chest, must fill it with silver and handmade linens, embroidered pillowslips, things for the bed, things for the table, decorative things. Resurrecting a skill learned in childhood, I took up crewelwork once more, and began learning needlepoint against the day when I would need sofa cushions. One day, whispered my inner home economist, I would yearn for such things.

I had gone to weddings, received the carefully penned thank-yous on creamy paper engraved with "Mrs." at the top. Once the engagement rings were on their fingers, women who last year drank gin from jelly glasses and never changed their sheets visited the stationery counter at Saks or Tiffany's and followed Emily Post in all respects. Women who had discarded *Seventeen* and *Mademoiselle* in favor of *The Nation* and the *Village Voice* now read *Modern Bride* — surreptitiously, of course, the way men read *Playboy*. My women friends no longer talked politics, only etiquette. Florists. Where to find a judge who'd marry a Congregationalist to a Jew, or a rabbi who could co-exist with a priest, or any official at all to join two atheists in holy matrimony. Which bakeries made acceptable wedding cakes at acceptable prices. Which hotel charged what per head for a reception. Next thing, the baby announcements would begin rolling in. They had already rolled in, in startling numbers, from friends, relatives, and acquaintances back home. Now the rising tide of rag-content paper steel-engraved or inscribed in a fine italic hand was engulfing New York City. "I'm learning to write," a friend announced. She'd once had literary ambitions, but this time had taken up a broad-nib pen and was practicing italic lettering.

I inventoried my possibilities, the eligible men washed up on my shores like sea creatures, the flotsam and jetsam of cocktail parties, Fire Island, and happenstance. Allen Gillian and I had more or less ended our relationship. He told me he really did hope to persuade Carol to marry him and thus it was time for us to stop fooling around. I was deeply hurt and yet knew I had to get serious about finding a husband. I gave up the highly impractical idea of rescuing Antonio Piazza from the arms of the Almighty. Even if I managed to do it, I'd be married to a perpetually regretful man who would think birth control a sin and would want a dozen children.

Time to get hardheaded. First, and most promising, were the twin lawyers, Jamie and Hal. I had met them at a party celebrating someone else's engagement. Both telephoned me regularly, drank up our household liquor, invited me out occasionally for a meal. Though they were identical twins, I could tell them apart, could even distinguish their voices on the phone. I did not want either of them to know I was his brother's girlfriend. I spent weekends with one and then the other, made love with both of them because they expected it, and because I wanted to. I had begun to love this image of myself, casually going to bed with this man or that. How wonderfully remote from my upbringing! How wonderfully remote from the sort of novel I liked, where sex was so serious and carried spiritual as well as physical consequences.

But the transition from my Paris self — where I had specialized in a kind of promiscuity of the mind — to this easy promiscuity of the body failed to make me happy. Turning my back in bed to Jamie or Hal as he fell asleep or got up to find his clothes, I would often be teary-eyed, would wonder why he was so relentlessly matter-of-fact, so determined to remain unthrilled, why he never said anything beyond a few monosyllabic requests or cries of satisfaction, matched by my own dutifully rendered cries of satisfaction. "Intense" was the word Henry Robinson had once applied to me, and oh yes, I was abundantly endowed with those qualities that frightened men, that eagerness for permanence, that thirst for more than I was currently receiving. I found myself wanting to pull at Hal's or Jamie's arm, bring him back into bed, aping the gesture of that rosy, powdery, ample-thighed Venus tugging at the arm of Mars, the Titian Peter and I had joked about in the Metropolitan Museum. But this was foolishness. They were modern professional men. I was a modern professional woman. What terrible, destructive thing did I seek?

I wanted Hal or Jamie, these perfectly presentable, sensible, well-educated young men, to utter some sequence of words that would satisfy me. I didn't know what. Occasionally I would think back to the delights I had imagined as a child, the body bent backwards in a kiss, Juliet on the balcony, some grand and mysterious undertaking. I scolded myself for being a miserable believer in romance novels, a collector of clichés. An abnormal, unfeminine, desexed woman unable to accept her destiny and in need of psychoanalysis. I had read a book — *The Lost Sex*, it was called — about modern women like myself: we had cut ourselves off from our X chromosomes, from our hormones, and from our destiny as women, that is, as multiparas and submissive wives. We would surely pay an awful price, in the cost to our own health and that of society, and it would serve us right. The book made me angry: I knew that I was being bullied, used. And yet I had no immediate answer for this argument. I didn't want to be the lost sex. A man, a plan, an orgasm: who could wish for more than that?

Perhaps marriage would reverse the flat-earth trend. Maybe married love was more compelling than I thought or had observed, maybe it grew and complexified and twisted into marvelous shapes and colors. Would I marry Jamie or Hal? I compared them as if I were picking out blenders in Macy's basement. Both were quite presentable: friends and family would be impressed with what I had caught. Jamie was sweeter-tempered, a more adept and gentler lover. He smoked a pipe (endurable). Hal was wittier, less predictable, but I sensed some nasty trait of character underneath. And he smoked cigars (unendurable). How would I manage as a lawyer's wife? I should need to have dinner waiting when *he*, whichever he it was, came in at ten o'clock. I should have to deal indefinitely with his (their) parents, a rich Long Island couple, Jewish, with a Cadillac and a sailboat, who would instantly dislike me because my parents were Protestant and my clothes bargain-basement. My parents would dislike either of the men because of their ferocious, Manhattanite articulateness, their urban manner, their lightly worn but alarming religion. But then Mama and Daddy would recognize security — "He'll always be able to provide for her" — and they could die in peace. (If money was the object, why not marry both of them?) Jamie or Hal, he would expect me to keep his shirts in order for business travel. He would not want me to have a job myself. Both, in different contexts, had already expressed the opinion that being a wife should be job enough for any woman. I would need to organize cocktail parties for his associates, talk with the wives.

Wifedom looked like a mountain I could never climb, a weight I could never lift. Why didn't Hal and Jamie simply hire maids? When we had children, I would be pressured by his family to become Jewish and by my family not to. If I converted, I would never really be accepted into the new religion but would be forever on the blacklist of the old. I decided that of the two of them I would prefer Jamie, and that when the time came I would convert. Whither thou goest I shall go, where thou lodgest, *moi aussi*, thy people, my people. I recalled that Ruth, gleaning in the fields of alien grain, made this pledge to another woman, not to her husband.

My problem was solved when Hal discovered that I had been sleeping with Jamie. He broke off with me at once, whereupon Jamie announced that perhaps the differences between him and me were too great.

But I took heart once more. The boyfriend who had inspired Carol to shop for major nightwear and think about the china pattern had proved out, had stuck around, and she told me he was it. If he asked her, she would marry him. He often spent the night in our tiny apartment. They tried to be discreet, but I could hear them making love on the other side of the wall. She kept her ecstasy fairly quiet, but he sometimes could not repress appreciative yelps. On Sundays they slept until mid-afternoon, and out of consideration I went around in slippers, never played the phonograph, and tried to make coffee very quietly.

Carol had no intention of marrying Gil or having any fur-ther relations with him except those of a casual friend, and she told him so. I knew he was sorrowing, confused, and so was I. He began taking me out for long drives once more — he mourned for Carol, sang the blues, while I pretended to be heartbroken over Jamie or Hal or someone else I had been tracking. One Sunday afternoon, as Gil and I drank coffee in my living room, Carol and her man arrived, and Carol flashed her left hand under our noses: a diamond. Squeals, laughter, embraces, jumping up and down until the landlord on the first floor pounded angrily on his ceiling. They talked of marrying the next year. I was to be the maid of honor. I wondered what Gil thought of all this, but he looked unperturbed. He told me later he was glad — he was over her. I was sick. How would I do without my Carol? How would I pay the rent without her? Why did she have to be first?

But only six months later, at the age of twenty-seven, I found my fiancé, my man who asked to marry me, who said he loved me, Gil, of course, who'd been there all the time. Like me, he was past the peak age for wedlock. Even before his crush on Carol, he had been engaged and had his heart broken. I knew all about this unhappy history; indeed, his entire unhappy history, wildly and gamely clad in humor, was woven through his conversation, providing a mournful, self-deprecating un-dertone that caught my ear, aroused protective feelings in my heart. Here, I reasoned, was a man who had known pain and therefore could never inflict it. I knew too about the lost jobs, the interviews that hadn't quite worked out, the near misses that had characterized his life. Here was a man of talent (I had read his short stories, his two attempts at a screenplay) wasting himself on journalism and promotion copy. Maybe I could do something about all that. Rescue an artist from the wicked toils of commercialism. Why not? It was a role I fancied.

Week by week, I learned to wait impatiently for his calls. "We're only friends," we assured each other. "Two lonely people biding our time." But I had finally reached a point where I did not need to be swept away. I needed only to experience one small symptom of love — the casual kiss in the car, the veal scaloppini I made when he could not afford to pay for dinner, the lovemaking after. It was like hearing the first bars of a song and automatically supplying the rest. I sang the song because I knew the words and couldn't keep from singing it, and because it was time.

"When whippoorwills call, and evening is nigh . . ." He liked the cute, bouncy stuff about hearth and home, rose-covered cottages, a boy for you and a girl for me. "My romance doesn't need a thing but you." I knew those songs too. If falling in love was supposed to be a precipitous plunge, this was not it. Rather, I let myself down slowly, hand over hand. I did not at first love this man as hopelessly as I had loved Joey Cash or as intensely as I had loved Henry Robinson in Paris, nor did he satisfy my utmost sensibilities, as Peter Klein had done. But I could help him, and that would be the same as loving him. I could make life all right for him. He could make life all right for me. I decided that I loved him. He was not my ideal, nor was I his. But imperfections become lovable in themselves. "Love is not love which alters where it alteration finds, or bends with the remover to remove!" We drank scotch and cooked steaks and made love at his fifth-floor walkup, not emerging from Friday evening to Sunday night. And gradually, the romance of the weekends began to stick, to carry over into Monday morning,

Wednesday afternoon, Thursday night. I began to tell myself, with confidence, then with joy, that I now loved Gil. I could hardly wait for the weekends.

Sometimes while he slept I would look around his disorderly bedroom, the piles of laundry to be done, the papers unsorted, the books that needed a bookcase, the tiny Olivetti portable typewriter with which he earned his living, the floors tangled with stereo wires and connections and jacks leading from preamp to amplifier to tuner to woofer to tweeter to an electrical outlet that seemed to have twenty plugs jammed into it, and I would think, "Oh, yes, I can fix this. Here is a task for me. Balance his checkbook, match up and fold his socks, put the books in alphabetical order by author. File all the rough drafts by title and date. That way he'll be able to find what he wants." And no doubt as I slept, he surveyed the room and thought, "Ah, she will soon get used to my disorder, my chaos. She will come to love it as I love it."

Above the sidewalks, with city grit drifting in his open windows, with dishes and frypans stacked in the tiny sink and the detergent bottle empty, we shared stories about our childhoods, searching cooperatively for common ground. His youth had been harsh and unhappy, and I deliberately, reciprocally, darkened my own narrative. Yes, my parents had squelched me, failed to nurture me as I deserved, had saddled me with neuroses that I was only just beginning to work through. This was untrue but was the conventional wisdom of the day, the only respectable thing to say, and besides, it seemed disloyal to Gil for me to have had a happy childhood. It was corny to have had a happy childhood. One needed at least stupid, preferably ferocious, parents. He no doubt shaped his narratives as artfully as I shaped mine. I was determined not to frighten him off, to be feminine and sincere, to bank the curves of my hardheadedness, my lust for absolutes, to respond gently and maternally to his strong points as well as his flaws. I noted but decided not to worry about the long silences and bad moods that occasionally engulfed him, the unrealistic dreams he had about the cars we would drive, the houses we would own. Warp and woof, we wove the cloth, busily, industriously, two artisans at the loom.

The engagement ring he gave me — a handsome diamond that he had inherited from his grandmother — was having its third trial. (I gazed at the stone on my finger, pleased by this small caldron of pure light captured in a calyx of tiny platinum prongs. How beautiful! Would I now be honored at afternoon teas, pick and choose outfits for my trousseau? Get my name in the paper?) The ring connected me to the world, rendered me proper, compensated for failures at the same time that it set limits to my ambitions. "Getting married," he joked the night he offered me the ring, "is a good way to put an end to a beautiful friendship," and neither of us paused to decipher the darker meaning of the words. (He was always joking about one thing or another.) I was ready to be his wife. Maybe I'd have to support the family. Wear the pants, like George. Yet that seemed less odious, somehow, than the ready-made slots lawyers and doctors had waiting for their wives. It would free me up. I need not become his hostess and social secretary. I tried not to think of his being out of a job. Ah, but I would help him, I would steady him. He needed the motivation of a wife and children.

About this time my father had a heart attack and I was called home. I had already told my parents the news — they could strike me off their worry list, because I was getting married. Gil was unable to come with me — he had two assignments due in two weeks, hadn't started either of them, and couldn't afford the plane fare. But my engagement was swallowed up in my parents' disaster, which had only just begun to unfold. Waiting for me alone at the airport, my mother, at forty-eight, looked elderly and worn out. "Your daddy isn't himself," she told me as we climbed into the ancient Dodge and drove to the hospital. "I doubt he'll ever work again. They've already filled his job with some young man. The doctor talks about disability — you know, payments from the government. But those won't cover our expenses, I don't think. I have to go to work." What she did not tell me was that she too was having alarming symptoms and was scheduled to undergo some tests as soon as my father was out of the hospital.

And my father, sitting up in his hospital room, his thin form swaddled in a new seersucker bathrobe, his bony ankles protruding above his hospital scuffs, was a strange gray color. He briefly admired my engagement ring, then told me grimly that his working days were over. He'd never be able to fly to New York for the wedding, as he might once have hoped to do. He didn't approve of fancy weddings, which were in any case now beyond his means. "Get married at city hall," he advised. "A justice of the peace was good enough for your mother and me, and it should be good enough for you. We are happy you are settling down. Thank God for it. I probably don't have much longer to live." (Here my mother burst into tears, and I protested, but he continued.) "I hope to meet Gil, but if I never meet him, I expect you've chosen right. Time you started on life's rocky pathway," and he laughed. Shocked not by his words but by his pallor, by the cane he now needed just to walk across the floor, by his shortness of breath, I told him he was not to worry about anything so trivial as a wedding.

That afternoon, as we went to and from the hospital, preparing for my father's homecoming the next morning, my mother suddenly detoured past the new county library building. "Seems like I run into Cora Lena Brown every time I go out on the street. She even came to see your daddy in the hospital. Brought him some reading material. She asks about you all the time. Always says how much she misses you coming into the library, what a good little patron you were. I want you to go in there and show her that ring and tell her you're going to get married. She would be just thrilled to see you."

But I didn't want to show Cora Lena my ring. I was tired, terrified about my father. I wished I hadn't brought the damn ring. Was this the right moment to brag to Cora Lena about my engagement? "I haven't had time to talk to you about it," I muttered nervously, "but I have doubts. I'm afraid. I'm not sure we're so well suited, actually. I thought maybe you'd . . ." My father's bony ankles, his panting breath as he moved across the floor, rose in a stabbing image in my mind. I had no right to get married. Somehow the notion, once I voiced it to myself, was comforting. How could I leave them, the two people in the world who truly did love me? "You're going to need my help, Mother," I said.

But taking aim at her parking place and fighting the stiff steering wheel of the old car as if grappling with an opponent, she heard only my last statement, or chose to respond to the offer of help rather than to my confusion about my prospective husband. "Now, don't be foolish. You have your life in front of you. Daddy and I can take care of ourselves."

Cora Lena, now gray-haired, had given up her yellow pencil with the rubber stamp at the end in favor of a hulking machine that went *shunk* when she ran a library card through it. The librarian's station was at a great distance now from the open shelves. No longer did Cora Lena know exactly where everything was shelved. There was a card catalogue; the Dewey decimal system reigned. You had to do the ransacking yourself, without her supervision. She no longer knew what every kid was reading. But her eyes were as bright as they had been fifteen years before when I first applied to her for a copy of *Jane Eyre*. She rose from her swivel chair and threw her thin arms around me.

"Well, look who's here. I am so glad to see you, honey. I went to see your daddy, and I know you are so anxious about him, but don't you fret. He needs to take it easy for a while, and he'll be on his feet once again. Tell him I've saved some mystery stories for him. Your mama tells me grand news about you. That's what we need to concentrate on now. Oh, imagine how happy this has made your mama and daddy. What a gift!"

"Show Cora Lena your ring!" my mother insisted, poking

my arm, and I offered my left hand, which the librarian rested in her own palm as she eyed the diamond.

"Ah, lovely. Just simply exquisite. What an enormous stone! Why, imagine how hard he must have worked to get this for you! Lucky young man. His name is what?" Her face glowed with generosity and joy.

"Uh, Allen Gillian. Called Gil. He's a journalist, a newspaper reporter and writer. I met him in New York. The ring belonged to his grandma, he didn't work to get it."

"Well, I do say. You are the beatingest girl. Smart as a whip, naturally curly hair, fine grades in college, a scholarship to France, a wonderful job on a magazine, and now this. You have everything a young woman could possibly want. I know how happy you must be, all except for this worry about your poor dad. I am thrilled for you, just thrilled."

I smiled, choked, said nothing, and groped to lay hold of my identity. Cora Lena had once been a kind of conspirator with me against the flatness, the ordinariness of small-town life. In some crevice of my adolescent soul, I had admired her lean and hungry and bookish life, her defiance of all pressures to marry. Now I stood before her with a diamond on my finger. I was about to marry a man she certainly imagined as an important newspaperman (for I knew Cora Lena had extrapolated upward, not downward, from my neutral statement about Gil's profession.) She imagined that he and I adored each other. Did not a diamond on the left hand signify that we did? Somehow this glamorous creature standing in my shoes had evolved from the bookworm who used to appear at Cora Lena's desk, applying for permission to swallow all two hundred volumes of the county library, especially those with dirty parts. I could no longer see the continuum between my present self and that child or teenager with the fatal crush on Joey Cash or the ten-year-old swooning over Frédéric and George in the Paramount Theater. I no longer knew which one of these characters was fictitious. I saw the admiration in my old friend's eyes, read her belief that she and I together had accomplished something, and deeply wished to be the person of her imaginings.

My father stabilized; I went back to work and wedding plans. My prospective mother-in-law was thrilled with me. I was her dream girl; she could stop worrying about her boy. She wrote to me weekly from Florida, commanding me to call her Mother, or Edwina if I couldn't manage Mother, sending recipes for Gil's favorite cakes and pies and for making roast beef gravy the way he liked it. She had always wanted a daughter, had given up all hope of Gil's ever marrying. Now I was to be her pupil in a school for wives, the recipient of a thousand gifts to adorn the home she wished her son to live in. Did I not know how to make a proper pastry? She would teach me. Where did I plan to buy the furniture? (Nowhere; we were dead broke. She recommended teak.) Was my favorite color blue or red? (I had no favorite color. But I answered "blue.") When could I come for a visit? She volunteered to manage the wedding for me. I fought her off as best as I could.

I persuaded the minister of the Church of the Ascension on lower Fifth Avenue to marry us, even though neither of us was Episcopalian. Carol agreed to be my witness, as I would witness for her two months later. I bought a pattern and three yards of white satin and made my dress myself, turning down Edwina's offer to accompany me to some fancy bridal salon. We would have a small wedding cake and champagne at home afterward, and then go briefly and inexpensively out of town. My mother and mother-in-law and a few other wedding guests arrived from out of town. As my father had predicted, he was unable to attend.

The November day that we had picked for the ceremony proved unexpectedly bright and mild, a few leaves still red and yellow on the trees, a brisk wind blowing. Five minutes before the ceremony, in the anteroom with Carol and the rector, I was stricken. Sweat broke out of every pore — soaking my underarms, staining the satin, threatening to demolish my carefully arranged hair. My voice vanished, and I thought of the little town a thousand miles away where even now the newspaper presses were starting to roll out an account of what was about to transpire in the Church of the Ascension.

No writeup of this wedding would make it into the *New York Times,* of course, but at home the spools of newsprint were already spinning as inexorably as history. This ceremony was already on page one of the society section of my home-town Sunday paper. I was married, whether I wanted to be or not. The item, written and submitted by my mother, described my short white satin dress with its matching jacket, my bouquet of white roses, my lace mantilla, my matching pumps with the little bows on the toes — for that newspaper, you had to tell about everything the bride wore except her underpants. The article identified Carol Perkins as my only attendant, and Mother had been eloquent about her exquisite blue chiffon frock with dyed-to-match pumps, her blue silk picture hat, her nosegay of daisies.

And indeed, there Carol Perkins stood, wearing that very hat, fixed dizzily in my vision. "Now don't you get sick here at this crucial moment," she was pleading. "Your groom has arrived. He sure looks hung over, but he's all ready." She turned to the rector. "Is there someplace to get a glass of water? I think she is passing out."

"I don't want any water. Carol, for the love of God, let's get out of here. I don't want to get married."

The organist had already begun to play. I could hear the strains of Henry Purcell's trumpet voluntary. This was the fashionable wedding music of the moment — nobody wanted Mendelssohn anymore. (The voluntary turned out later not even to be by Purcell, but how little we knew!)

"I can't. I'm not doing this!"

"Okay, okay. I believe you." She flung aside her daisies.

"I'm going out to get a taxi. Grab our purses. They're in that little closet in the hall. I'll meet you by the side door. If you don't want to get married, you damn well don't have to."

But the rector pushed Carol aside, seizing me by the shoulder with efficient fingers. "You can't back out of this now. All brides are nervous. You'll feel better in a minute. Stagefright. You're afraid to walk out there." I stared helplessly into his cold eyes. I knew it was true — not that I was merely having stagefright, unless he meant a stagefright so global as to engulf my remaining years, but that I must go ahead and do what I had bargained for, that running out the side door of the church was a piece of treachery no woman would dare commit (except in screwball comedies, of course). I was not up to such an act of childishness, of spitefulness. What would Gil say? What would they all say? I thought of the rosewood box with the hinged top where my wedding-gift silver was accumulating, carefully wrapped in soft brown cloth to keep away the tarnish. Ten butter knives. A cake server. Five iced-tea spoons. Each would have to be wrapped and sent back with an apologetic note. Better just get married.

"I am starting the procession toward the altar, and Carol is going to follow me, and you are going to follow Carol," the rector commanded, and the authority of God and man was in his voice and at his back. I looked into his face and felt resolved to do it. "You both just get behind me and start walking, just like we rehearsed it yesterday. Step, close step. Step, close step. Get on with it. The poor organist has already started over twice. Your guests are getting anxious. The groom and best man are waiting. They'll think you've lost your mind. Come on."

And so I went out, my roses quivering, step, close step. The few friends and relations we had invited had bunched themselves together loyally in the front pews, and I could hear my mother sobbing ever so quietly. I followed Carol into the nave

of the century-old church, the very church I had imagined being married in, dressed in white and clutching flowers as many
New York City brides had done before me. At the altar, I listened to the readings from *The Book of Common Prayer,* the
well-wrought sentences, radioactive as uranium, grave with authority, words designed to corner their prey. Earlier that week,
the rector had required us to come for instruction, had described the duties and pleasures of Christian marriage, the
sanctity of the four walls of home, of sexual love within those
bounds, the chains of marriage that united you. These chains
would heal the wounds of life, he said, and would eventually
not feel like chains at all. I had resolved not to fail.

". . . therefore is not by any to be entered into unadvisedly
or lightly; but reverently, discreetly, advisedly, soberly, and in
the fear of God," he was saying now. "If either of you know
any impediment, why ye may not be lawfully joined together
in matrimony, ye do now confess it."

"I confess I am not good wife material," I wanted to cry out.
"I have been spoiled by too much reading and by the movies
and by listening to the opera on Saturday afternoons. I have
seen too many movies. There is something in the air these days
that tells me not to do this. I have a different notion of what life
should be than the duties of a sanctified household. My ideas
about love are insane." But I held my peace, assenting quietly
when asked to love, comfort, honor, keep my husband in sick-
ness and in health, and, forsaking all others, keep me only unto
him.

And the minister went on, "Give thanks always for all
things unto God and the Father in the name of our Lord Jesus
Christ . . . Wives, submit yourselves unto your own husbands,
as unto the Lord. For the husband is the head of the wife, even
as Christ is the head of the church . . ."

I thought of turning to Gil. "Our love is hardly all-consuming. Yet we look to each other for love, not knowing, each of
us, how to give or receive it. I want some transcendent thing I

cannot even describe, you yearn for comfort, a housekeeper, and someone to laugh at your jokes. I fear, my darling, that marriage is about money, not love. Why does this cleric in his black suit not speak of that? Or of the divorce that seems so regularly to occur after children arrive and then there are three of you or four of you? We are not marrying each other but an institution. Ah, why should we expect it to be about love?" But I remained silent.

". . . a man leave his father and mother, and shall be joined unto his wife, and they two shall be one flesh. This is a great mystery . . . Wherefore they are no more twain, but one flesh. What therefore God hath joined together, let not man put asunder . . . O God, look mercifully upon these thy servants, that they may love, honor, and cherish each other, and so live together in faithfulness and patience, in wisdom and true godliness, that their home may be a haven of blessing and of peace . . ."

I walked up the aisle wiping my eyes as the church bells pealed, and we received congratulations, both of us still giddy with fear. Edwina told me that a bride's tears at a wedding were a good prognostication. I had managed to do the thing that society demanded, that my upbringing dictated, and that my reason required me to do. Oh, I would try my utmost to make our home a haven of blessing and of peace. I would change the sheets every week, stand at the sink scouring my cookware, give nice little dinner parties, eschew my bad habits: I would never dream of flirting with another man or behaving like the heroine of a novel, not even a Great Novel, and as soon as we got back from our wedding trip, I intended to quit smoking. Yet as I changed into street clothes after our small reception, I was wracked with apprehension, once again playing a solo in D minor on my paper and comb while the philharmonic thundered onward in the key of C.

12

THE PECULIAR
INSTITUTION

Gil and I found a rent-controlled, one-bedroom walkup on a cobblestone avenue in the West Village, rumbling day and night with trucks, not far from the Hudson River. Our living room windows looked out through the upper branches of a ginkgo tree, the tough guy of New York City flora, impervious to auto exhaust and dog urine. And in this place we set out to create our haven of peace. We were no longer twain but one flesh, a union blessed not only by God but by the federal tax code, smiled upon by choirs of angels and the Internal Revenue Service as well as our relations and insurance company. Surely marriage would prove to be a vessel for love rather than a substitute for it. And indeed, Gil and I began to love each other, to delight in being married, and even to confuse one emotion with the other. He had refused to wear a wedding band, but I went whole hog. Mrs. Gillian, Mrs. Allen Gillian. Like my adolescent self in love with Joey Cash, I practiced writing my name, developed a rather splendid capital *G*, had "Mrs. Allen Gillian" printed on notepaper, changed my bank account, notified the utility company, changed my magazine subscriptions, informed Social Security. Let other women keep their so-called maiden names.

We enjoyed the legality, the availability, the inevitability of sex, and like all newlyweds learned that inclination is not eternally mutual or simultaneous. I learned the practical skills of intimacy — blessed skills, really: how to sleep with a man when sleeping is the chief object, how to put up with the odd noises another person makes, how to get over being embarrassed by the noises I myself made (the clearing of the throat, the blowing of the nose, the inopportune fart, the clipping of toenails, and all the details of physical life that one may keep secret from a lover but not a husband), how to replace uncomplainingly the cap he has left off the toothpaste, hang up the towel or washcloth or sock discarded by one's beloved, to sleep in an old shirt or nothing and forget the peignoir. I learned the inequalities of wifedom: he never put the milk back in the refrigerator or wiped up spills but reprimanded me when I idly ate lettuce leaves from the salad bowl with my fingers as we lingered at the supper table. The bachelor who had been willing to wait two weeks, if necessary, for the next visiting girlfriend to wash his sink full of dishes now noticed how the plates were stacked in the cupboard and had opinions about detergents, was fussy about his clothes and inveighed against the scent of furniture polish, the look of wash-and-wear shirts.

These were, to me, unwonted (but not unwanted) masculine traits. All men were like that. I listened patiently. I coveted an identity as a proper wife, a true acolyte of Athena, goddess of the spinning wheel and of the hearth, the taskmistress born from the head of a male god. I would spin and weave. A born-again matron, I ironed his cotton shirts, though he begged me to send them to the laundry. I went into the butcher shop, requesting this cut or that because "that's what my husband likes," watching sternly while the slab was trimmed to my order. I was now an associate editor with a whole researcher and half a secretary of my own, and my salary had been correspondingly improved. But I began believing that my life, or the significant part of it, ended in the morning when I left for work and began once more when I entered the apartment at night carrying two pork chops and a pound of green beans.

I had never expected my mother-in-law to be a presence in

my marriage, but she was frequently on the phone, in the mailbox, and arriving at La Guardia airport with sheaves of recopied recipes in which she intended to rehearse me. Pie crust. Meatloaf. Roast beef gravy. She and Gil had never been particularly close, he said, but she was deeply infatuated with the two of us. I gave in to her commands and called her Mother. "I already have a mother," thought I sourly, but Edwina seemed as much a part of the marriage package as the double fitted sheets. My own mother was now working full-time as a department store saleswoman and looking after my invalid father. She wrote little notes once a week, and we telephoned, but otherwise my parents did not intrude on our new household. Meanwhile, like some zealous Vichy functionary, I collaborated openly with the invader, chatted with her about spot removal and how to extract the most use out of everything from nylon stockings to tea bags. Surely I could do these things, know these things, remain on good terms with Edwina without losing my wits.

French cuisine attracted me now the way the French language once had done. But while the language had served as an escape hatch from the humdrum, the cuisine as practiced in my decrepit Village kitchen was a trap door to servitude. Julia Child was the current queen of the kitchen, a saboteur of female liberty in the tradition of Fannie Farmer and a dozen other such instructresses of America's aspiring brides, assiduous devisers of new labor to cancel out our labor-saving devices. (The egg beater, invented to spare housewives' arms in the nineteenth century, was followed instantaneously by the invention of angel food cake.) Julia's goal, she stated, was to teach the servantless American housewife to cook at the level of a trained French chef. Real French chefs earn a wage and have a staff to bone the chicken and prepare the lemon zest, and they don't have to clean up, either. But no matter. *Mastering the Art of French Cooking* replaced all my other reading. I worked to run a proper kitchen, *à la française:* I learned to make stock, threw out my garlic powder. I hid my electric mixer in the bottom drawer: only a wire whisk would do. Mrs. Child said you'd never get your egg whites to the maximum height if you were so lazy, so unconcerned, as to use a mixer.

My oven had two temperatures, hot and cold, and my refrigerator was older than I was, but I studied the science of cooking techniques, of inserting the boning knife just so between the chicken rib and the meat, of injecting lardons into otherwise unpalatable cuts of roast beef, clarifying butter, assembling stews that required a day to prepare, binding up dried herbs in cheesecloth bags. Even butter had to be served as a curl, not a pat, and required a tool for making the curl. Even snapping a bean had its rule. Vegetables I had once been on casual terms with turned into demanding strangers, not something to be hurled into a pot and boiled. To make a pâté was insufficient; one had to track down cornichons. It was so pure, so ethical, so high-minded: no shortcuts. Nothing, *nothing*, was easy.

All in the name of wedded love, I absorbed the philosophical niceties of preparing fish fillets and soufflés, marveled at the cleverness of provincial French cooks who could extract flavor from a stone and never wasted a morsel or a scrap, the correctness of the plain balloon whisk, my teacher's bibulous insistence on plenty of alcohol — in the recipes and at table. Good wine, too. If you cooked with cheap stuff, you'd get cheap results. No cheating, girls! Groceries, formerly a haphazard concept augmented by moo goo gai pan and rice noodles in takeout cartons, were now a formidable item in the weekly budget, not to mention wine, whisky, gin, and vermouth brought up the stairs in corrugated boxes, with the empties to be carted down again in an astonishingly brief interval. Cooking dinner for a few friends became an obstacle course, two evenings' shopping, all day Saturday cooking, all day Sunday cleaning up — not counting detours to Macy's basement for springform pans, proper boning knives, and costly heavy-bottomed casseroles. But I achieved a level of skill enabling me to cook and serve a four-course dinner for eight, including a successful dessert soufflé. I even felt triumphant as I scrubbed sauté pans on Sunday afternoon rather than reading. I had turned into Julia Child, or an amalgam of Julia, Edwina, and my own mother.

And I still reported for work Monday morning, having polished the last soup spoon at midnight Sunday and wrapped it in tarnish-repellent cloth. Sometimes I sat at my desk and wondered who I was. Was I the married self with a mother-in-law and Green Stamps? The woman with an editorial job and a recent promotion behind her, who got paid for what she knew, what she thought, rather than reams of neatly typed columns or stacks of neatly stitched garments? My work took on a surreptitious character, something I needed to hide from my husband. Adultery of the mind. Deep in my books and papers at the office, profoundly lost in them, looking at my watch only when it was past quitting time, I would mentally apologize to Gil, confess to him my sin of spiritual neglect, the solecism of having forgotten him not merely for several minutes but for several hours. I would grow anxious over the faint impropriety of joking or lunching with one of the men I worked with, the hint of flirtation that I squelched but never instantly. Why did men feel more at liberty to flirt with a married woman? How exhilarating it was at last to deal with men as if we were professional equals. But I was resolutely and absolutely a faithful wife.

Gil adjusted uneasily to my onslaught of haute housewifery, which after all was more my idea than his. He liked the food and adored having a drink while I prepared dinner, but he soon began to complain of my compulsiveness, of my determination to do the dishes after dinner rather than leave them for some future date, of the money I was spending, of the dangers of getting fat. "Smells like the goddamn Lower East Side in here," he shouted one evening, arriving home as I was sautéing garlic — thus launching a tearful quarrel that lasted into the night. He did not hear the voices in my ear, did not see the presences that eyed me and lectured me as I went about my daily tasks — my mother, my cousins, my married friends, women's magazines from ages past, Hannah Klein, and now Julia and Edwina, all of them boarders in our small apartment, perched on the kitchen counter, lurking in corners, inspecting table settings, spotting dustballs under the bed. "Not correct to snap green beans that way. Use a knife." "You'll chip those dishes if you aren't more careful." "Your silver needs polishing — you can't put it on the table in that condition." They drowned out whole choruses of poets and novelists. I forgot about Chopin, obliterated George Sand and indeed all French literature from my memory. I forgot Paris. I forgot how to speak French. What good had it been, or done me? I didn't need it now.

I also obliterated from memory all other persons I had slept with or lusted after or consorted with, blotted out Peter Klein, Olivia, the lawyer twins, Henry Robinson, and particularly Bill James with his piles of books and his feverish insistence that life was lived most keenly via words on paper. Me, a partaker in adultery, dalliance, brief encounters, homosexuality, greed, the intellectualizing of physicality, the obsession with language, the reading of novels that could not legally be offered for sale in the United States, and other forms of subversive activity? Not me; I was a woman with no past. I was not now nor had I ever been ambitious for passion, fornication, or adulterous liaisons. I was clean. I had arrived at my destiny. "Now you are a little married woman," my mother had told me anxiously on my wedding day, sensing in her kind and generous heart that I was in for a hard time of it.

In spite or because of his growing discontent with the march toward perfection, Gil settled into the role of cared-for spouse, a role his upbringing had taught him to play just as my mother had trained me to keep house. He offered little help with household tasks, only occasionally looking over the top of his newspaper as I wrestled the grocery cart up the stairs at eleven o'clock Saturday mornings. I wanted no help, and actively discouraged it. I didn't want my husband in the kitchen or gathering up laundry: he was too fragile, was far too busy, was struggling too hard with his work. He needed to sleep late weekends because he often worked all night. No man, indeed, ever worked harder or sought work more diligently. I was willing to hold down two jobs if he could successfully do one. Anyway, homemaking was not a job but something verging on the sacred.

Sometimes I wised up and grew apathetic, cynical, bored with my own efforts at conformity. And some nights after I had gone to bed alone, exhausted after a day's work and an evening's housewifery, Gil would sit in the living room drinking scotch and listening to love songs. When this happened, if I wasn't angry with him or already asleep, I would get up and rejoin him, sitting on the floor, leaning against his knee, and wondering if I were still included in his vision of eros. "My romance doesn't need a thing but you" acquired undertones of parody. "I get a kick out of you," Ella Fitzgerald warbled, but did he get a kick out of me? The love songs now seemed to be about some other couple. Occasionally I would weep against his trouser leg, but I never succeeded in explaining (least of all to myself) what the tears were for.

Another point against me: I was too emotional, always weeping, always overly dramatic. Oh God, perhaps I *was* the lost sex. Perhaps the combination of salaried employment and a literary education had screwed up my hormones, deprived me of my feminine nature. "My first mistake," I told a girlfriend that winter, laughing as I spoke, "was learning to read. Illiteracy would be a good quality in a wife. Except for cookbook English." Whatever the reason, sexual love seemed increasingly irrelevant to both Gil and me, and no doubt it was my fault. In all, no wife ever collaborated more willingly in her own demolition than I.

As our discontent simmered, we tried to smother it with things, littered our two-closet apartment with them. Edwina displayed relentless largesse: planters, canisters, chafing dishes.

Everything she gave came packaged with her own social aspirations, none more so than an enormous silver coffee and tea service with a sugar bowl and cream pitcher on curvaceous little legs, an emblem of the sort of life she imagined us leading. Arranging all this paraphernalia on its enormous silver platter, itself with clawlike appendages, I envisioned myself presiding importantly over coffee and tea like some matron in a Marx Brothers movie. One lump or two, Cornelia? The trucks and taxis lumbering past our open windows deposited a shower of grime on the silverplate. I sometimes covered the thing with a sheet and promised myself that I would soon locate a huge cardboard box in which to hide the set forever.

Edwina was concerned that we had no furniture apart from the shabby, makeshift couches and chairs we'd rescued from the gutter, board-and-brick bookshelves that we had pooled from our premarital apartments. She wanted us to have a decent sofa and club chairs and a rug and a proper bedroom set, and she was working out a plan to make a substantial down payment on our behalf, with us contributing so much a month. ("It will teach you the value of money," she said.) When she came to visit, she slept in our bedroom while Gil and I moved to the foam-rubber sofa. Gil never resisted her, even when she said pointedly that married women ought not to have jobs. Making a home should be fulfillment enough, she said. And though some part of me believed that this was so, I also crazily resented her saying it.

"Why don't you defend me against your mother? Why don't you tell her I have to have a job? Tell her I do it for the money," I asked one night when Gil and I were quarreling in whispers in the living room as Edwina slept in our bedroom.

"Look, don't take it personally."

"But it is personal. It's goddamn personal. She talks like my paycheck is optional. It isn't. I'm not trying to fulfill myself."

"What do you expect me to do? Give her a lecture on economics? Hell, you invited her. You're the one writing her all those cozy little notes, exchanging recipes and all that shit." But I hadn't invited her. I had merely neglected to tell her not to come.

I was earning the living, or trying very hard to earn it, for expenditures now exceeded income. A reasonably sophisticated urban couple past our first youth, Gil and I tolerated and indeed welcomed any sort of unconventional behavior in our friends, and in spite of our proper dinner parties scorned anything we perceived as middle-class or ordinary, but the idea of having upset the traditional breadwinner model was so terrifying that neither of us could discuss it beyond a few allusions to the situation. Having taken on the job of family bookkeeper, since Gil had no talent for balancing a checkbook, I concealed our difficulties from Gil, who was only just scraping by on freelance writing, chiefly of promotion copy. Sometimes his checks, even for work completed and accepted, were three or four months in coming. Sometimes they never came at all. Assigned work that had taken weeks of his time would be rejected without so much as a kill fee, sometimes even without explanation. One company he worked for went bankrupt. It hurt him deeply when we were short of money, when I had to put off paying bills. Because it seemed counterproductive to be frank, I hedged the truth about our income and outgo, lest the truth push him into a fit of despair or a weekend of drinking.

Curiously, my new role as hunter-gatherer brought me not honor but shame. What a man would have taken pride in was a disgrace for a woman — syphilis would have been easier to own up to. Even to each other, we hardly alluded to the role reversal, except when Gil laid dreamy plans for the future — the top copywriter in the game, stories appearing in the little magazines, Hollywood calling, the Aston-Martin in the garage, the apartment on upper Fifth Avenue, a pretty daughter in private school, birthday parties — sweet, seductive visions of paradise in which my salary would be superfluous, something to be banked against college expenses or European vacations. I loved his visions, loved the details of them, the inclusion of material and artistic success, the ease and comfort he envisioned for me.

But the horrid truth emerged in quarrels. Gil, not I, would pull the pin from the grenade and toss it: "You have the say-so around here, I guess. You earn the money." This accusation would disable me with grief. It was true, I was emasculating my husband. I was a ball-breaker, a take-charge guy, I wore the pants, and if I wept upon being reminded of the truth, I was dubbed Stella Dallas. We dried our tears and doused our rage with lovemaking, whisky, food, movies, friends — whatever came to hand. True to my prewedding resolution, I gave up cigarettes, and he did too, and we praised each other for saving hundreds of dollars that way, even as the liquor bills were rising.

In rational moments, I put myself in his place: a writer who for some reason (certainly not lack of effort or talent) never held a job for long and could find only work writing promotion copy or other dreary tasks — which he nevertheless tackled with enthusiasm and hope, laboring all night to meet deadlines, like a student condemned to study for finals all his life. In the ecology of the New York communications industry, he was a day worker, hired by the hour, a man whose ambitions seemed to undo him, sell him down the river, rather than advance him. A perfectionist for whom nothing was ever perfect, nothing ever good enough, nothing ever finished. I loyally believed in his dreams, mourned for his suffering as if over his wounded body. I waited patiently under his various crosses, hoping only to bind up his wounds.

All that felt right to me. Womanly. What I had been taught to do. And yet there was this vexing matter of funds. I had suspected that marriage was all about consumption, which was why I now was doing endless shopping and carrying, cleaning and disposing, bookkeeping and toting up — jobs that had hardly existed for me until now. I didn't mind the work, but what was this taboo against a wife who earned? Who were

192 ~ LOVE'S APPRENTICE

these pundits in the press who waggled their fingers at working wives, waxed vociferous in their condemnation of working mothers? Why did my salary, so inadequate that we were now falling back on bank loans, embitter my husband, bring me to despair, tie my tongue when I wanted to explain to Carol or my mother that our first months together had been tense, that we were off to a precarious start?

I tried to think of some literary precedent, of some heroine who'd hunted woolly mammoths for her spouse/lover or who had otherwise upset the social and economic order that had prevailed for several thousand years. Nothing came to mind, not a single book or poem. Elizabeth I? But she sat placidly on her throne, wearing a tight gown and a wig, while Sir Francis Drake committed acts of piracy for her. Hippolyta, queen of the Amazons? A bit ludicrous for a person scurrying into the subway every weekday morning at eight forty-five with a sandwich in her tote bag.

When the time came, I prepared our first joint income tax. My w-2 form struck me as treachery, cheating, a kind of adultery, something inadmissible. Yet we'd have been unable to pay our rent on Gil's earnings. I handed him the 1040, dreading his outburst, wondering if our circumstances were somehow my fault. But he merely signed it, almost without inspecting it, like the deeply wronged spouse in a nineteenth-century novel, determined to ignore what he could not correct.

By our first anniversary we had learned the importance of pretense. I kept telling myself that I must redouble my efforts. If I took better care of him, if I tried harder to be a good wife, he would do well. He too was continually picking himself up, redoubling his efforts, renewing his touching, indestructible faith in his future. Neither of us yet perceived the risks of self-deception à deux.

Marital quarreling ought to be taught in the schools, along with household management. Domestic squabbles have themes

and variations, first and second movements, crescendos, dimin-
uendos, codas. They modulate thrillingly from minor to major,
have form, tone, coloration. "You work too hard. Your compe-
tence is deadly, you make me sick trying to be perfect, and if
you achieve perfection, where does that leave me?" was one
theme of Gil's accusations, and I would fling back some version
of "You have no right to criticize me. You profit from the very
qualities you condemn." I would tell him that he, not I, was
killing himself with perfectionism. Character analysis got us
nowhere. When one of us needed privacy, the other thirsted for
companionship. His pace, his rhythms of eating and sleeping
and working, were slower than mine, or at least different, and I
tried earnestly to adjust. (He really preferred going to bed at
dawn; I pronounced myself a born night person, but I drooped
after midnight, and I had to report to work at nine-thirty.) My
attempt to adjust to his requirements produced an emotional
state equivalent to a low-grade fever.

We accused each other, rightly, of having smothered those
two old pals who used to stay up all night. "We used to have
fun together" was one lugubrious statement guaranteed to turn
down the volume momentarily. In separate trenches on our
Maginot Line, we learned to be wary — he of my flaring temper, my baroque and self-dramatizing manner of expressing my
grievances, my tears; I of his silences, of his irony, of his sar-
casm, so deeply disguised as to be undetectable at first, a knife
so sharp that the incision to the bone hardly required a bandage.
And most of all, I hated his retreats, for he would dive so
deeply into his interior jungle that I could never reach him, no
matter how persistent my cries. "You must always be first to
make amends, you must never let the sun set on your anger,"
Edwina had counseled me. But Edwina had no idea how wide
and deep our anger was growing, like a fiery lake. Gil and I had
learned the opposite of Edwina's lesson, how to keep anger
smoldering darkly from one day to the next.

We honed our fighting styles, becoming adept with verbal

thrusts into the soft spots. On the whole, I favored the daylight bombing raid, while Gil specialized in sneak attacks: I was the Great Power who flew the flag in full view, the imperialist ambushed by a guerrilla with grease on his face and palm fronds on his helmet. In spasms of renascent love and mutual thirst for a future together, or compulsive sexuality, or mutual dread of separation and divorce — for how, after so brief a time, could we admit to failure? — we hammered out truces, even armistices. We regained our vision of happiness: I would wake in the morning and grow tender over his sleeping form, would remind myself that this man was mine, that it was us against the world, that he must, must have loved me when he asked me to be his wife. I would imagine becoming pregnant, imagine the children we would have together. The less suitable we proved to be for each other, the more stubbornly we stuck to being married.

How could I turn my back on such a vision, walk out the door and be obliged to start this whole weary process of courtship and marriage all over again? By the time I found another man, perhaps I'd be too old for babies. And when I wasn't looking, perhaps when I was laboring at the sink or perhaps when I wasn't even in our apartment, my smiling face, my slender form clothed in the tweed jacket and skirt he had chosen for me in Better Sportswear at B. Altman, the suit with the sexy drape to the fabric, would assert themselves as his own dear wife, the vision of all he needed or hoped for or wanted. Of course it would all work out. How could it not? And thus, arriving from work with a bag of groceries, I'd find him in a celebratory mood, his spirits patched and glued together, his heart repaired, his love ready to see service once more. Anger would be unthinkable.

Off we'd go around the corner to the Blue Mill, a sturdy Village landmark with leatherette booths, waiters with white napkins over their arms, large drinks, steaks, chops, crisp home fries, bowls of hopelessly overcooked string beans, carrots, and peas, ketchup bottles and Lea and Perrins right on the table, all of which came as a relief from soufflés and *boeuf à la mode.* We'd hold hands, laugh, start out with a dry Rob Roy and order some red wine for the steak. Then off to some nearby spot for Charlie Mingus or Miles Davis or some other jazzman, or uptown to the Metropole, a crowded, thousand-decibel Times Square bar where for the price of a drink you could listen all night to the music of Woody Herman and his Thundering Herd, a long row of sweating musicians packed onto a small platform above the bar, Woody with his checkered jacket and his melodious clarinet driving them onward while the trumpets screamed. Duke Ellington occasionally played at a big nightclub called the River Boat, too, on the ground floor of the Empire State Building — a forest of tiny round tables with white cloths, a cover charge, and the Duke smiling his elegant, sardonic smile, his face lined with age now, as crowds sauntered around the dance floor and waiters scurried here and there with pots of black coffee to fortify the drunks for the drive to the suburbs. How hard all these people worked for us! A few dollars at the door, and the greatest composer in America led the band in "Satin Doll" while you ate terrible food and drank one whisky sour too many.

Gil and I would sing and giggle as we made our way home afterward, with him clutching the wheel of the silver car and barely able to tell a red from a green light, both of us about to wet our pants from laughter and alcohol, truly united at last, reveling in togetherness, though not precisely the togetherness that *McCall's* and other women's magazines were energetically marketing at this epoch. Rather, the togetherness of heartache and booze and precariously founded hope. But who else could I have this much fun with? A guy who knew all the jazz spots and had an exquisite collection of old 78s. A guy who gave me an open-reel tape deck for Christmas rather than the angora sweater I had spotted in a shop window. Who else had a husband who even when plastered piloted his silver sports car through Manhattan traffic and into the one remaining parking spot in our neighborhood? It took a lot of liquor to dampen our doubts, but so what?

What other girl could he find who adored Woody Herman rather than Woody Allen, a girl quick to get angry but quick to forgive, who remembered the names of saxophonists and drummers, who knew Johnny Hodges from Gerry Mulligan, remembered what kind of horn Roy Eldridge played, thought Duke Ellington superior to Leonard Bernstein or even J. S. Bach, if it came to that, a game girl who didn't mind going to work on three hours' sleep? And for a few days after these outings the ceasefire would hold, strong and sure, and my fears for the future would subside. Sober, or at least not too drunk, we would make love. It would be our chief evening activity. I would go into the working world next morning like a woman with a great secret, like Saint Theresa having known ecstasy, wondering whether people in the subway could read it on my face. Then, after a day or so, the sniper's bullets would whine through the air once more and the Cong would attack by night. By our first anniversary, I had stopped hoping for a lasting peace.

A second heart attack carried off my father a year and a half after Gil and I were married, and two years later my mother died of cancer. Being orphaned in my early thirties reduced me to deep sorrow, gave me a feeling of homelessness and rootlessness that made me even more determined to preserve the home I had — ginkgo tree, truck traffic, 1930s refrigerator, and all. Now that my parents lay under twin stones a long journey away, I could not think of running from my home to theirs when my evenings with Gil were unbearable. My hometown seemed impenetrable to me now, a place where I must be invited as a houseguest. A small life insurance policy and my parents' modest house had been my inheritance, plus five thousand dollars in World War II savings bonds, made out in my name and stowed in the safe deposit box. I cashed in the policy and sold the house, transferring the proceeds to my name and Gil's. All this constituted our first savings account, a comforting sum even after I paid off our debts. Before my parents' deaths, divorce had seemed the best option for Gil and me, though the thought was too horrible to be voiced. Absorbing my mother's hard-won financial legacy, I now internalized her emotional one. I was more determined than ever to be a strong, faithful, nurturing wife, as she had been to my father — as her mother and grandmothers had been all the way back to Ur.

Certain privileges accrue to orphans, along with the inheritance (if there is one) and the whiff of abandonment: a sense of irrevocable adulthood, of having no one to answer to, and of having the tiller in one's hands for keeps. This at least enabled me to gather strength against Edwina. For starters, I packed away the silver coffee and tea service and refused to bring it out even when she came for visits. Having been cast as an adult, I was determined to be one. I nevertheless had profound regrets, not only about my parents' early deaths but about my failures as a daughter. I had been a prickly and contentious handful — headstrong, as my father called me, a restless misfit, plotting sedition and yearning for escape. Now I was striving to be a good wife. I had always imagined turning my parents into grandparents, making up for my shortcomings as a daughter by presenting them with a grandchild or two. That chance was gone forever, and if I didn't hurry up, my chance of having a child would also be gone. Ironically, it was their death that might enable me to produce that grandchild. With some money in the bank, I could imagine quitting work for a few months.

Of course, I would have to return to my job after the baby came. I wondered what it cost to hire help, some pleasant woman who would take my baby to the park. My desire for a baby took on a ruthless clarity, unclouded by any of the duplicitous fears I had brought to marriage. In the 1960s, having a first baby at thirty-five was still regarded as a dangerous anomaly — I would be an "elderly primipara," in obstetrical parlance. Better elderly than never.

My former roommate and bridesmaid Carol had moved to California right after her own marriage, and we seldom saw each other, but almost weekly we exchanged letters. She had a two-year-old son now and was expecting another child. Reading my accounts of married life, Carol had begun urging me to leave Gil and get a divorce. "You don't need to live like this. It isn't the nineteenth century. Get out while you can." I remembered her in the vestibule at the Church of the Ascension, commanding me to grab the pocketbooks while she hailed a taxi so we both could beat it. Easy for Carol to talk. She had what she wanted — a baby and a half, and though she was still working part-time, she could afford to quit when the new baby came, quit forever, stay home and drive the carpool and be a participatory parent at nursery school and see to it that her children knew how to read before they were five. Carol's husband was doing well. At least he was the major earner in their house. If Gil and I divorced, did I have time to find another father for my unconceived babies? Did he have time to find a mother for his?

In any case, the idea of having a baby had begun to unite Gil and me, to distract us from warfare. He wanted a child too. He renewed his professional efforts, got put on a small retainer as a copywriter, with office space as part of his remuneration. The sports car needed five thousand dollars' worth of work to keep it running, so we sold it for a few hundred dollars. (He turned the keys over to the new owner with tears in his eyes. I felt as if I had deprived him of essential nutrients, taken ten years off his life.) Unable to afford more space in Greenwich Village, we moved into an apartment with a tiny second bedroom in a less expensive part of town, cut down on the entertaining, stopped going to jazz clubs, drank less. I could see now that alcohol was our enemy, not our friend, an element that would destroy the family we wished to create. It was a consumer of work time, a destroyer of the peace. I suggested quitting altogether. I refused to buy any more liquor. I banned cocktail hour and wine with dinner. Gil said that was a puritanical, idiotic idea, a product of my small-town upbringing, but at least he cut back. Together in the larger bedroom, we lay arguing — good-humoredly — about names for the baby. I preferred William to Henry. And Jeffrey was better than Geoffrey, but Gil said it was going to be Geoffrey because that was really the proper medieval spelling and you shouldn't streamline it. We never picked a boy's name but agreed on almost any number of names for girls.

We eventually had two babies, both daughters, which we both deeply wanted, if only to avoid the battle over William vs. Geoffrey or Jeffrey. I held my job until the very last moment in both pregnancies, never for one moment needing or expecting anyone to give up a seat on the subway or bus for me — and in the epoch when our first child was born, nobody did. Obstetrics had progressed to the point that I expected to give birth fully awake, not automatically to be given an anesthetic. The Lamaze technique of breathing and panting, used to prepare the mother for remaining aware and in control, was in vogue. As with love affairs and cooking, my instructions for giving birth had arrived from France. Indeed, Lamaze birthing seemed somehow to inhabit the same realm as *Mastering the Art of French Cooking* — pure, precise, and ethical. But also obligatory: if you couldn't or wouldn't do it, or if you preferred a hospital where the babies didn't "room in," you were in the same category in my social circle as a woman who served canned vegetables and bottled salad dressing at a dinner party. The cook who refused to cut corners and could get a soufflé to rise merged fuzzily in my mind with the mother who produced a healthy baby and was cheerfully present to meet it at birth.

Fortunately, I could and would do Lamaze, could hardly wait to get my hands on the book, not to mention the heady propaganda manuals of a breast-feeding organization called La Leche Society. You had to give the breast, La Leche commanded, in parks, on trains, in planes, on demand, and without embarrassment; you also had to quit your job if you had one, because nursing mothers had no business working. It was up to the father to provide the money, said the society. Also to fend off dirty-minded or disapproving spectators when the wife was breast-feeding on public transportation or in restaurants. (The booklet featured a drawing of a capable-looking young father casting menacing glances at an approaching crowd while baby smacked away at mama's nipple.) Well, I couldn't quit my job. The Milk Society would have to take me as I was.

Gil and I attended night classes during the pregnancy, counting the seconds between imaginary labor pains with the sweep hand on his watch, learning the techniques of "effleurage," or massage, and preparing to be a team when the day arrived. These weeks were undoubtedly when we came closest to the ideals *The Book of Common Prayer* had recommended. When I woke him one spring morning at three, the day our first daughter arrived, we rehearsed Lamaze in the taxi on the way to the hospital. For four hours he dutifully timed contractions and I dutifully puffed and panted. Then the real labor began, and method went out the window. I noted that giving birth involved being quite naked and bottoms-up in front of a lot of other people, and I marveled that I did not even mind. I yelled once or twice, but in fact the birth was easy. As natural as promised, even with a doctor and a resident and two nurses in attendance. Lamaze had less to do with it than luck and physiology, plus the unexpected enthusiasm Gil and I mustered for the process.

Sarah, bald and as purple as any newborn, looked up at me with my father's greenish hazel eyes, startlingly, as if he had been resurrected for the occasion. If this eight-pound female infant had spoken to me in his voice, I should not have been surprised. "Mine," I cried, "mine!" and startled the attending physician by clutching this morsel to my chest and laughing aloud, from sheer tenderness and joy, on the obstetrical table.

Later her eyes took on a lighter hue, and she began inexorably to look like my mother. The euphoric sense of possession, of ownership of this small person, intensified.

Margaret also woke us in the middle of the night, four years later. We no longer cared about Lamaze, and in any case she was born half an hour after we got to the hospital, so that timing contractions and doing effleurage would have been irrelevant. The team in the birthing room knew I was a veteran mom and paid less attention to me. Anyhow, triplets were being born in the next cubicle. Gil and I more or less delivered this baby by ourselves, or so it seemed. Margaret's eyes were deep blue; she arrived without any particular morphological credentials, bringing her own particular face into the world. The cocky sense of possession I had had with Sarah was now replaced by awe. How, thought I, have Gil and I managed to produce this singularly beautiful baby?

They retrieved Margaret from my arms and put her into a little clear plastic case a few feet away while they prepared me to go down to the ward. I gazed into her eyes and she into mine, as hopelessly infatuated as two creatures have ever been on earth. I managed to wait out the time until I could lay my hands on her, give myself over to pure lust, look at her hands and feet, inspect every inch of her, tell her I would love her until I died and then some. I didn't need anybody to show me how to feed her and change her or to explain that the soft spot on her head would harden. I knew already. I wanted to get out of there, to go home and show Margaret to Sarah. She gazed back at me with the sturdy survival instincts of the second-born. Later she grew a head of blond curls that might have been inherited from either side of the family, and refused to resemble anybody but Margaret.

What turned me delirious on both occasions was that I fell in love with the newborns. I had expected, of course, to love them, but not with such intensity. Babies are equipped biologically to seduce and command their parents, fathers as well as mothers, grandparents, and other bystanders, and our babies were as practiced at seduction as any. Never had I fallen for a man in such a manner. I could understand why breast-feeding had for many years been frowned on, out of fashion. After all, could such pleasure — the comic smacking noises of a baby at the breast, her impatient need, her helpless satisfaction afterward, the brazen intimacy — really be legitimate, could it truly have medical sanction, provide needed calories and nutrients and immune factors? How, I wondered, did Gil or any other father endure this, or the blatant infatuation of mother and child? Every other love I'd ever experienced, between the covers of a bed or a book, now seemed a triviality — Casanova, Romeo and Juliet, Keats and Fanny. All past disappointments healed miraculously over. Whatever had been required to achieve this, whatever I had to do to support this, would be well worth it. All my wants were fulfilled; indeed, my wants hardly seemed to matter. (I wanted, for example, to sleep through the night, but rose in my nightgown at the first whimper.) Gil and I called a truce and sat down at the peace table. For the first few months, at least.

No rake or roué can ever have known the delight that came of bathing these tiny bodies, kissing the fingers and faces, coaxing the smiles, quieting the distress, satisfying the hunger and thirst, replacing the crib blankets at three A.M. All the words once applied only to lovers now came tumbling out of my mouth for these infants: honey, darling, sugar, sweetheart. And impulses so sweet and voracious that they had to be curbed: Oh, I could kiss you all over! Oh, I could eat you up! No love song could express it.

At home with my daughters in the first disordered days after their births, I no doubt complained about being awakened at three A.M. and then again at five-thirty, never having time to wash my hair, not even having time to get dressed in the morning, of being terminally exhausted, but what lover had ever wanted or needed me so sincerely? What lover had ever looked upon me as the source of all nourishment, wisdom, life? How curious the relationship! I was the articulate, ambulatory, literate partner, capable of spooning carrots out of little jars and mashing up bananas. Yet it was the baby who ruled, who woke me from my sleep and persuaded me to take her in my arms, who decreed when the household should sleep and eat, how our time should be spent, whether or not the beds would go unmade for a week and the groceries unshopped for, who rearranged all my priorities to suit her needs. And would continue to do so, more so, the older she grew. I wondered, as I knew Gil did, how any marriage manages to survive this ultimate adultery, the infidelity that can never be undone or repented of, this transfer of allegiance that cannot be explained away in the office of some marriage counselor. The few remaining pleasures of our marriage faded like a radio station on a long car ride. Sex became a nuisance, an impediment to sleep, an act that might interfere with baby care, a nicety I could easily dispense with, like making our bed or cooking dinner. Of course, falling asleep with a baby in one's arms was more satisfying than falling asleep with a spouse, not only for me but for Gil, rousing in each of us a tender, incurable passion, as if holding a baby were the ultimate in illicit encounters.

After a few short months at home, however, I was obliged to turn Sally, as we eventually called Sarah, and then Sally and Maggie over to a daytime baby sitter and go back to work. I did so with a heartsick sense of abandonment — not so much the feeling that I was abandoning them, although I felt I was, but a kind of jealousy about the continuance of their fascinating lives from morning until evening each day without my presence. Would they utter their first word, take their first step in my absence? Many a morning I wiped the tears from my face as I left for work; many an evening I ran all the way from my subway stop, hoping to be present for some landmark event in their lives.

In time, as passion must do, my passion for my children lost the first edge of intensity and transformed itself into a usable, lively devotion. Having babies late in life is not bad: I was deeply grateful for them. My mother had had no control over my arrival — babies were simply what happened to women who got married at nineteen. My children seemed to have been imported from a foreign land. Furthermore, I was old enough to know that babies don't last. For inevitably the baby smiled, sat up alone, drummed upon the high-chair tray with a spoon, expressed her unalterable preference for peanut butter over string beans, toddled fearlessly across the floor, climbed out of her crib alone at an early hour and woke me by patting my face and demanding pancakes, outgrew May's summer sandals by July 1, broke out of my protecting grasp in the playground, climbed recklessly to the top of the jungle gym, laughed at me from above as I stretched my arms, entreated her to climb down, and pleaded with her not to take such chances with her precious little bones: evidence enough that one day the child would follow her own will and test her strength in other ways and gradually vanish altogether.

With children in the house, the years are theirs, not yours, and middle childhood and early adolescence are a blur in my mind, except for the picture albums, Christmas tree after Christmas tree, Easter basket after Easter basket, and the journal I sporadically kept. During this time, my first job ended as the magazine faltered and then went out of business, owing to a growing shortage of readers who cared about history and the arts. I hustled work, wrote about any subject for anybody who would pay me, never turned down a freelance project, interviewed for a dozen jobs, and finally got one, just in time to avert financial ruin. Gil continued to labor twelve or more hours a day, not counting the hungover mornings.

When Sally was ten and Maggie six, we moved to the suburbs — a split-level tract house in Long Island, in a development called Flower Manor, relentlessly bulldozed and built, nearly identical house after nearly identical house, in 1956, the year I finished college and ought to have been moving into just such a house, pregnant, with a young, ambitious husband, his ties conservative and his hair cut short. But here I came, twenty-odd years too late. Courtesy of Edwina, to be precise, who had begun to fear that Gil and I actually would get a divorce and who thought to prevent it by giving us the down payment on a suburban home, a present with even more implications than the silver tea service. All she asked in return was unrestricted visiting rights. Was I for sale? Indeed, I was, along with the split-level. Until now, a proper house had been not only beyond our means but beyond my imaginings. I had supposed I would raise my girls in the city, protected little urban schoolchildren whose whereabouts I would always know, who would go regularly with me to performances of the New York City Ballet. But the suburbs meant normality — children running free in back yards and later, when they got driver's licenses, in automobiles.

Whippoorwills called, evening was nigh, and everything in the house was blue: inlaid blue carpets, walls, woodwork, kitchen counters, linoleum, bathroom wallpaper. The two toilets, one upstairs, one down, were blue. In a kitchen drawer I found a neat manila envelope filled with instruction booklets and leaflets for the various appliances, which had been installed when the house was built. Instant archaeology, like uncovering mysterious frescoes on a wall: here, in faded color in the pages of these little brochures, were women whose hair had been set in pin curls, women who tended the cookpots on their General Electric ranges wearing presentable dresses with aprons and high heels and sparkling Pepsodent smiles. My automatic wall oven, I read, would permit me to prepare a roast beef for my husband's supper while playing bridge all afternoon. All I needed to do was put the roast in the oven, set a few dials, and go my carefree way. The automatic roasting mechanism no longer worked, I discovered after a few tries. But oh, to don my frilly apron and shirtdress and take charge of this romantically blue kitchen, to make dozens of chocolate chip cookies according to the recipe in the oven booklet!

Oh, to position my hat on my head, back my Studebaker out of the driveway, and spend the afternoon at a bridge table while the roast sizzled in the oven! In the evening, when I returned, the dog would fetch the evening paper and Gil would sit down at the table after kissing me. However, we had no dog, and our present plan was that Gil would stay at home with the girls, writing copy in a basement office, and I would commute to my new job in town on the 8:20 train with bankers and lawyers and chief executive officers, administrative assistants and middle management personnel, a growing handful of whom were now female. That woman's world of 1956, with cookies and aprons and smart ovens, not to mention Studebakers, had vanished as definitively as ancient Crete. It was 1979: sixty percent of all women with small children now had jobs. I had read that we were likely to earn sixty cents on the dollar compared with a man's wage for identical work.

The former owner of our blue heaven, a kindly woman now widowed and moving to Florida, made touching gestures besides the booklets in her attempt to bequeath us her way of life — she left us a hammock and a birdfeeder in the back yard. Sally and Maggie loved the hammock, my journal tells me, as well as the back yard. And they liked having separate bedrooms. The first night after the movers departed, I watched them cavort in the moonlight in the small back yard like the baby raccoons in one of their storybooks. Through a fog of fatigue, my hands skinned from taping and untaping cardboard boxes, my sweatpants and sweatshirt for once actually soaked with sweat, I suddenly imagined my world had set itself to rights. In spite of everything, Gil and I had a house. A house in the burbs. He would be happy, I would be happy. The kids had a back yard to play in. I had a standard kitchen with an automatic oven, albeit an antiquity, each child would have a closet for her own clothes, and the school bus would roar its nice, normal, orderly roar on our street every morning. The ship had docked at Ellis Island, and we had emerged from steerage. America — I had come to America.

But that all wore off fast, according to my journal, a fits-and-starts chronicle of suburban life.

Yesterday Sally came in from school sobbing. [I was still home, for this first week, getting everybody settled before I started commuting to work again.] She has one friend, from across the street, and they sit together on the school bus. Two older girls called them lesbians because they like to sit together. I asked Sally if she knew what that meant, and she said the other girls had explained it in detail. Nothing so cruel in this world as a pack of little girls.

~

Gil has set up shop to be a freelance writer working at home. I have begun my daily commute to the city, my new job. It only takes fifty-five minutes, and I rather like the train. Crowded as it is, the train is a private place. As an economic model, this new life Gil and I have constructed for ourselves ought to work, if only Gil could get over the idea that it's unmanly of him to have me earning the bread. If only I can earn enough to support this house and buy the kids enough sneakers and brand-name jeans. If only Gil's despair and anger would lift. If only. If only.

~

The autumn weather is spectacular, blue sky, crisp air, and the berries on the little Washington thorn tree in the front yard are so very red. The onset of winter saddens me. More so as the years pass. A day like today could be filled with joy. Ah, wedded life: a perpetual war. But here are sweet Maggie and her playmate under the thorn tree in their sweaters, like fairy-folk from some late comedy of Shakespeare. I played in the sunshine too at that age, and no doubt my mother looked through the glass in the front door and wondered what had happened to her youth, feared the future, and asked herself why she'd ever gotten married in the first place.

~

By the time my kids are grown, I hope marriage has been outlawed. Or at least put on a contractual system — i.e., all marriages automatically dissolve after five years unless renegotiated voluntarily for another five-year period. During that fifth year, at least, life might improve. I wonder where Olivia is now. Suppose she and I had actually made our foolish pact. No Mr. and Mrs. on the engraved thank-you notes, no tax breaks. No rights of survivorship. No in-laws. How pure that kind of marriage might have been, unpolluted by the regulations and constraints of God and Man, of banks and governments. A marriage between two men, or two women, or two lovers of whatever affectional persuasions, unrecognized by society, doomed to secrecy, condemned to survive on its own merits. The only form of true marriage, possibly, uncoerced so long as it lasted, and simple enough to dispose of when one grew weary of it.

As my own marriage deteriorated in this landscape of backyard barbecues and hammocks and separate bedrooms for each child, this place where every family possessed two cars and anguish had been declared unmentionable, I sometimes brought up the subject of divorce. Gil refused to discuss it usually, but then maintained that he could not live apart from the children and blamed our failure on me. I was too critical. I demanded too much. "How the hell, anyway, are we going to afford a divorce?" A good question. Divorce, of course, is for the well-off. Our joint income was barely enough to keep one household going. We had no money for lawyers and separate residences. Where would college money come from if Gil and I divorced? Where would it come from anyhow?

But something else was mixed in too. Slammed up against an

economy in transition, in which a wife had to earn a salary and figure out how to remain a wife, where a woman could no longer proudly identify herself as a housewife and mother, I nevertheless bought into Gil's desperate accusations that our problems were my fault, that I had somehow deprived my husband of his rightful role. Yet what if I had been a traditional woman, standing at the kitchen door in my apron, wringing my hands and waiting for him to solve our economic dilemmas? It was the ancient problem George Sand had ranted about: if you're weak and dependent, that destroys your husband. If you're strong, that destroys him too. In our unhappiness, neither Gil nor I could perceive even the simplest of truths.

And with all my eagerness to be a modern woman, I had one foot firmly nailed to the floor of the past. Divorce meant failure, abandonment of one's duty, weeping children, holidays spent apart. No woman in my family had ever been divorced. Not even a second cousin. Neither had any of them finished college, or left home, or spent a year in France, or (so far as I knew) enjoyed unsanctified couplings with persons to whom they were not wed. But breaking precedents like those were easy compared with breaking up a family. And Gil knew how to hush me up when I said the nasty word that began with *d:* "Yeah, you'd like that. But nobody would benefit from a divorce but you. The kids and I don't want a divorce."

Gradually, mercifully, in our first year in Flower Manor, Gil and I quarreled less, perhaps because I was commuting and thus we saw each other less. When I got home, around seven, I took possession of Maggie and Sally, questioning them about their activities, overseeing baths and bedtime. Though I did not recognize the development as threatening, merely as an immense relief, Gil and I began to go whole days without speaking. I don't recall making an issue of it, but I moved into the spare bedroom. Gil did not object. I myself came to love the solitude. I would check to make sure the children were slumbering on their pillows, then return to my room and fall willingly asleep.

The moonlight came through my curtains; soon my lover arrived in a perfectly tailored suit and elegant tie, but when he lay down beside me, he would be quite naked. And then in the trough of night I would wake up, floating on a cloud of eroticism and desire. My nameless, bodyless dream lover would be gone, a vision painted in oils, in Technicolor with Dolby, a dream that replayed itself just behind my retinas all day, crept up on me like a headache or a relapse into addiction. Perhaps ten thousand married women had had the same dream that same night. (It floated over us like the weather. We should have resisted it, denied it, shut our ears to its seductive background music.) The nights, unlike the ragged, pressured, all-consuming days, were beautiful.

"Oh, if only the lover would vacate my dream world, damn him," reads a journal entry from this epoch. "It is too tormenting." When I awoke once more, it was daybreak. I was indeed freezing: the blankets were on the floor. The tears on my cheeks and my fingers, the tears I now drank, were mine. Alone in bed? How could that be? Had my lover been some strange conflation of other men — my father, the first man I'd slept with so many years ago, Henry Robinson, Peter Klein, Gil, my husband, bitterly and drunkenly asleep in another room and now, alas, my sworn enemy, my traitor, as I was his treacherous enemy? How had this come to pass?

Maggie began to have night terrors and would arrive and curl up against me at two or three o'clock, too frightened to weep. I always held her close, begged her to talk about her nightmares. "I dream of you, Mommy," she would confess, her tears flowing. "You always look so angry in my dreams, you look at me as if you don't love me anymore, but I know it isn't really you, only somebody that looks like you." And I would comfort her, blame myself for her dreams, wonder whether I had grown so haggard internally that my own child felt it and feared that the anger would turn against her. Children see all, know all. It did not occur to me that her world was creaking on its pinions because I no longer slept with her father. Of course, she never mentioned this as a source for her bad dreams. She would soon be asleep in my arms.

Sometimes, lying awake beside her, I would take inventory of my lost loves, my missed chances. I wrote them down mentally, as if recording my medical history for some solicitous nurse. Joey Cash. Married, two kids, teaching high school mathematics, of all things, in Columbia, Missouri. To my astonishment, I had encountered a woman at a party who'd gone to Oberlin with Olivia and kept up with her. Olivia was in Memphis with three sons and a successful husband. A lawyer, the fellow was. Rich, too. Family dough. Yes, I might have known! Bill James, after our student days in Paris, had simply disappeared. I had invited him to my wedding, and he had written a brief, polite refusal. My next communiqué, the announcement of Sarah's birth, was returned: no forwarding address.

Henry Robinson, good faithful Henry who had never completely forgotten me, had made a point of keeping up with me, as if his honor were involved. He had worked for four different corporations now, a cash register company in Dayton, Ohio, and similar enterprises that took him back and forth to France — the world of Franco-American business he had dreamed of inhabiting, to my ill-disguised contempt, while we were students. He and his wife, Alissa, were the parents of twin sons, born the year that Gil and I had married. We had even seen them occasionally, when they stopped off on their business trips to France. His red hair, last time I had seen him, had begun to gray. He had long since shaved off the auburn beard I had once found so enticing, had put on weight. (I was no longer bone-thin either.) When we exchanged looks, there was merely friendship in his face, or not even that. Perhaps I had in fact fabricated that night of love with Henry.

Peter and Hannah Klein now lived in Chicago. As they had been about to leave town, a decade before, Peter had invited me to lunch — an expensive lunch in a midtown French restaurant.

I still remembered the vichyssoise, veal citron, *crème brulée*. At the time I was pregnant with Margaret. Peter had been kind, truly concerned about my professional progress and the problems of working during a pregnancy with a small child at home, solicitous about my fears of failing on one front or the other, my sometimes tortured perception that I could never manage to be in the right place. He was saddened, of course, to hear that Gil and I weren't getting along very well in spite of the forthcoming baby. He had shaken my hand, kissed my cheek as we parted. There were two Peters, I concluded, the mentor who taught me to write and in whose bed I had spent one momentarily joyful night, and this one at the table, whom I had never even kissed, this kindly father who looked wistful as he told me goodbye. I had wished him well in the splendid new position he was moving to Chicago for. We set off in opposite directions, and I turned to watch the back of his raincoat disappear in the crowds of Fifth Avenue. Now I wondered bitterly if he thought of me still. Had he ever told Hannah? Had there been other young women besides me? I would smooth the hair of my sleeping child, wondering what she'd ever know of me.

Antonio Piazza actually had died two years before of a heart attack in the upstate New York parish where he worked. The news had taken a long time to reach me, but a friend of mine from the old days had finally heard of his death and telephoned me from California in great agitation. "Tony is dead. Actually collapsed at the altar in the middle of mass. A soul that flew straight to heaven, I bet. You know he was in love with you, don't you? Before he was ordained, I mean. He talked to me one night about breaking his vows for you, but he feared for his immortal soul. He was in the end a priest." I scoffed at the notion that Antonio had loved me, and yet somehow it compensated for the sorrow I felt. Had he really feared that loving me would send him to hell? The pope won that tug-of-war. But I could still picture this lanky acolyte singing Petrarch's sonnets to tunes of his own composition, a troubador worthy of the medieval courts of love. Death had taken him; and indeed the others had also been obliterated as if by death. I would imagine myself with Tony, defrocked, both of us madly happy. I would rehearse being his wife instead of Gil's. Tears would come. Such melancholy, figurative chewing of the fingernails would put me back to sleep as dawn broke. Reality would set in when the clock jangled. Unpaid bills and mortgage notes would fall through the air and bury me.

At breakfast one morning, Maggie (junior high) and Sally (high school) searched the house for socks, bookbags, and sweaters while I in my ragged terry bathrobe stirred a pot of oatmeal, washed some glasses (I had forgotten to turn on the dishwasher), poured orange juice and milk, boiled two eggs for egg salad sandwiches, assured my daughters they were old enough to be making their own lunches for school and I wasn't going to do it anymore after this week, and et cetera and so on, though in fact I only continued to do these things because I dreaded the day when I should finally have to stop. In every other gesture and detail I rehearsed the fleeting, comforting, predictable drama of getting up with two kids, improving their moral outlook, fixing them a proper breakfast, and sending them off to school — this paradise, this heaven I had dreamed of when childless and single with no prospects.

But my nights of dreamy lust and regret tormented me, as if some illegal drive-in movie screen had been installed in my own kitchen, with speakers attached to each side of my head. Standing at the sink, cracking eggshells and scraping the scorch off the toast, I found it difficult to conjure with desire. Tears of shame and rage began to roll down my cheeks. The ancient paradox of my childhood seized me once more, the need to mother one's children, whom one adores and would cheerfully die for (ah, if only one were merely called upon to die), the need to have one's husband and household rise up and call one blessed, to be above reproach, to sit in dignity on the PTA board — this destiny, this calling, this sacrament that is mocked and riven by the heresies of literature, by the mythology deep in one's memories that thumbs its nose at womanly enterprise, by the terrible imperatives of one's own body, one's lust, one's intensity, one's neediness. Or at least my own lust, intensity, neediness, my disinclination to submit to what my life had become.

Maybe it was only me; maybe the housewife next door didn't have wet dreams or seek absolutes. I leaned against the refrigerator and sobbed, until finally Sally, or perhaps it was Maggie, or both the children, looked amazed and troubled as children do when their mother, wearing an old bathrobe, collapses against some major appliance in tears. What's wrong, Mommy? They were afraid, naturally enough, that I'd tell them I'd only six months to live and then they really would have to find their own mittens and make their own egg salad. God, I loved them. They were only a breath away from becoming women themselves. Sally already dreamed of marriage. I put my hands on their respective knit caps as they crowded into my arms.

"I'm okay. I feel fine. Don't know what came over me. I gotta get ready for work. You're going to miss the bus, scat right out of here." Relieved, restored to standard time and daily life, they were out the door. Forty-five minutes later, as always, I stepped aboard the 8:20 with my newspaper and cardboard cup of coffee, in a raincoat identical to the other raincoats. A trained commuter now, I had my own techniques for locating a seat, for enveloping myself in my newspaper, for putting other passengers on notice that I was hostile to all possible fellowship and must not be disturbed. My dream of lust with a virtual stranger rattled in my mind, a stone in a tin can, a fatuous ditty ringing in the ears like tinnitus, over and over.

I was past fifty. My mother would have said I should stop thinking about love. By this stage of marriage, even devoted couples have forgotten about love. They have cable TV and VCRs instead. Maybe they rouse themselves once a month or so, or once a year on some Saturday night when the kids are sleeping at Grandma's: the second honeymoon syndrome, the romantic weekend at some hotel that offers discount rates and one bottle of complimentary champagne. (Even had we been able to afford such things, I wouldn't have gone.) Then back to Monday night football. What need had I for love? I had no time for it. I could live without it, as generations of women before me had lived without it after menopause. Had most definitely wished to live without it! I had a responsible job, two growing children, a house, and a whopping nine percent mortgage. Love was for other women. And yet I could not give up dreaming of it.

Love was an inconvenient, embarrassing emotion that woke you at dawn, interfered with the day's routine, caused you to terrify your children at the breakfast table, gave you the mean, down-hearted, jailhouse blues when you ought to have been thinking of local politics and which candidate to support in the congressional race. It hoisted its images before your eyes and loudly mocked you as you located your gloves, belted your raincoat, stuck your newspaper in the recycle can, and headed for the subway station. Nevertheless, I wanted it.

According to the feminist philosopher Andrea Dworkin, whose work I had just read, sexual intercourse was rape. "What intercourse is for women and what it does to women's identity, privacy, self-respect, self-determination, and integrity are forbidden questions," she had written, "and yet how can a radical or any woman who wants freedom not ask precisely these questions? The quality of the sensation or the need for a man or the desire for love: these are not answers to questions of freedom; they are diversions into complicity and ignorance." Yes, perhaps. Yes, undoubtedly. Yes, oh, decidedly. Sex was brutal, or in any case had been brutally used, a weapon against women, to be sure. But was the penis, in all its perversity and ludicrousness and beauty, any less a source of grief for men?

Oh, complicity was indispensable, even as it deprived you of your freedom. Love made you part of life, made you one with the she-bear or dog or snake coupling (whether ecstatically or painfully) with her mate, a creature of her own hormones and Darwinian imperatives. But, mysteriously, the act also rendered you human — virtuous, in some lyrical and absolute sense of the word, some sense to be divined in Keats's poetry or Chopin's music. One was rendered open, in mortal danger, and therefore capable of love. I was at an age when decent women abandon love, yearn for the pleasures of a separate bedroom, grow weary of the burdens of marriage, realize that expensive cosmetics won't help a bit, that antiwrinkle creams don't work, and that anyway they are utterly disqualified by menopause, thicker middles, thinner hair. But not me. I would keep trying.

13

REVOLUTIONARY
ETUDE

This anguish I feel, the uncertainty, the longing, even the guilt, I think of as excitement, as the romantic element of my life. The equivalent, for me, of what men seek when they go to war. The opposite of security, the tension that keeps you alive . . .

— *a letter from the narrator to a friend*

The adventure began with the phone ringing — at the other end of the line a man I used to know at my first job, a century ago, it now seemed, one of those faithful-to-his-wife fellows who flirted easily, gently, whose admiration wore a genuine air but knew how to bide its time. Where had he come from, this man I hadn't seen in years? From out of town, of course. He now worked in Los Angeles. "Would you be free for dinner next week?" Two decades before, when I was still a new wife, he had teased me with the same suggestion. "Lunch perhaps, if you get lucky, but never dinner," I would answer tartly in those days, making him laugh. "Tartly" — a double-edged word. I had taken pleasure in his teasing, and in the undertones I assured myself I would never, ever truly respond to.

This man was no androgynous genius with long eyelashes, no seductive and talented art-critical fellow, no child in need of a mother, no hero with a romantic past, no promoter of civilization, not at all the sort of man I had ever responded to, but a muscular, athletic man, a head taller than I. Interested in bodies, not literature. Now I was meeting him for dinner, as if in a fantasy, as if in one of those tormenting dreams. At six o'clock I left my office — my present workplace, the real one, with real papers stacked on the desk — headed for the hotel bar where we were meeting, and found that the sidewalk had turned to ice: plumes of cold rose visibly from the concrete, the burning breath of dry ice, and the wind cut like a boning knife. I wore only a thin silk dress — a clinging print with a row of small buttons down the front — and a thin coat too, the only decent-looking coat I owned. (Could I go to meet a man for dinner in my old fleece-lined raincoat? No.) I clutched a scarf around my head to shelter my hair. I had spent half an hour in the ladies' room arranging my curls, applying makeup. I had no stocking seams to check, no slip straps to adjust, but I seemed to be emerging from the ladies' room at the movies in my childhood, going past the candy counter, seating myself in the darkness, waiting for the curtains to part like a bathrobe, eager for the great male on the screen to take me by the hand.

I hurried toward the subway stop, dabbing at the freezing water on my cheeks, wiping it away with bare fingers. My eyes ran icicles. Birds froze under their feathery coats, city horses shivered in their carriage trappings as they waited beside Central Park, the feet of little subway mice froze to the railings, bronze and marble statues in the parks surely shuddered and split, so heavy was the cold. A mysterious night on which to find a lover to warm me, prepare a feast of delights for me and lay it at my fingertips, then melt into my dreams like the blending of flavors or fragrances. Rose into violet, Keats had said in "The Eve of St. Agnes," a poem about a young virgin acquiring a lover on a winter's night, which I had once partly memorized. Afterward, like the virgin in the poem, would I flee away with this lover, leaving Gil, abandoning my children? A tempting thought. I waited impatiently on the subway platform, and the train roared out of the tunnel, clanking and shrieking, and bore down toward the platform. One step and I'd be on the tracks, but instead I stepped through the doors, no longer minding the cold.

Climbing the subway stairs near where I was to meet my dinner date, I realized I was late. What if he only meant to have dinner, what if he didn't ask me to spend the night with him? What if he did? I had taken the precaution of warning my family I was spending the night in New York. Uncertain, I stopped off at a nearby shop and bought a nightgown in a floral pattern, with a dainty little yoke of lace, a cloak for lust as well as shyness. I bought a toothbrush at a drugstore. Indoors the next minute, in the hotel bar where he was waiting, I found him drinking whisky, toying with a cigarette — the paraphernalia of wickedness. He looked anxious. I could see he had been watching the clock. He seated me ceremoniously at his table, bent over me to kiss me politely. How beautiful he was! His hair had grayed, he was heavier than twenty years ago. I liked all that. He took my hands, warmed them. What a piece of work is a man! How noble in reason! How express and admirable! In action how like an angel!

"What is in the package?" he asked me, alluding to the little flowered bag that held my new nightgown, but I refused to tell him. "Oh, just something." He ordered a drink for me, and we began to talk, quite certain where the talk was leading. He had just separated from his wife, he said. I knew that this was true, not a mere come-on. I said I hoped to separate from my husband but that I was having difficulty doing so. The landscape of love had altered. The map of love was different now. Men and women were equal. Married women could have love affairs if they wished, and I wished. Women's magazines that had once been full of recipes and decorating tips now added advice on how to deal with love affairs. You must try to understand, they always admonished, why you/he wanted to be unfaithful. I already understood.

We thought we'd go around the corner for dinner and left the warm room. I noticed the sound of my heels on the frigid sidewalk, and shivered noticeably in my thin silk dress and lightweight coat. "You're freezing, my love," he said. "Let me warm you." I turned into his arms as if for salvation. "Will you come to bed with me?" he asked, and I put my arms around him, kissed him in full view of a half-dozen pedestrians, who were too cold either to rejoice or to disapprove.

Next we were in a crowded elevator, afraid to touch each other lest someone notice, and then in a room with a large comfortable bed. I was trembling; my hands were cold again. He pulled my dress off — the buttons slipped out of their buttonholes miraculously, at one touch. "I'll hang this up," he said. "You'll have to wear it tomorrow." And he put it on a coat hanger with such tender care that I smiled. I wore only my underclothes, like a child being stripped down for an evening bath. Of my bra he said, with infuriating knowingness, "This kind unsnaps in front," and then he peeled off my stockings. After an amateurish struggle with his tie, as though I never had untied a man's tie before — and in fact I could not recall having done so — I unbuttoned his shirt and slipped it off his shoulders. My eye fell on silk linings, impressive labels, and other marks of fine tailoring. There was a low-key, delicious scent about him. Yet, oh, he was flesh as well, hard, desirable flesh, and how gentle he was. Not an old-fashioned man, out to please himself, but a New Man, wishing to please me. (Hear me, Ms. Dworkin.)

I meant to hang up his shirt, his tie, his belt, his trousers, with the same consideration he had shown for me. But he was not looking for a wife to hang his trousers up, nor did I wish to be the good girl who had just bought herself a modest nightgown. Not Constance Chatterley hoping to achieve an all-natural, no-additive orgasm but a ravening heroine in a dirty novel. Look on page 93. Just read what's on page 250! The doublet is doffed, stays loosened, the heroine moans with passion, the hero's lips rapturously seek the plump curves emerging from her deep décolleté. Watch for me by moonlight, look for me by moonlight. I'll come to thee by moonlight, though hell should bar the way! The stubble on his face, like briars, kept me in touch with reality, kept me from drifting off in a stupor of delight, from which I might never have returned.

But after a few hours' sleep it was time to find the toothbrushes, shower, dress, and go. We had forgotten dinner, so he sent for breakfast. Famished, I downed my orange juice and two cups of coffee, devoured buttered toast. Then he said, "I love you. When I first saw you years ago, I loved you. I have wanted you ever since. I will always want you. Even if I don't see you for another ten years, it changes nothing."

Easy words, and I needed them. Cheap or expensive, I would purchase them. I felt vaguely threatened by the idea of never seeing him again, but what he said soothed many an ancient scar and wound.

"Yes, I love you too," I said, spreading jam on another piece of toast. "We can love each other in the best way. This way. No legal documents. No groceries to shop for, no life insurance." We shall never be caught in the terrible coils of marriage. We'll never be angry. Never quarrel. Indeed, this is love. Perhaps the only possible version of it. Perhaps the only version I wish to know.

And thus began a romance of a type that is as old as marriage itself but seems new and revolutionary to the participants. It occurred in episodes, and always in hotels. I could never go straight up to his room, of course, because the desk won't give out room numbers. But the switchboard would connect me to him from the phone in the hotel lobby. The second time we met, it was spring; summer, the third time. I shivered slightly in the dark, cool elevator, though it was ninety outdoors. I was anonymous. I was jumping into a dry well. If anybody were looking for me that night, I'd be unfindable. If the man who opened the door to room 3105 turned out to be somebody besides my lover, somebody who stabbed me or strangled me, he'd need only to destroy the cards in my wallet and nobody would be able to identify the body, not until they somehow located my dentist and checked my teeth, or until my family was brought to the morgue, somehow, to check me out.

But these were silly thoughts, born of guilt. The thoughts my generation thinks when conducting an affair. Twenty years hence would my daughters, speaking softly to their lovers on the house phone, think such thoughts? But I didn't want them to meet men in hotels! The elevator stopped at the thirty-first floor, and I emerged. The corridors led this way and that, carpeted corridors, where 3105 might be. I hesitated, faltered, rummaged in my purse for my reading glasses — oh God, had I left them on my desk? — but finally I found them and inspected the tiny plastic plaque on the wall. I had come the wrong way.

In an instant I would be in his arms. A silly expression, but I used it mentally: "I am in his arms." And how my blood rose, how dizzy I became. A teenager again, as I of course told him. And he said it was the same for him. In room 3205, directly above our heads, were they also growing younger? I promised myself that this attraction wasn't merely physical, not just lust, certainly not at our age. We weren't just here for sex — not me, surely not me. Oh, what a good lover he was, how exquisite. Being postmenopausal made it all the easier to be with him. No worries, no pill, no mess, no goo. My own body was the contraceptive now, an improvement over the others: nothing to remember, swallow, or apply. I was not sorry to be rid of monthly bleeding, not at all. What had seemed to an earlier generation a fitting marker to the end of love struck me as a marker for the beginning of it, love freed at last from the evolutionary chains.

After a couple of hours, love would turn easily to conversation. First, his divorce. Yes, they were living apart now, it was official. His daughters (both grown) had been apprised. They were angry, but they'd come around, he was certain of it. In any case, they had no choice. I would tell him that I had talked things over with Gil for the twentieth time and that Gil had refused to listen to reason. Gil did not want a divorce. He intended to fight me. We'd then consider possible strategies for me, carefully avoiding any discussion of what we might do, together or separately, after the divorces were final. And then we'd drift to books, the office, tales of former loves, of first loves, of the first time each of us had made love, of the reasons we were having this affair now. Funny aunts and uncles we both had, funny things they had said. What had been on the op-ed page of the paper that morning. We chose our words carefully, chose the stories we told each other, spoke of our respective childhoods, of our wonderment at the high-tech world we now inhabited.

Then we went on to the next phase: room service, something to drink. I fled to the bathroom when the knock finally came at the door. The room service man had no doubt seen everything, but he wasn't going to see me sitting in bed at nine-thirty P.M. I inspected myself in the bathroom mirror, my tumbled hair, my cheeks pleasantly ruddy from excitement and from the stubble on my lover's chin. I emerged, wearing my skirt and shirt but no underclothes, to find a youth in starched white jacket arranging the dinner that he had trundled in on the cart, opening the bottle of white wine and placing it in an ice bucket. He left, and we devoured the roast chicken, ate the slender green beans, poured dressing on our salads, drank the wine. For dessert there was strawberry-banana ice cream. We assured each other it was the best ice cream, no, the best thing we had ever tasted in our lives. I didn't care how many calories it had, nor how much fat and cholesterol.

When I lay down with him again, he was no longer interested in love. I pretended it was okay. It wasn't. I wanted more. Not for the sex, for the reassurance. But he fell heavily asleep. It was eleven-thirty. This was the night I had anticipated for six weeks. I had thought of it daily, derived my energy from it, my sense that I was still attractive and worthwhile. Now it was over, or mostly, and I was queasy, unhappy, and bored. I slept by quarter-hours, or so it seemed, as I dreamed and woke to the warmth of the body of the man beside me, disturbed by his occasional snores. (Did I snore? Oh God, please not. But who could be certain?) I knew not to expect a decent night's sleep in these circumstances. This must be the way soldiers slept on a battlefield, waiting for dawn. The way the sick woke in hospital beds in the interminable night. Once or twice I was awakened by his muscled arm falling over me, causing me to stir with desire until I realized that this was the leaden gesture of unconsciousness, an artifact of the wine consumed.

No night is blacker than the night on the thirty-first floor of a first-class hotel. At five on that June morning, the air began to glow as if penetrated by the chemical glare of streetlights. But it was daybreak touching the half-drawn drapes and the translucent curtains that confer a spurious grace, an illusion of luxury, on the sealed windows and industrial walls of the hotel. At that moment, the pampered customer thrust from an uneasy sleep can clearly detect how ruthlessly the decor has been slapped on, the textured paint of the walls, the cheap furniture veneered to resemble costly antiques, the lushly pleated draperies over the stingy little window, the pallid, inoffensive artworks in tones to match the bedspreads. In the meager but increasingly insistent light, the clothing mounded atop the other king-size bed became intelligible once more, things with buttons, cuffs, and crumpled collars. The dinner cart too took shape. We should have pushed it out into the corridor. Stale butter mingled with chicken scented the air. What remained of the strawberry-banana ice cream had turned into a toxic puddle.

I inspected my watch: five-thirty. The digital radio alarm was set for six. He must get to the airport this morning, I must get to work. And to be sure, I must show up at home this evening. But it was still the present. The event I'd lied and cheated to arrange was still in full flight. Dawn had not quite broken. Emma had come to Rodolphe's chateau, running through the fields. Anna lay next to Vronsky. As any attentive reader of Tolstoy knows, Anna didn't enjoy the sex much, and

Flaubert left me in doubt about Emma, but I enjoyed it, and the minutes were flying. He must be gone by six-thirty, maybe six-forty-five. A car service would be waiting for him downstairs. Even then, he might miss his plane. He must shower, dry his hair. His blow-dryer, I noticed last night, was neatly arrayed on the vast marble counter, along with his electric razor. Did I dare wake him? No, he was too exhausted. And a man is not always delighted to be awakened for love first thing in the morning. Nevertheless, I moved closer and insinuated my hand under his elbow and onto his chest. If he had saved time for all that grooming, he could make some for me.

Suddenly his feet were on the floor. I watched his unsteady walk through the cool white light. He shut the bathroom door. I heard the water run into the pink washbasin and, additionally, the splash of urine in the toilet. Then the flush, a pause, and the vigorous scrubbing of teeth, the expectoration. A good sign.

I pretended to sleep, burying my head in the pillow, and I did sleep, long enough to begin a dream. Then I felt him curling around me, his cold flesh in need of warmth. Sweet, fresh, cool. His arms were around me, his fingertips grazed my chest some-what purposelessly. I feigned luxurious, sensual slumber, mov-ing toward him just a little. Sighed but not loudly. His hands fell away. He had dozed off. I turned, exasperated. If he had had an agenda last night, I had one this morning. He was soft, languid, flaccid. Adam on the Sistine ceiling. I set about arousing him, knowing that he knew whose pleasure I sought, knew that my concerns were selfish, not tender, knew that I wanted to sit at my desk all day recollecting the perfection of this morning en-counter, the urgency of love that caused people to have inter-course at dawn even though they felt terrible and might miss their planes.

Soon, obediently, resignedly, he pulled me toward him and kissed me. Though I sensed that his head was splitting, as in-deed my own was splitting, soon he was able to fulfill my ambi-tion, and I rode with him, approaching my own climax with reckless ease, the sensation that swiftly peaks and vanishes, then I went with him again, insatiable, ready for more. Multiple orgasms, multiple achievements! I could climax four times to his one. How nice to be at this stage of life finally. My lover was cooperating with me, trying hard to reach his own climax, anxious to be done with this, bound by the nature of his masculinity and his anxiety, fighting his headache, his need for coffee, the waiting airplane, the possibility of failure.

Then somehow the sheet got tangled around his feet — he began struggling to get loose — and the clock began to beep, beep, beep. Hampered by the bedclothes, he lunged to quell the clock and hurled himself overboard onto the carpet. He crawled back heavily into my arms. A large bundle. Sweaty, exhausted. There was no time to begin again.

"It's just the comedy of sex," he said, sensing my anguish. "You get your feet tangled in the sheet. The clock goes off instead of you." He left the bed, and the next sound I heard was the shower. Soon would come the terrible moment — the goodbye peck on the cheek and the door closing behind him, with its discreet noise, like a Cadillac door slamming, *shunk!* Alone in the bedsheets in room 3105, anonymous, without identifying numbers or a proper bathrobe or maybe even toothpaste, since I had forgotten mine and he had no doubt taken his, even though he knew full well I had none, because I had borrowed toothpaste from him last night.

He kissed me hurriedly, promised to telephone, and then he was gone. I sat up. I mustn't call room service and ask for a pot of coffee, because he had checked out and turned his key in. Officially there was nobody in this room and nobody to bill the pot of coffee to. I got up. The bathroom was littered with wet, abandoned towels, and little puddles stood here and there. Otherwise it was quite vacant. He had, however, left the toothpaste.

At seven o'clock, fully dressed, I let myself out the door stealthily, only to meet the maid with her cart of toilet paper and towels and sheets, plastic packets containing shoeshine kits and shower caps. I said good morning. Then, waiting for the elevator, I turned and inspected her. Dark, short, rotund. She worked here invisibly, unnoticed by those she served. Her only mark upon our lives was the cleanliness of the rooms, the beds made according to a certain protocol, the covers turned down at a certain hour of the afternoon, the two little chocolate candies placed primly on the pillow. Who had decided that customers required chocolates at bedtime?

Now this woman suddenly eyed me. She knew why I was here, knew that I had come smoothly up the elevator after calling on the house phone and that the man I slept with paid a single rate. She saw girlfriends every morning, several of us. When she saw the twenty-dollar tip I had left on the bedside table, she would know that it was meant as an apology — for the messy dinner cart, for the lies he and I told in order to have these nights. She would change the sheets, run the vacuum, refill or replace all the plastic bottles of shampoo, and see whether I had carried off the complimentary sewing kit. In the elevator, I thought about a fellow I knew who collected hotel bottles of shampoo and conditioner and shower caps in pink plastic envelopes and shoeshine cloths and sewing kits, swept all these items into his suitcase before leaving the room. He kept them in a hall closet at home, as if accumulating something of value.

The lobby was already swarming with businesspeople leaving for meetings, seated at enormous tables in the dining room where they superciliously ordered black coffee and dry toast after their breakfast companions had specified eggs Benedict and sausages. Out on the street I pictured him in his airplane seat, tightly buckled and maybe in the air, maybe thirty thousand feet above my head already and hurtling westward by now, with his briefcase open and a flight attendant bringing him coffee. An ordinary day. It was too early to go to work. What could I do between now and nine o'clock? I would walk to my office, carrying my briefcase. I would stop somewhere for breakfast, take some aspirin, buy the newspaper.

I would sit at my desk all that day and wait for the phone call: "Sure did love seeing you." While I waited for his voice on the other end of the wire, I would squeeze the juice out of the memory — carefully doctoring it up, cleansing it, and expunging it of mishaps, missteps, pain, forgotten toothpaste, ringing phones, orgasms you weren't quite sure you'd had, interrupted sleep, his satiny snore, his inevitable airplane, the possibility that this was the last time.

This was love, the sexual revolution, a revolution that had somewhere along the way acquired its guillotine, its Robespierre. Oh, yes, the liebestod was now within reach of all ages and social classes, regardless of gender, sexual preference, or educational attainment. In the customary hubris of the educated class, of mature, well-manicured white heterosexuals, we hadn't even used a condom. But there was a disease in people's blood now that didn't give a damn if you were educated and white and heterosexual. Gay cancer, people had called it nervously in the first years, but it had proved not to be cancer, and no respecter of persons. It killed the poor because they were easy game, and it killed gay men because they happened to have fallen ill with it before anyone else, but it did not hesitate at anybody. AIDS was an acronym we had all recently and reluctantly learned to recognize: acquired immune deficiency syndrome, a disease that no antibiotic could touch. Syphilis had been leisurely, sporadic, waxing and waning, allowing its victims to grow old before it ate away their noses, drove them mad, and killed them. AIDS claimed its prizes young, dispatched them in the prime of youth, deflowered and tortured them, a foul set of teeth that chewed away at the most basic, most private, most intricate bodily defense and rendered it defenseless.

Emma need no longer shop for a dose of arsenic in the pharmacy next door, nor Anna fling herself under the onrushing iron horse, nor Juliet take the dagger to her breast. Tragedy, banished so briefly in the mid-twentieth century, had come back in style by the late 1980s. Sexual intercourse was no private matter: I was the partner of every man or woman my jet-set businessman had touched, and they all were partners of my partners. God, when had we begun referring to lovers as partners? Limited partners? Partners in what? Were George and Frédéric partners? Anna and Vronsky? Ingrid Bergman and Gary Cooper? Jack Kennedy and Marilyn Monroe? I didn't want a goddamn partner. I wanted love, not this casual flirtation with boredom and humiliation on the one hand and death on the other. Dying for love was one thing. Dying from it, another.

He would telephone. If not today, tomorrow. If not tomorrow, next week. Yet I knew that the love he had offered me was a fabrication. I had thought it sufficient at the time. A high point of my life. "He can never leave me," I had assured myself, and perhaps in some sense that was so, because I had no real need for him. I could hardly be abandoned by a man I did not really possess. My old vice had resurfaced, the need to turn raw life into a romance novel. Perhaps I could always remind myself of his passion, and in that sense I would always love him. But literature no longer seemed enough. I had taken a wrong turn in the road. Inclination River, into which I had dived like a skinny-dipper on a summer day, was inexorably emptying into the Lake of Oblivion.

Indeed, he did telephone. Once to say that his divorce would soon be final. Once to say that his next trip to New York had been postponed. Then he called to make a dinner date. But something odd was in his voice. The fact was, he finally admitted, he had been seeing someone else. She worked as an executive secretary, he added, emphasizing the "executive," as if I might more easily comprehend the attraction that way. We had never vowed exclusivity, of course. But I sensed that he had fallen for his new acquaintance. My reactions flickered uneasily from annoyance to rage, from a sense of abandonment to unfounded indignation, and then I unexpectedly laid hands on a deep sense of relief. What I had begun to imagine as an endless series of hotel-room dates had been canceled, erased from my appointment book. As an inexperienced young woman so long ago, I had exulted over each encounter with love, satisfactory or not, had unfailingly mourned each parting. Now I was glad to be free. I was my solitary self once more. I politely declined his invitation for the next week, invited him to keep in touch if he felt like it, and said goodbye.

I thought of Gil. How we had stumbled together into the mansion called marriage, a rickety old relic, its atmosphere polluted, its rules confused, an institution now failing on every side, with matrimonial law and divorce kits the growth industries of our age. How hard I had tried to reclaim this ancient dwelling, to remodel it to suit a woman who worked and a man whose professional dreams never materialized, how hard he had tried too, how complete our failure. Before marriage Emma Bovary had thought herself capable of love; but the happiness presumably conferred by love eluded her. She tried to understand just exactly what people meant in this life when they used words like "felicity," "passion," "abandon," words that sounded so pretty in books. But my daughters were not yet women, and I had responsibilities. For the moment, home was the only place to go.

14

CODA

It is New Year's Eve, foggy and rainy. Our house has been filled with people since mid-December. Besides Edwina, a cousin and her two children came for Christmas and only departed yesterday. More bodies than beds. Though poised on the edge of madness or murder, I always make a nice Christmas for my family. Gil set up a tree, and I dragged out the box of Christmas ornaments. Besides finances and stoicism, they seemed the chief factor holding our union together, for we had collected them over the years and would never be able to divide them up. Who would get the little handmade angel, the birds' nests and toy soldiers bought at the nursery school bazaar so many years ago? Christmas is the equivalent of the law of gravity for the Peculiar Institution — Christmas, Passover, the high holidays, anniversaries, Kwanza, Chinese New Year, or whatever else has been devised around the world to keep husbands and wives from dissolving into quarks and neutrinos and unpredictable particles and wheeling off into space. You'd leave in November, but Thanksgiving is coming up. In April, but it's your kid's birthday.

My own bedroom is occupied by Edwina on her customary holiday trip. Thanksgiving to New Year's. At eighty-three, she has grown selectively deaf. Hears what you wish she didn't hear but nothing else. I take care to shout courteously at her, because otherwise she feels discarded. "It's hard to be old," she says, in a rage, when she can't make out our conversation. "I'm sick of it all. I wish I were dead." She has never considered a hearing aid. I not only have to shout but have to remind others to shout as well. "Grandma can't hear you."

I had three hours' sleep last night. Gil forgot to tell me that our Sally, now twenty and a college student, was spending the night with a friend, and I sat up until four, waiting for her to come in from the party she'd gone to, wondering why she hadn't called. Sally always calls. Gil finally got up to pee and told me. Today I am a dullard; I consider napping, but recoil from the idea because then I'd never get to sleep tonight. Sleep doles itself out to me in stingy little doses. I want my dose past midnight. My mind is a great vacancy inside my head, which feels like a burned-out building. But it takes no brains to do dishes, pick up, plan meals, do the wash, fold the clothes.

In the middle of the afternoon Sally and Maggie appear, hungry and rushed. Their chief anxiety, as usual on New Year's Eve, is how to have a good time, how not to be left out of the evening's pleasure. Sally for once has a solution. She and three of her girlfriends have all been invited to a spectacular new dance club by four young men, a mass date. All the girls soon arrive, and the house is wonderfully alive with shrieking, with the trying on and casting off of various skimpy little dresses, dark stockings, high-heeled sandals, dangling earrings, so that soon every chair and tabletop is festooned with sheer, dark, gorgeous finery. The dresses are smoothed over bony young hips, the skirt tails flipped and swirled, the shoe straps buckled and unbuckled, silky hanks of hair pinned up in tortoiseshell clips or fluffed out in aggressively kinky masses.

In my jeans and old shirt, I admire and advise, feeling some-what anxious about the lacy, brazen G-strings kids now wear instead of panties, their cruel little underwire bras that cut their ribs with every breath, just as my panty girdles of bygone days tortured my upper thighs. (Everything they wear has been ordered, at extravagant prices, from a store called Victoria's Secret — the secret being how to charge so much for so little. Sally's socks, with a designer's name on them, now cost ten dollars a pair, and this morning at the clothes dryer I folded ten pairs for her and six for Maggie. Maggie too has ten pairs, but four are under her bed, I believe. Where have I gotten two hundred dollars, plus tax, to spend on socks?) The girls apply and reapply their makeup. The bathroom is littered with makeup brushes, mascara, emollients, exfoliation creams, blushers, tweezers, lipstick in every shade from deep brown to white — most of which belong to Sally. I exclaim "Ooh, ahh" as they glue false eyelashes on their lids.

This afternoon my younger one, Maggie, is not within their happy circumference. She is jealous of these twenty-year-olds with lacy underwear and plump breasts and driver's licenses and solid plans for the evening. She has been arbitrarily excluded from a party she very much wanted to attend. Her friends habitually practice these sadistic arts. It's a totally suburban thing, as they might say. She thinks she can get an invitation to a party in the next town, but that would mean forty-five minutes of driving each way for me, and I urge her to find alternatives. She locks herself in her room and begins a round of telephoning. The older girls, who need the phone, pound raucously on her door, call her a bitch and a brat. I exhort, "Please don't call Margaret names. I can't bear it." I remember telling the girls that in a house where people practice courtesy and love one another, an extra phone line is unnecessary.

At twilight Maggie emerges, calm, with a plan in mind. She is going to an all-girl party at Kathleen's, whoever Kathleen is. It is the first time I have heard "Kathleen." They will watch the broadcast from Times Square, she says, and may she please take one of the two bottles of champagne in the fridge, because Kathleen's parents haven't any but will permit the six girls to share one bottle if Maggie brings it. Ah, innocence. Ah, parental supervision. Of course she may take the champagne, which is only cheap stuff anyhow, and of course I can drive her to Kathleen's. Now, if I can survive dinner with Gil and Edwina, perhaps the rest of the evening will be my own.

About seven, the twenty-year-olds depart in clouds of perfume, bare-shouldered under their school coats, clacking on their strappy high heels, their legs provocatively sheathed in sheer black with sparkly things on the calves, their earrings dancing and swinging. No, they won't have too much to drink. Yes, if the boys have too much to drink, they will call a taxi. I tuck a twenty into Sally's tiny handbag. "Go to sleep tonight, Mom," she commands. "We're grownups." The door slams, and I summon the household to dinner. Maggie, on the telephone once again, declines dinner. Gil is angry with me for unspecified reasons, angry with his mother because he wishes she would go home, and angry with his daughters because they have not consulted him about their plans for New Year's Eve.

"But you've been locked in your room all day," I point out helpfully. He pours himself a glass of wine.

The three of us settle down at the kitchen table and pass the serving dishes.

"How jolly we are this New Year's Eve. My, my. How happy we should be!" says he, employing the heavy irony of the heavy drinker. Edwina and I stare at our plates. No wonder Maggie refuses to come to the table. I envy her having refusal rights. I welcome the interruption when she asks to be driven to Kathleen's. Gil offers, but I beat him to the car keys. DWI, in addition to everything else? In the car, Maggie assures me that the one glass of champagne will be her limit, that Kathleen's parents will be present at all times, and that she will telephone me no later than one o'clock. Always the prudent mother, I ask her to write down Kathleen's phone number. She complies, then sits sullenly beside me, her lovely head emerging from a ragbag body. Her jeans are tattered, the pockets in her outsize, thrift-shop duffle coat ripped. It would enrage her if I offered to mend the tears; she refuses to wear the presentable coat I bought her six months ago. She prefers rags, the poverty of plenty, for how else would she and her peers deny that they have a good school, solvent parents, enough to eat? The rags show their contempt for the privileges they wallow in. Up yours, Mommy and Daddy! Your rotten middle-class values, your utility bills paid on time, your mortgage escrow, your mutual fund! Fuck it all! Whew. That's what I think too, babe. Down with propriety!

I drive her to an address two miles away. I don't know the house, but this is a suburb, not a town. You aren't supposed to know anybody. Upon my return I find Edwina and Gil in front of the TV in what we call the den, where wild beasts slumber. Relieved that they are out of the kitchen, I clear up the dinner dishes, load the dishwasher, pour in the detergent, press the button. I love the swish of the hot water inside, the idea that the machine is swishing and laboring instead of me. I have formed a passionate relationship with my household machines. I am fascinated with the noises they make, the time they take to do things, the demands they make on me in spite of being labor-saving devices. Starting the dishwasher has the force for me of a vesper bell tolling. *Deo gratias.* I am bone tired, entitled to a rest.

An aria from *Lucia di Lammermore*, Maria Callas singing, tinkles out of the cheap kitchen radio, perpetually tuned to a classical station. Lucia, don't marry that bastard your brother has fixed you up with, he'll drive you nuts! Then they announce some pianist, unknown to me, with three of Chopin's nocturnes. Tears come to my eyes. What chords are those, what notes of grace, what wild ecstasy? Whose house did Chopin live in when he wrote those nocturnes? Ah, yes, Nohant, George Sand's house. I have not thought of George for ten years. Now I recall that she went to the island of Majorca with Chopin and her two children: it never stopped raining, and she had to sop up the puddles and try to keep the bedding dry. When his cough turned lethal, she had to search for a doctor willing to treat him, ransack the village for anything fit to cook, deal with the angry neighbors, who realized the skinny little Polish musician had brought tuberculosis to their island. I imagine her mopping, cooking, changing sheets, drying her tears and everybody else's, remembering the lost pleasures of the bedchamber, trying to find five minutes to work on her current novel — for they were out of money. Of course it was her lookout to earn some. At least, I thought, she wasn't *married* to Chopin. At least Madame Chopin *mère* hadn't come along. Tough life, isn't it, George, wearing the pants?

The house is suddenly silent. Edwina and Gil have both gone to bed. I switch on the TV in the middle of a James Bond movie. Wonderful! I adore Sean Connery. Elegant, witty, sexy man, sidestepping bullets, rescuing women from danger, always ready for love. Every housewife's dreamboat. He complains about nothing, he takes his girlfriend out to dinner, and he has no mother. James Bond never had a mother, not ever in his life. He sees to his own shirts, his own packing. Nobody figures his taxes for him, pays his bills, or hangs up his towel in the bathroom. His power for me — and I am swooning as I once did over Cornel Wilde but for different reasons — is that he draws his creature comforts from casinos, airplanes, and king-size beds with gaudy headboards in various hotels. He doesn't *live* anywhere. No home, no wife! He needs women only as companions in the casinos and in the king-size beds. Never in his life does he ask why there's no clean underwear in the drawer or chide his companion for spending too much money.

I take up my needlepoint. I stitch neatly away on the white part, hiding the ends perfectly on the back side. James is sinking into pink satin sheets with a beautiful spy. Serenity overtakes me. This is the best New Year's Eve ever. Maybe James will stay in bed with that woman, or keep his beautiful self on the TV screen, until Maggie calls for her ride. I decide to take Sally's advice — I won't worry about the older girls. They'll either get home safely or not, and it will be morning anyway by the time the cops call.

Then I hear footsteps: Edwina lumbers back downstairs.

"I have an idea. I'm going to wake Gil up to watch the ball

go down at midnight. Why, what's that you're watching? Where is the New Year's Eve show?" Seizing the remote, she switches to the Waldorf, to Times Square. James had just been taken into custody by some terrible thugs in black suits. Three of them. "What's that in your hands? Oh yes, that needlepoint. I prefer cross-stitch. Why don't you do cross-stitch? You can make your own patterns. I do little dogs."

"I guess I'll just stick to the needlepoint. I like these flower-garden patterns. Why don't you just leave Gil alone? Let him sleep."

"No, I feel too guilty bringing in New Year's without my boy." She sits beside me weeping, fumbling for tissues and sticking the wet ones up her sleeve. Eventually she mounts the stairs once more. I instantly flip back to James, but the credits are rolling. Nothing else is on. The house is still. My eyes burn, and that place between my shoulder blades feels as if a serrated knife has been plunged into the muscle. If only this day were done. If only Maggie would call. I see that I have put purple stitches where the green ought to be, and I discard my needle-point. I doze. I stretch out but jerk awake at one-thirty, half frozen. The phone has not yet rung. Well, surely Kathleen's ob-servant parents won't object if I telephone at this hour and say I am on my way. Ten rings, and finally a woozy male voice: "Don't know where the hell they are. You tell me. Left hours ago, in a cab. Whadda mean, calling at this hour." And he hangs up.

I return to the kitchen table, angry, helpless, trying to think of another house to call. Goddammit, Maggie promised never to do this again. Not to make up stories. Not to stay out past curfew. Not to act like a suburban adolescent. I make myself a cup of tea, then throw it viciously down the sink. I hate tea. Thin, cursed, ladylike tea. Milk or lemon? One lump or two? My mind is full of savage thoughts, but I whimper. I think of young boys careening around drunk, of Maggie in the front seat. I tell myself that she didn't really lie, that the situation was misrepresented to her, that she simply fell in with the crowd. Desperate for something to kill the pain, I work the crossword puzzle, then find yesterday's paper and work that puzzle too. I wish I could eject Edwina from my bed. I fantasize about going in there to my bed, yanking the old lady out of the blankets, throwing her on the floor, and telling her to prepare for a quick ride to the airport.

I try to imagine some punishment bad enough for my daughter. Strangulation; ah, my hands around her neck! Then I bend over her in a hospital bed, on a gurney in the emergency room. Drugged, drunk, bleeding to death. My darling, my child, my baby whose steady gaze in the first moments after her birth I still recall, her tiny hands, the relief I detected in her blue eyes as she focused on her mother's face. By now the rain is icy, I hear the tinkle of sleet against the windowpanes. Is she out in this? Call me, my Maggie, let me come and get you! I begin to sob, then dry my tears and take up my pencil again. A five-letter word for vessel. Crock?

At three-thirty, past exhaustion, rage, anxiety, but suddenly furious with crossword puzzles, I hear a noise at the back door. There is Maggie, a drowned stray, pale, her hair streaming. Is she drunk, stoned, destroyed? I cannot tell. She is tiny in the rain, trembling from top to bottom, no hat, no gloves, her bodily form undetectable inside the ragged clothing.

"I am such a jerk!" she cries. I can hardly understand her, but I pull her into the kitchen and put my arms around her. Maybe we can talk this out. Then, footsteps. Edwina! Goddammit! Edwina must not see Maggie. For my sake, she must not see her. But here we are, three generations of women in one kitchen. An American matriarchy. An American quilt.

"She's been raped. Margaret, tell your grandma what happened." Edwina somehow manages to get her hands on the child, but Maggie escapes. I hear the key turn in the lock to her room.

"You mustn't punish her! This is nobody's fault but yours."
Edwina shakes her wattles and waves her hands.

"I'm her mother and I will punish her as I see fit. Go back to
bed and stop interfering. Why are you casting me as the villain
in this play? At least I sat here. Her daddy is asleep. Go back to
bed!"

I hear Maggie sobbing through her locked door, and I finally persuade her to let me in. The youngsters had left Kathleen's house and gone to a large raucous party. "I didn't know,
they never told me that's what they meant to do," she insists. I
believe her. She drank beer, smoked pot, and then fled when
two police cars pulled into the driveway and the party animals
scattered. She walked three miles home in the dark, icy night,
with cars flashing past her, forcing her toward the ditch. She has
not been raped. Has simply had a taste of privileged adolescence in the burbs. She weeps in my arms. I weep too, then
towel her hair, get her into dry pajamas (ragged, of course,
since she won't touch the new pair she got for Christmas), massage her hands, remind her to remove her contact lenses, kiss
her goodnight, pat her bony shoulder until she appears to fall
asleep. Then I wrap myself in my old comforter and fall asleep
on the couch in my jeans and shirt. It is four o'clock, the tail end
of night.

When I awake at eight, my first thought is Sally — oh, yes,
she has come home, along with her friends, and I didn't even
hear them open the front door. A female body, divested of its
finery and covered with a quilt, is on the other couch. Pantyhose, dresses, bras, dangle from banisters, festoon chairs and tables. I pierce the ball of my foot on an earring lying prong upward on the throw rug. The puncture bleeds only a little. When
did I last have a tetanus shot? When I was fourteen. I peek into
Sally's bedroom and see that she and another girl are sleeping
in her bed, swathed in sheets and blankets. Yes, yes, it is my
daughter's head under the bedclothes, I recognize its contours,

the wisps of curly brown hair, the just-visible line of the silky eyebrows. Mine, mine. The head I have kissed, fondled, brushed, de-nitted during various louse epidemics in grade school, applied gobs of henna to, yearned over. Soft on its pillow, not smashed on the dashboard of her boyfriend's car. There is one more New Year's Eve child in a sleeping bag on the floor. All bodies present and accounted for, and none in plastic bags. The females have made it home, and the males are not my concern. But God save them, I hope they got home too, wending their way through the minefield of adolescent life.

I shut myself in the kitchen and make coffee, hoping they will all sleep until midafternoon, especially Edwina and Gil, but mother and son join me, wanting breakfast. Edwina tells Gil that his daughter is a victim of rape. Unable to muster a polite riposte, I shout that she is not to mention the word again. She storms out of the kitchen. Gil and I begin the year in combat. His mother is unbearable, he says, and I am unbearable too.

As the battle escalates, I ask him, for the hundredth time, to grant me, to grant himself, at least a break in the horror, at least a separation, if not a divorce. Uncontested, amicable, so that we need not each hire attorneys and squander what few assets we have. I offer him the house. Alimony. Anything but custody. He looks interested. Then, suddenly, I hear a cry. A kid in a sleeping bag somewhere is quite sick. On top of dehydration and hangover, she has hard menstrual cramps, and last night's champagne and cheese crackers are coming up. She screams and sobs. During the next hour I hold the basin, empty it, fetch cold cloths, say comforting words, and search for the ibuprofen. I commandeer Gil's bed and put the sick child in it. Then I tend the one on the living room couch, who isn't in much better shape but at least doesn't have cramps. Eventually the two sick girls return to sleep, Gil says it is unbearable here and he is going for a drive. Edwina, I note with pleasure, stays behind her locked door.

Energized by the thought of freedom, I make a plan. Next

weekend I shall search for an apartment for the girls and myself. After all, the kids are nearly grown. I see myself happily alone, nobody but me. I ransack the house for laundry. I stand dumbly before the dryer, waiting for it to ping. I iron what needs ironing. I mend some underthings, a profoundly comforting female task that connects me with my mother and grandmother and the good women of the past, thrifty homemakers patching up the holes of life with a darning needle, but I badly botch the job and am forced to pick out dozens of tiny stitches.

Maggie arrives in the kitchen as I assemble a lasagna for supper. She is remorseful, full of love, bright and healthy again after twelve hours' sleep. "Mom, I'm sorry. I will never do that again. I will never worry you again." She eats a slice of toast, drinks milk, retreats to the TV. Sally's friends sleep until good health is restored and eventually gather up their pantyhose and sandals, makeup brushes and bangles, and go home: late-model cars driven by fathers and mothers and brothers screech up to the curb to collect the girls, one by one. Tomorrow is a school day, a work day. Sally will be on her way back to college, Maggie will go to school. I shall travel to my office, I shall sit at my desk, do what I am competent to do. My fingers will fly over the keyboard, I will speak intelligently into the phone. I shall produce something my boss can sell for money. By noon I shall have earned my day's salary, and then I shall lunch with a business associate and work all afternoon. Speak in well-modulated tones, counsel the young around me, train the new hire. I shall have covered up my roots by then, my hair will look fifteen years younger than I am, my colleagues shall call my name blessed. In this realm a cause produces its effect. *Je travaille, donc je suis.*

At the table that evening, Gil announces to his mother, his daughters, and me that within the next few weeks, no later than February 1 at the outside, he will be moving out. I wonder where the cash is coming from for his new apartment but am too overjoyed at his news to inquire about details. Actually it will come out of our joint savings account. Separation will be constructive, he says bitterly. Perhaps he'll make it a legal separation. Then a divorce. His face is haggard, ashen. He casts a glance on me that says I have killed him, that I am a murderer. I have shattered the family unit. I need not imagine, he warns me, that he is going to let me off easy. Oh, perhaps I am a villain. As usual, it is hard for me not to buy what he is selling. I turn my back.

Edwina weeps, protests, demands that I put a stop to this. Maggie and Sally comfort their grandmother or at least try to quiet her. They comfort their father but openly support his plan, to the point that he is offended. (Odd, how this situation turns the children into psychiatric social workers. How ably they take on the task!) Edwina heads for bed, Gil goes off to begin packing, the children begin stacking dishes. I tell them I can do the rest, and they vanish gratefully. As the house settles to silence, my heart is light. I scrape and rinse and stack meticulously. I cover the leftovers and stow them away, wipe down the counters, put away the placemats. The last dishtowel is hung to dry, the table is ready to receive breakfast, the dishwasher begins its first rinse. All is in order. Clear.

Half of all marriages end in divorce. That leaves half that do not. A good divorce demands the same virtues, I realize, as a good marriage. Consideration, concern for the other party, an ability to negotiate, confidence in the future, plus just the right amounts of coercive monetary pressure. I don't imagine we're up to it. Well, good divorce or bad, Gil and I have at last taken the first step. I cannot rise from the table. I lay my head upon my arms. I am a curious creature washed up on the beach, a clump of algae, a specimen of the jellyfish phylum with no head and no central nervous system, Coelenterata rather than Chordata. The dishwasher, cranking into its final rinse, its coda, provides the background music, slosh, swish, like ocean waves pounding on sand.

I think idly of that column in some magazine, *Good House*

Cleaning or *Woman's Home Psychiatrist* or *Better Wives and Gardens,* entitled "Can This Marriage Be Saved?" Written by professionals with strings of M.D.'s and Ph.D.'s after their names, a kind of diagnostic manual of marital woes. Controlling, enabling wives. Insensitive, impotent husbands. Debt and lies. Squabbles over money and kids. Neglect. Infidelity. Mutual rage and despair. But to a psychiatrist there's no such thing as rage or despair, only mental disorders ready to be mended. Ready to be talked to. For a price. Yes, every marriage can be saved. The answer to the question is never negative, for the social edifice would collapse and advertisers flee and circulation fall by half if a women's magazine admitted that some marriages are not worth saving. All it takes to save a marriage is penitence, remorse, sensitivity training, unfailing sympathy for your spouse, and sexual intercourse every Tuesday and Thursday night. But Gil and I cannot be saved. I had swum through the current to the other side.

15

DIES IRAE

> If the past is cut off from the present by a series of obstacles — hills, mountains, chasms, contrasts — it also has ways and means of restoring contact — roads, paths, and streams. The past is all about us, unrecognized and insinuating, and we are caught in its toils without always realizing it.
>
> — Fernand Braudel, *The Identity of France*

"I'm going to Europe in January to visit my sons, one now very gainfully employed in Brussels, the other in Frankfurt. As you know, Alissa died last year. I intend also to call on her sister, who has lived for years in Aix-en-Provence. I always liked that side of the family and hope this won't be my last visit, though it may. I have some keepsakes to deliver, photographs, a couple of rings, and such that I am reluctant to consign to the mails," Henry Robinson's letter began, my first letter from him in perhaps ten years. The return address was unfamiliar, but the penmanship was not. Handwriting lasts even longer than faces, at least up to a point. How long it had been! I skimmed through the letter: he was inviting me to meet him in France.

Two or three times Henry had brought his family to New York and had visited us briefly, first in our disorderly, cramped two-bedroom apartment, then in our less disorderly suburban house. Alissa seemed perfect in every detail, Henry's dream of femininity: soft gray eyes, the manners and accent of the upper-class South, a woman at home with herself and her role, as southern women often are. Intelligent but noncompetitive, not thirsty for equality, not roaming the streets in a tailored suit and aerobic shoes, not twisting and turning in her own hot ashes the way I did. I had liked her, envied her the clear mission, the handsome husband — for he had shed his gangliness and facial hair and he dressed very elegantly — with the solid job. I could tell she made good coffee every morning, was admired for her beaten biscuits, knew how to turn two boisterous little boys into soft-spoken, properly dressed, courteous little citizens without for one moment threatening their sense of male superiority. I imagined, with a touch of envy, that she must be a skilled lover, according to the old mythology about the underlying sexiness of proper southern women. But what did I know? God, how marriage sealed people off, forced them into pretenses. I had never really known this woman, except for those visits with Henry and the children and her dutiful Christmas cards and various announcements concerning the twins — out of high school, out of college, and then married. She had been a pleasant phantom — Henry's attractive wife.

Four years before, Henry had phoned to announce that Alissa was ill. Lung cancer, terminal. I instantly began writing notes, awkward, cheerful notes on cards with Degas or Monet reproductions on the flap. Perhaps such notes are helpful: I won't know until my turn comes. At first Alissa replied. Then, after many months, one of the Robinson sons telephoned to say that she had died. I sent flowers, and yet another note. She was only fifty-five. I had reached the epoch of widows and widowers. Of having friends who were going on alone.

"I may not have told you, in the confusion following Alissa's death," the letter now continued,

> that I took her body back to be buried in the Georgia countryside. An empty gesture, perhaps. Increasingly I had come to feel I should never have married her in the first place. It's been nearly four years since the funeral. This will be my first visit to France since a couple of years before she died.

In February, after I visit my sister-in-law, I'm returning to Paris. I've taken a small apartment in the Marais, near the Place des Vosges. I wondered if you might join me for all or part of the month. I never got around to all those museums when we were kids, you know. And now there are more of them. No strings are attached, but I have dreamed for many years of revisiting Paris with you. I never thought of telling you. Just one of my fantasies. Call it a second chance.

The apartment belongs to a bachelor friend of one of my sons. Two bedrooms, a living room, kitchen and bath. I have become a pretty good cook, and we can economize by eating in occasionally, if you like, and I promise to do the dishes, too.

But of course I could join him, out of curiosity if nothing else. I had nothing to prevent my going except my job, and I was due a vacation. Sally and Maggie were young women now, having love affairs of their own. I stood at the sidelines, their fierce partisan as always. But there's little advice you can give a daughter of twenty-odd years. What on earth did Henry have in mind? Mutual nostalgia? Something permanent? Somebody to share the grocery bill — a roommate? All he wanted, he said, was for me to give him three or four days into February, so he could settle in, learn the French for "fuse box" and "leaky faucet," in case of need. He wanted to get supplies laid in, be ready for me, he said. I was charmed by his careful planning. Better that he, not I, should cope with fuse boxes and leaky faucets, especially French ones. I wondered if I could still speak French. I booked a plane ticket and let him know.

At the end of a workday I went to the airport wearing jeans and a jacket under a warm raincoat. I traveled light, with no more than I could carry over one shoulder. Goodbye to owning things: just a few skirts, sweaters, turtlenecks, a pair of nail scissors, some makeup, a bottle of aspirin in my nylon bag. No sets of matched luggage with fasteners that snapped like mousetraps, no trunk going on ahead with books and extra clothing. The smiling cabin stewards and deck chairs and dining rooms of the Compagnie Générale Transatlantique were a dream, a recollection out of a period film, like the momentousness of a voyage that used to separate one continent and one identity from another. I was lucky to have experienced that.

But I could settle for the present: an airborne bus, one of a score of flights from New York to Paris that day. I swallowed most of the flavorless dinner, napped in the rigor-mortis position for three hours as we roared eastward toward daybreak, and awakened as the flight attendant deposited a cup of coffee and a plastic container of orange juice on the tray in front of me. My hair was fuzzy, my mouth sour. I wondered if I could get into the lavatory before the seatbelt sign flashed on. Then we ran into the sunrise and in red-eyed, sleep-deprived rapture, peering through the window of the coasting jet, I spotted the wintry stubble of Ile-de-France lying under the morning sunlight like a map.

I arrived at Charles de Gaulle (like John F. Kennedy, no longer a man but a terminal) at seven o'clock and went through customs. Henry had offered to meet me. Quaint of him. I had told him during our last phone conversation that I was perfectly capable of traveling from Charles de Gaulle to rue Roger Verlomme, but he insisted. Now I anxiously scanned the crowd. No Henry. I wondered if this were a dream. He would never come for me. He was in Chicago or Minneapolis. Had he forgotten? Fallen ill? Should I simply set out for Paris? I had the address, the telephone number. I had done careful research on ground transportation. My French might be out of date and I had never been in this airport before, but I was no tourist. I knew what to do.

I spotted a tall, gray-haired, serious-looking man, showing his years, bundled up in overcoat and gloves. I shied away, as from a blind date at the door. But it was Henry, now next to me, his arms around me, Henry kissing me, *à la française*, three proper pecks on the cheeks. I searched my memory for his other face, his bearded twenty-two-year-old face, in order to link it to this one. He had aged well, had kept his character. What must he see in me? Had it done any good — the hurried application of toothbrush, lipstick, and comb just before landing? I quickly overcame a spasm in the heart, a shooting pain in the mind. Is that you, Henry? Is this me?

Shouldering my bag in a kindly gesture that turned me oddly infantile, an old-fashioned girl with a man toting her bag, he suggested a taxi, which I declined. I wanted to bounce along the streets in a bus, walk on French sidewalks, buy a carnet of *métro* tickets, be just another person in the morning rush. The air stank with jet and automobile exhaust, but it was French air, and the sun was about to break through the fog. So we climbed aboard a *navette*, which Henry told me was the word for "shuttle," and afterward went into the *métro*. "I'm not going to go to sleep until midnight," I told him. "I don't want to waste even an hour."

We emerged at a stop near enough to the Seine that we could stroll easily onto a bridge. It was sunny, but the morning fog still lay on the river, like breath condensing in chilly air, half concealing the gray stone walls. No cityscape can match the sweep of the double-sided Parisian river skyline, the mix of palaces, government buildings, department stores, spires, book-stalls, embankments, bridges, trees, traffic — the creation of many hands in many epochs. Catching the sunshine, the dark, ancient walls rose up as if from my own past, and from the city's, all the way back to Lutetia, the Roman village with the river for its moat, Paris waiting for barbarians.

My bloodstream and brain being set for the middle of the night, I listened to Henry dutifully, hardly making sense of the words. "You'll hardly believe how Paris has changed! Overgrown. Overheated. More materialistic than Los Angeles. Worse than us. More gadget-ridden. Filled with unbearable little Parisian yuppies. Unbelievable prices! Nine bucks to get into the Louvre, a glass of beer five dollars. The quais ruined by the highways, the stink of car exhaust!" He smiled. "Welcome to the City of Light. I don't mean to complain." I had to grab his arm, look into his face. The walls of Paris threatened to fall down on me. And who was this man leading me along? Did I know him at all?

As we turned northward into the streets that would lead us home, I wondered if some arthritic French pride in ancient possessions had taken the place of creative genius and egalitarian rage. Perhaps the city had aged as human beings age, become a stiff and crusty old dowager with no creative juice and a rasping, critical voice. A dowager with her monumental past recently sandblasted and scraped and spruced up, her trees perfectly pruned, her greenswards scientifically trimmed, and several thousand smartly uniformed *agents,* trained in crowd control, to keep traffic flowing. No more the wild, passionate Paris harboring illicit lovers of myriad inclinations and barricades and rebellion and students hurling paving stones. Not a city anymore but a work of art, a hothouse of nostalgia, of history as carefully pruned as her trees, a pantheon of high culture, and ready for business. Eternal Paris, dead or alive. A thousand years from now the Seine would still flow under the bridges, whereas Henry and I faced an acute shortage of time.

We walked into the Marais — "marsh," the word means — a palimpsest of palaces and ancient mansions, *hôtels particuliers,* monuments and ruins, *tabacs* and cafés. Once this quarter had been home to the Valois kings. In a house on one of these streets, Mademoiselle de Scudéry had drawn her map of love. Hundreds of years ago, somewhere around here, the greenhouse was invented — the garden under glass supplying the king's table with fresh fruits and vegetables in winter. And of course — and small wonder — a revolution had begun nearby.

We reached our destination. Henry's apartment was up four flights of stairs in a narrow old building. The hall lights had to be switched on at each landing: still chary of electricity, the

French. Henry unlocked the door and set my bag down in the entryway. (A similar house not far from here, whose topmost windows glowed at night, had contained, in my youthful imaginings, my life and love and work. I had stood in the street below, certain that a fire crackled in the grate, a bottle of red wine was on the table. Was my dream at last coming to pass?) Henry showed me around: a bedroom with a huge armoire, and the bathroom was spacious, with plenty of hot water, he assured me, an improvement over the old days. The heating system worked too. He had left, I noticed, plenty of space for my things. The double bed looked lumpy but was covered with a goose-down puff. The pair of double windows looked out on an interior courtyard, rooftops, and chimneys. The smaller bedroom was dark, with an even more dangerously lumpy single bed. The living room had a sofa and two chairs; white curtains covered the windows. The kitchen was decrepit but workable. Even with the window closed, you could hear the beguiling racket of the street, and the sun poured in through the curtain.

"Will it do? I'll stow your things in the big bedroom."

"Yes, it will do." Did I want this man? Have any use for him? Did he really intend to sleep in the other bedroom? Was he waiting for my invitation? Reluctance overpowered me. It had been a while since I had touched a man. I had given up looking. I did not want to begin a love affair at this age. I wanted peace. I would remain his companion. No strings attached, he had promised. But if he did want to be my lover, could I say no? I had only ten days here. Why had he asked me to come?

Never mind. I wanted breakfast. He set a fresh baguette and a straw basket of oranges on the kitchen table, measured out coffee into an electric pot, steamed the milk. Henry's hands were broad and sturdy still, but the skin of them betrayed him: blue-veined, freckled, fragile, the knuckles distorted. Yet this kind of skin had its own beauty, the finite beauty of all living things. My back was as straight as ever, my gait as quick. My once tangled, unmanageable hair had thinned; so had my lips; my eye sockets had become rather prominent. I was older than my mother had lived to be. Henry was a grandfather. His gray head pleased me. His smile was as eternal as some master drawing. With a sharp knife, he sliced a round off the end of one orange, cut the peel into crescents, bared the sections one by one, guided the knife precisely between the white part and the skin, separating the wedges with his fingers. A few drops of juice dripping through his fingers, he offered me the fruit. Like something from the House of Lanvin, the scent of orange overpowered the coffee and fresh bread.

"Where did you learn to peel an orange like that? You do it exactly the way I do."

"You don't remember that I taught you? I can't believe you've forgotten. We were in that student restaurant where we went so many nights. The food that evening consisted of potatoes with a side dish of macaroni and a piece of cauliflower. Something like that. *La cuisine blanche,* you used to call it. The only dessert was an orange, which at least wasn't white, and you said you'd never heard of oranges for dessert until you came to France, only for breakfast, and you began attacking it with your fingernails. Like Americans do. I'd done the same thing in the dining room of the *Normandie,* on the way here. But the waiter at my table had showed me how to use a sharp knife. How to eat an orange like a civilized person. Thus is French culture transmitted." He laughed. "And I showed you how to do it. You aren't supposed to forget the first time you learned to peel an orange."

"Would you like to know the most persistent thing about you?" I asked, prompted by something in his face or gesture. "The thing I do remember, the thing that would make me recognize you in hell? It isn't oranges."

"Yes, and then I'll tell you the same thing about yourself."

"You live in hiding. You never show yourself on the surface. I was always trying to discover what you wanted, what you were thinking, but I never could. You are a snail in its shell. I imagined some amount of pain and suffering at the interior."

"Alissa used to say the same thing, not always so kindly." They had had a troubling, unhappy marriage. Less elegant and composed than she had seemed on visits, Alissa had not been suited to life in the Midwest. She had gradually grown depressed in her role as a businessman's wife, especially a man whose business took them — or him — frequently to France. She had needed psychiatry, then hospitalization. In the end, he said, she forgot why she had married him. They planned to divorce once the boys were grown, an amicable divorce, allowing her to return to Georgia. He would visit occasionally. But just as this looked possible, she fell ill. Henry had a sense of duty. He watched her suffer for six months, which shattered them both. "I wanted to tell her I regretted having married her, that everything was my fault. But you don't say that to a dying woman. So instead I told her I loved her. She only smiled. In the end, she begged to die. Our sons didn't get there until her very last month. It was not a good death, not for her, not for me. Such terrible regrets."

He laid down the piece of bread he had cut. Poor Alissa. I had wondered, long ago, why Henry had wanted her instead of me. I would have liked, now, to hear her version of what he had just told me. I took his hand in mine, as one would do for any friend. A large hand it was — I made an effort to remember the younger version. Like my hand, it was wrinkled and spotty. Had seen some use. I assured him that he had done what was required of him, that he had been, in fact, a husband. But I could never know whether he had been or not.

To distract him, I asked what trait he found most constant in me.

"You won't like this. But I promised. It's your neediness. You were the neediest person I knew. It was written in your face. Still is."

Needy? Me? He was right, I didn't like it. Henry went on. "Maybe your ideals about men, about love, were too elevated to begin with. Maybe you wanted more than anyone could supply."

Thirty-eight years earlier, I thought I needed Henry. At least he was a candidate for the post of needed man. I might have married him, if he had not left me in the Gare Montparnasse that afternoon. Now we were sixty. I had never found anyone to satisfy my thirst for love, my promiscuity of the heart, my lust that was only incidentally physical. "Feeling that I was born for the opposite sex, I have always loved it and done all that I could to make myself loved by it. But if anyone calls me a sensualist he would be wrong, for the power of my senses never drew me from my duty when I had one." This had been Casanova's summation of his restless life, whether he spoke truly or merely to serve his own ends, and now was mine as well.

"Whatever you needed," Henry said, "I wasn't equipped, emotionally or any other way, to satisfy you when we were twenty-two. You were good to come along with me that night after we ate ourselves sick at that four-star restaurant. You surely guessed that I was a virgin." He smiled. "Love, like haute cuisine, is wasted on the young."

"I was so near to being a virgin myself that I could hardly tell the difference. For my purposes, my dear friend, you were a great lover. I have only the tenderest memories of that night, and I cried for a whole day at least after you left Paris. And I figured I'd probably gotten pregnant. That was nearly the only folly I'd avoided up to then." But neediness has its uses. It had kept me alive. Been the fuel for my internal combustion machine. It had brought me to Paris. Perhaps it was why Henry had remembered me all these years. What else could it have been?

He gave me the last section of orange, gently wedging it into my mouth, sweet, acidic, delicious. I relished the sudden pressure of his fingers between my fingers and his palm against my palm, the rush of memory, tenderness, and desire, all of which included him but spread far beyond him. I was once again a child leafing through my father's small collection of erotica, fingering the first book of love I ever read, from which Casanova had emerged, plumed hat in hand, sword at his side, his ruffled shirt bosom slightly soiled, his boots muddy. He had asserted that the goal of love was pleasure, that it is a thing of delight, consensual and mutual. Against morality and good sense, I had believed that love is worth what it costs. As a young woman, I had come to France to learn the arts of pleasure, to craft some definition of femininity that did not snuff out my identity, my wits, and my desires: an American, naive and unaware, well-meaning, a mind in need of a thought.

Now I was at the opposite end of my adulthood. Other men and women my age and Henry's were playing with their grandchildren, taking up a hobby, wondering where their lives had gone. We two sat contentedly at a kitchen table four floors above the Paris streets. That evening our windows would shed a brilliant light toward the sidewalk. We would cook our dinner, drink wine. Perhaps someone on the sidewalk would look up, trying to imagine the scene in the warm light above, would picture a fire in the grate.

But it was still morning. I was tired, out of sorts. Too early to do more than touch each other's hands, kissing lightly, trying out each other's arms, which now we did. I tried not to want him, tried to persuade myself and him to wait until night. But what was the point in waiting? We had only ten days and ten nights, and this day lay before us like a beatitude. I grew fearful of his heart and mine ticking away, the blood flowing perhaps too thickly through our arteries. "I've aged," I said apprehensively. "I haven't?" he replied with a smile. To begin a love affair in one's seventh decade, in broad daylight, takes courage. Two bodies no longer young and beautiful, sexual function no longer guaranteed. But desire, oddly enough, was more power-

ful than at age sixteen. "In me thou seest the glowing of such
fire that on the ashes of his youth doth lie, as the deathbed
whereon it must expire, consumed with that which it was nour-
ished by." Why should a pair of sixty-year-olds wait until
dark?

Not bad, after all, to be freed of youth and its terrible obli-
gations and ambitions, those pots and pans and silver patterns,
mortgages, the possibility of having children. We were not
obliged to set up housekeeping and be respectable. No aisles to
walk down, no vows to exchange. No life insurance. We could
be lovers so long as we were underneath these eaves, with no
other duties than pleasure. Time moved more swiftly for us
than for any Renaissance love poet measuring the brevity of
passion in sonnet, ballad, or villanelle. "This thou perceivest,
which makes thy love more strong, to love that well, which
thou must leave ere long!"

That afternoon, the chill February sun shone through our
windows. Paris waited below like a beloved body to be explored. Henry and I had paintings to see, walks to plan, seats to
reserve. Wednesday, Thursday, Friday. Oh, it would last forever. At dusk there were groceries to buy and dinner to cook,
standing in line behind French women with their rolling carts
and babies and dogs. Like a leitmotif, for the next ten days we
kept losing things, searching for them, miraculously relocating
them all. Emerging from a movie theater or a café, we'd miss
his scarf, my scarf, our map, his *plan de Paris*, my gloves, as if
these losses were a mnemonic device, a key to the lock of the
past. "*Voici mes gants, voici ton écharpe*," we'd tell each other,
like first-year French pupils, brandishing the item we had just
retrieved.

We walked every narrow street, visited every arrondisse-
ment, crossed the bridges, watched the children on the slides in
the Place des Vosges while their guardians chatted on cell
phones. We read the writing on the walls: here the heroes of
1830 took the barricades for *liberté, égalité, fraternité*. In the

square now named for it had stood the Bastille, the royal prison and madhouse, the storming of which had marked the beginning of the end of kings. The Marais was, and is, the Jewish quarter. From these very streets and houses, the French police had rounded up the Jews fifty years before, imprisoned them in a nearby stadium, then shipped them to Germany to die — a fact the walls don't mention. Up in Montmartre, against another wall, in 1871 the Communards were lined up and shot. In another place, in 1944, under heavy fire, one hundred glorious heroes had laid down their lives for France, slaughtered by Nazi machine guns. Give me your heroes, Paris, spare me your traitors! Don't mention collaboration and the militia. Remind us persistently that you invented the Rights of Man.

How could one not love a people who had, in fact, with all their flaws and failures, invented the idea of liberty and equality, who had perfected the idea of love, whose language had given us the key to understanding the human heart? The *carte de tendre*, the emblem of gallantry and frivolity, served as the road map for every love story that followed it. A year in Paris, so long ago, had taught me that love was a construct, a fabrication of the mind. Without that Rosetta stone, would I have succeeded in reading love when I found it?

Just like Americans, of course, the French were a maddening, self-congratulating, murderous lot, guilty of crimes against the high-flown principles they professed. (At least we two peoples had this much in common. Could we not make peace with each other on these grounds?) As in my student days, I could have knelt down to scoop the dust of Paris in my hand, to finger the grime through which George Sand had walked, knocking the ash from her cigar. And yet the George Sand proper to this stage of my life was not the woman in pants who slept with a dozen men in the Quartier Latin and Montmartre and curled up under Chopin's piano listening as he played. She was that hefty, spit-curled matron in the photograph that had startled me when I came upon it in the college library. She was at her family home, a day's journey from Paris. Hadn't smoked a cigar for years, took long vigorous walks, bathed in an icy stream each morning, undertook the schooling of her granddaughters, wrote dozens of letters to her friend Flaubert, whose *Madame Bovary* she had admired and defended when they threatened to put him in jail for having written it. Flaubert addressed her as his "dear master," and the two of them grumbled cozily together about the immorality and folly of the young, the crassness of modern times, the degradation of politics. They never spoke of their wild youth, of the writers and poets and musicians she bedded, of the belly dancers whose love he purchased while touring Egypt, the French mistress and poet he spoke harshly to and never married.

Nevertheless, I could imagine what George's counsel might be now: "Hear what this man is saying. He loves you. Don't waste time doubting it. I invented the modern woman, it has been said. Now it's time to invent another. Be as ruthless as you wish, tell him whatever you wish, hear whatever you wish in return. Never mind your duties or your job or what your mother might have said about your adventures. Make love all night and all day if it suits you. You can subside into respectability, if you so desire, after you get home."

Gradually, as day followed day and turned into a week, our lives took on a kind of permanency. We developed habits, became predictable, discovered that we liked the same music, the same food, morning rather than evening baths. We liked green beans. He cooked delicious dinners, laboring over the details, mincing onions and garlic, stirring rice and broth, uncorking the wine. At breakfast I would peel and slice mango and orange while he went below for a baguette and the newspaper. I had stopped thinking about the plane ticket in the pocket of my suitcase, responsibilities at home, my job.

One evening we set out to hear a concert: Mozart's Requiem in a Jesuit church on the Ile St.-Louis. I had dressed in layers — a blouse, sweater, and jacket, lined raincoat, a fine wool scarf around my shoulders, a short skirt, dark stockings; though I was past the age for such worries, Paris forced me to think of legs, shoes, scarves. Sexuality is an element of the air there, like oxygen. Or maybe the element is merely gender, for the French language admits no neuter, insists on gender: a pebble in the path, the river, the ticket window, the ticket itself, the sky, the curb, all are sexed, and not always according to logic. Henry too wore layers under his raincoat — sweater, tweed jacket, a silk muffler — and we hurried up the quai des Célestins and crossed the bridge onto the Ile St.-Louis, hurried through the narrow, high-walled streets, ancient façades propped up against one another, wrought iron balconies like lace insets, the blue slate roofs darkening under the night sky, the heavy courtyard doors occasionally open, revealing a motorcycle or two but retaining their seventeenth-century grit. "Nothing changes," the walls insisted. "To us, the centuries are irrelevant."

Henry carried his square brown guidebook, *Paris par Arrondissements, "L'Indispensable,"* as the cover claims. It lies satisfyingly in the hand like a lump of gold or a prayer book. Though we knew the quarter well, we suddenly felt lost. Under a streetlamp, Henry opened the book, his fingers traced the route. "Quai de Bourbon, rue St.-Louis-en-l'Ile," he muttered. "We turn left." He kept his reading glasses handy, pushed down on his nose, so that he might instantly decipher maps without having to fumble in his breast pocket for his glasses or ask me to fumble for mine. The cobblestones twisted my insteps as though I were barefoot, and my heels ticked like clocks, a vulnerable sort of noise, women's heels ticking on paving stones. The mist rose from the river, turning my hair to fuzz.

At the corner of rue Budé, Henry kissed me. I slipped my gloved hand under his elbow. Why not skip the concert and return to bed? I don't want to hear the Requiem. Mozart only wrote a little of it anyhow. It's a patchwork, it's a fake. He was dying as he wrote it. Time is short, Henry, kiss me, let's go home. George is telling me, go home to bed and skip the serious

music. But I didn't say it. I clutched his arm through his coat
sleeve. But he slipped his guidebook in his pocket, put his hand
over mine, and led us on, as if it were a mission we were bound
to complete.

The church of St.-Louis-en-l'Ile, a neighborhood sanctuary
frequented by women carrying prayer beads and market baskets
in daytime, is unremarkable, shabby, from the street. Nothing
tipped us off to the stateliness of the inner space, the dome, the
elaborately wrought ceilings, the forest of dignified Corinthian
columns. I came through the dirty little vestibule and was suddenly lofted upward by the exuberant stones. After paying a
large and uneclesiastical price for tickets, we found two seats in
the packed nave. "God is truly present in this place, please
maintain silence," advised a sign, and the deity was surely
among us. Also present were squadrons of musicians and a
well-dressed, mostly French audience. Heat, steam heat — un-
heard of in a Paris church in my youth — poured out of the
gratings on the floor, so that I had to shed my raincoat and
jacket. Saint Louis's church, named for the medieval French
Crusader king — yet another Parisian manifestation of power
in the name of a monarch whose power and pomp got him
sainthood. Church and state, combined and unbeatable!

The concert began, the great Requiem, the composer's own
funeral mass, left unfinished as his body failed him. "Requiem
aeternam," rest forevermore, rang out from the chorus. Here
was the canticle of the broken body, the body of Jesus on
the cross. Yesterday Henry and I had wandered through the
Louvre, had admired one of the greatest of all French paintings, the Pietà from medieval Avignon, in which the broken
body of Jesus lies bruised and dead on the lap of Mary. She is
worn and haggard beyond the possibility of rest, her anguish
too deep for human comfort. With its background of gold, this
painting once glowed in the gloom and darkness behind an altar; now it was pinned unmercifully against a white plaster wall
in the new Louvre, a mere cultural artifact to attract hordes of

foreign visitors. There was a savage crack across the canvas which underlined the mortality of the corpse and the deadly grief of Mary. Were they mother and son, or simply man and woman? Here was no hint of resurrection, or of eternal life: only the broken male body in the woman's arms.

"O hear my prayer: all flesh shall come to Thee," sang the choir. "I groan as one guilty; my face is red with the shame of sin." "That dread day is a day of tears on which each guilty soul shall rise to judgment. Then spare this soul, O God. Rescue me from the fires of hell." The music pierced the earth as though a trap door had sprung open and we all must fall into the flames.

I moved closer to Henry as the music soared into the vault. In this place, where God and nation joined hands to enforce orthodoxy, to uphold the sacraments, I was a heretic, a believer in every subversive myth from Tristan and Isolde to Romeo and Juliet, a seeker after a contemptible thing called romance, a woman with small faith in anything but the hegemony of language. In the beginning was the word . . . and the word was God. The word is in fact the one true and universal human possession, the paving stone we hurl at heaven.

And what was I, seated in church with my temporary lover? Church and state shook their fist in my direction. I had done no spectacular wrong, had lived responsibly, as a mother and wage-earner, had done no worse than many wives. But to profess a revolutionary ethic and lead a bourgeois life must be the greatest sin of all, worse than lusting after absolutes, worse than adultery. I laid my head on Henry's shoulder as the choir sang of hellfire. I loved him, and why not? He held on to my hand as though I were the only power that could save him from the flames. "Lamb of God, that takest away the sins of the world; give them rest. O Lord, Thou art merciful."

Out in the crowded streets, near eleven o'clock, we searched for a restaurant, reading a few menus, peering through the plate-glass windows, enticed by candlelight and half-empty wine bottles on the tables, and then we chose a place and wedged ourselves in among the late-evening smokers and brandy drinkers. On the advice of our waiter, we ordered whatever was left in the kitchen, which turned out to be crevettes, plump shellfish huge as lobster tails, in a delicious sauce, to be soaked up on bits of bread. Little white potatoes and zucchini on the side. And then two lamb chops. The white and then the red Burgundy Henry ordered went to our heads, made us laugh, rolled on our tongues. We shared a *tarte tatin*, the French version of apple pie, and thin, bitter, dark coffee.

Back out in the street, warm with the coffee and a cognac apiece, we hurried across the pont Louis Philippe, its street-lamps haloed in mist as they had been almost forty years earlier, when I had crossed the same bridge with a nervous youth who had kissed me lovingly, then withdrawn from my arms and chided me for being too intense. "Louis Philippe, citizen king," I said once again, and Henry laughed. The same passion arose in me here, forty years afterward. The streets were empty at one o'clock, as we made our way home. To silence the Requiem which still swirled in our memory, we began to sing old songs. *"Elle coule, coule, coule." "Non, je ne regrette rien." "Plaisirs d'amour ne durent qu'un moment, chagrins d'amour durent toute la vie"* — but I stopped Henry before he could complete the second phrase, the grim warning about the lasting power of love's anguish, the volatility of love's delights.

Back at home, we hung up our jackets and folded our sweaters. Each of us went calmly into the bathroom to brush and floss. Love at sixty is endowed with its own delights. You can hang up your clothes, smooth the bed, find your bathrobe. The desire is as complex and urgent as ever, but we took our time; the beauty we saw in each other lay partly in recollection. Regret stabbed us too. Why had we not spent our lives together? Why had we not met when we were fourteen? Why not have drunk some potion and lain down in each other's arms to die? Yet we both knew that love wounds, and not always to death. We knew all about anger masquerading as desire, could enumerate the irritating habits that pollute a bedroom like pesticides, the grudges, the failings of the bodies. *Dies irae, dies illa,* save me, call me. *Kyrie eleison,* Christ, be merciful. The voices, the tympani of Mozart's mass pounded in my head, with no knob to turn the volume down. Through the curtains, our window caught a patch of dark sky and framed the angularities of the rooftops and chimneys. A typewritten notice on the back of our apartment door, I had noted earlier in our stay, detailed the actions one must take in case of fire. But if the inferno broke out here, it would do no good to take precautionary measures — we'd be consumed like a pair of paper dolls.

That afternoon Henry had read aloud from a newspaper article about *la France profonde,* the part of France that isn't Paris, the part where old customs prevail, the France that all Parisians conceive to be the real France, the France that produces honest things, such as wine and plums, apricots and truffles. A France that, thanks to the European Union, is now passing away. But myths are more powerful than logic, and that night I said, "I think this is *l'amour profonde.* Apricots, good wine, plums." I am blessed or cursed with synesthesia — sex can seem identical to the way fruit tastes, or wine, or artichokes. Words mean more to me than flesh, and if love cannot be made flesh with words, what use is it? He assured me that I was still young and beautiful, that we would live forever, that we would return to Paris every year, that he loved me dearly and had always loved me. And would always love me. Even if only for one more day.

"Could we have a life together now?" he asked. "I'd stay here with you forever. I'm free now. At least we can both claim credit for staying married many years, for sticking to our jobs, raising our children, doing that which we ought to have done. As best we could, anyway."

Family values. Indeed, I had practiced them. But I didn't want a new marriage. "No, I don't want that," I replied, reduced to weeping as I said it. "I want this. I simply want these days with you. This intensity." I needed nothing to sanctify this, no laws, no papers. This was better than legitimacy. Love, honor, and cherish. Till death do us part, or until my plane takes off two days from now. We were beyond jealousy and beyond doubt. I could not have had this relationship with any other man. Who else had I known all these years? Who else had remembered me over a lifetime of marriage and invited me here? Impossible to lose this, even if we never saw each other again. Incomplete love, unsanctified love, might be the only complete and sanctified love there was.

Thus word and body fused, became indistinguishable, each of us inseparable from the other, like the lingering taste of wine in our mouths and on our breath, or the sound of the Requiem in our heads. Later, with rain dripping in the courtyard, I wrapped the sheet and blanket around us, secured the down-filled comforter around our shoulders, set a glass of water on the night table in case we woke up thirsty, and we fell asleep. Even in profoundest sleep, we did not let each other go. Awaking briefly toward morning, I found myself in the basket of his arms, heard his steady breathing, then fell into my dreams once more, or into his — I could not tell which of us was dreaming, which awake, where I ended and he began. I told the morning never to come, shoved it rudely away from us, vowed that we would never get out of bed and have breakfast. Alas, we could find no way to make the sun and moon stand still.

‿⦵‿

16

NOCTURNE

*Mon mal est different de tous les autres car, pour vous dire la
vérité, il me fait du bien et pourtant j'en souffre; je trouve du
plaisir dans ma souffrance. Et s'il existe un mal qui suscite
du plaisir, alors mon tourment est l'objet de mon désir et ma
douleur, c'est ma santé.*

~

Mine is different from all other woes, for truthfully it
does me good and yet makes me suffer; I take pleasure in
my pain. And if there is such a thing as regret that gives
joy, then my torment is what I desire, and my pain is my
health.

> — *description of forbidden love in a romance
> by Chréstien de Troyes, circa 1175*

I go to bed most nights as though embarking on a journey.
I will fall asleep but only to wake on the keen edge between
night and morning. A gray cat shares my bed, an ancient
dame, her skull prominent beneath the fur, eyes huge and yellow, some teeth missing. She wakes at three A.M. as I do, arches
out of her slumber, stretches, peers unblinkingly into my eyes.
Looking for something, patient, waiting. She was my daughters' childhood kitten and is determined to set a record for
longevity. Outside my uncurtained window, a distant light or
two, cats' eyes in the blackness. On the bedside table, my comforting, familiar clutter of books and papers: poetry; a couple
of bestsellers; *Jane Eyre* and *Madame Bovary,* lifelong companions; a learned work on ancient American stone circles a friend
insists I read; two childhood books, rescued from my mother's

house after she died; magazines folded open to interesting spots and set aside; the half-worked crossword puzzle that put me to sleep at midnight — a kitchen midden of the mind. Impossible, in that stack, not to find something that can set me at ease, the opiate of the printed page, like whisky for the alcoholic.

In the dark I wait for some wise guide to lead me toward the future, to shepherd me safely past the flames of the inferno, which glow brightly in the middle of the night. Jesus Savior, pilot me! Virgil led Dante; will he not appear and take my hand in his? I too should like to see the fires of hell beneath my feet. I too should like to walk past the wasted, ashen plains, to plot my path through those fiery winds toward Paradise, to see my enemies and old antagonists burning as I waft safely past in the arms of a master poet. Keats — I would choose Keats as my guide to all the strata of the earth, to heaven, and to hell. He died young, yet seemed to know the cosmos very well.

I double up my pillow. The cat digs her head into my shoulder. Apparitions emerge as I begin dozing once more. Out of one worn paperback comes Francesca da Rimini. Dante says she fell in love with Paolo, her husband's brother. Ah, divorce Italian style: old man da Rimini murdered the lovers in each other's arms. Their ghosts ride the tortured air of hell, united there as in life, whipping and whirling in the fuming, arid tempests of the inferno like laundry on a clothesline during a dust storm. Francesca, let it be remembered, was seduced by a book. Lancelot and Guinevere, she confessed — another odds-on favorite of mine, a love that destroyed a whole kingdom, killed off virtue forever, caused knighthood to go sour, ruined the fellows' games. Now as in childhood, I am on the lovers' team, not the king's. I recall that other Francesca, with her lover in Madison County. Under the bridges of Iowa, as it were. She kept her adultery brief and managed to escape the fires of hell. Is that a sign of social and intellectual progress? Probably. These tales have been passed from hand to hand; they will corrupt us forever. The cat is a gray reptilian coil on the quilt, a snake with fur and ears — no doubt a relative to the leggy serpent that slithered into Eden. I flip on the light, find my robe and slippers, patrol the rooms. It is four A.M. Should I return to bed or make a pot of coffee and begin my day? Neither. I locate a book and begin to read.

My marriage has resumed, or, to put it exactly, Gil and I occupy the same house once more. A live-in divorce, he jokes. He has been ill: two heart attacks. A long scar runs down the middle of his chest. Every day he swallows pink, white, yellow, gray pills of every shape and size. He sets them out in a line and contemplates them carefully before washing them down with coffee — forbidden, but he drinks it anyhow. I saw him through the heart attacks and surgery. Because there was nobody else to do it, and because our daughters needed me to do it. And because I care for him, in the distant, patient way that you care for a man you've known for almost four decades. He is, after all, the father of my children, I the mother of his. Sometimes, choosing our words very carefully, we lightly reminisce about the silver sports car, the amusement park funhouse and its leaky boat, the babies, the gray cat as a kitten. But we speak only of what won't scrape and sting. Do we love each other? Who can tell? We cohabit as an economic arrangement, a matter of detail and distances, of decency, of politeness sustained like one's balance on a bicycle. Old grievances sometimes flare. I sometimes haul out my heavy artillery, rusted and outmoded though it is. He conducts his wily ambushes, expert as always in verbal nerve gas. But we have grown bored with warfare as we once grew bored with celebrating anniversaries. We think of other things.

Our relationship has turned into something like a house, practical, usable comfort and shelter, providing a structure, security, predictability, as marriages are supposed to do. A quart of milk in the refrigerator, assigned chores, a small lawn to worry about, clean clothes in the closet. Tax records bulging in the filing cabinets. Does love dwell within this house? Who knows? Consider the dutiful visits to the hospital I have made, the balanced checkbooks, the taxes paid, the social security credits accumulated, the aluminum cans and newspapers correctly recycled, the donations made, the pair of us burying our differences to celebrate graduations, me stuffing a Thanksgiving turkey yet again, him seeing that the car gets its oil change. We married Sally to her beloved the other day. Maggie too has fallen in love. Perhaps soon we shall have grandchildren.

These arrangements are precisely what most people mean when they speak of love and marriage. Whatever is in our minds — be it affection, indifference, or murder, and all these reside there — church and state smile on us. Our names shall be inscribed in *The Book of Common Prayer*. I have been but an imperfect wife, O Lord, and O my goddess Athena. I have not lived up to your expectations, dearest Mother. He has been but an imperfect husband. But on our golden anniversary, if we remember to count the years ahead, I expect to receive congratulations from the president or the governor or at least the mayor. Possibly the pope.

My heart, however, remains its own place.

I saw Olivia the other day. After years of silence, she tracked me down through some college agency or other. Her letter, of course, had a return address I did not recognize, a last name I did not know. But the hand, of course, was still her hand. "I've no idea if you'll want to see me," she wrote. "The eldest of my three sons — aged thirty, twenty-eight, and twenty-two — is living in Manhattan with his wife. I'm planning a brief visit. My husband will be with me. He's a lawyer, quite busy and successful, and as you can see we live in Memphis. Perhaps you'd like to meet him and the boys. I hope you'll have an afternoon or evening free for me, just the two of us." She married young, while she was still at Oberlin, a man she came to love, though at the time she was unsure of her feelings. Nevertheless, she felt she owed a debt to me, an apology.

She had tucked a snapshot of herself into the envelope. Not the same face, the glossy hair still close-cut but white, the waist no longer slender. But the hazel eyes, still dominant in her face, retained that look of authority. I gladly accepted her invitation, suggesting that we meet in the lobby of a museum on a certain date in October. She saw me before I saw her. We kissed each other's cheeks, took each other's hands. She'd have known me anywhere, she said; but I'd have passed her unaware on the street. Is this you, Olivia? Is this me?

We decided to stroll along Fifth Avenue, and I acted as her guide. We were matrons now, invisible in the way that women our age are invisible, of no interest to the passing male but by no means so fragile and ancient as to attract concern. I was well dressed in a camel jacket and gabardine skirt, she in a handsome woolen cape. We were ourselves but not ourselves, each seeking and finding the eighteen-year-old in the other: the college freshmen of years gone by with poodle-cut heads and cinched waists, circle skirts and ballet shoes, the two who had met, embraced, parted, vanished, married, raised children, acted responsibly, and only rarely gotten drunk while listening to music. The two eighteen-year-olds had died, as if from a wasting disease. Now we were present at their resurrection.

"I don't regret our episode of love, not any of it, except the cruel way I broke off with you," she explained, though I had not asked for any explanation. "I knew you were vulnerable, an idealist, and I wrecked your life for a while. But I was terrified of your dream of a life outside the conventional world. I truly loved you, though I don't love women as a category. Nor men, either. It's my husband I love, not men. We have been happy, I suppose, in that complex, disappointing way that married people are happy. I remember when you and I meant to turn the world upside down. I have never been ashamed of that. I am only sorry that my life could not be lived at that level of intensity."

I said there was no need to measure love or make comparisons, or apologize for the inevitable. Gently, joyfully, I related that I had carried her with me wherever I had gone, especially to Paris. Since she had been the first to demonstrate love's duplicitous gifts to me, its riskiness, its body blows, her lessons had gone with me into the arms of men. We walked quietly, yet in a kind of rapture, agitated to a roil by the warm sunshine irradiating the concrete and granite, the yellow leaves so soon to vanish, the October wind with an edge of the razor in it. Recounting our biographies, we were serene, content. What had been unraveled had now been rewoven. The tears were dried. Later, after I had spent an evening with her family, we said goodbye with the tenderest affection.

I think of Olivia as I roam the house. We exchange infrequent but very long letters. Sometimes at night I reread them. Packed as they are with the details of daily life, they stay fresh and fragrant. They contain no hint of passion, except an occasional reference to music we still love (she plays Chopin's mazurkas to this day, she says, though only in private). Yet these plain letters from one woman in her sixties to another are full of passion, as deeply satisfying, with their finely wrought details of another woman's life, as physical love. Friendship too, when it endures for four decades, is a form of eros.

Now that she's ninety, my mother-in-law is still occasionally part of my night. Unable to break the habit, she still comes for long visits, a relic of my marriage: my legacy, my alimony, the wages of sin. Relentlessly, when I was a bride, she bestowed the trophies of True Womanhood upon me. "This is what you need. This will do the job. This is what love is. This is womanhood, all these things." Finally, and inevitably, Edwina herself arrived. "Take care of me. I can no longer do the job very well myself. I constitute part of your womanly duty."

At night, she too patrols the house, and sometimes raps at my bedroom door, clad in a blue nylon zip-front dressing gown decorated with cunning white ducklings. Her skin hardly looks like skin anymore, and the eyes have gone flat in their sockets. Nevertheless, the irises are still a piercing blue. She vacillates from rage to sweetness, her moods swinging crazily over the swamp of forgetfulness in the center of her mind. "I found the front door unlocked again. What's the matter with you? Do you just go to bed at night with the doors unlocked? They'll come in and steal the silver! You left the outside lights on too." Like the French, she cannot bear to see a kilowatt wasted.

"Go back to bed, Mother. No one's going to steal the silver."

Sometimes she tells her story: "There's a man who loves me, if only I could find him. He's in Florida now. He's so in love with me, and I'm in love with him too. Just take me to the airport. He'll be there to meet me. Years ago he told me he would always love me, care for me, the minute he was free. I dreamed of him just now. He was calling me."

"Mother, it's only a dream." She's even deafer now, and I am obliged to shout ever louder. "You can't remember his name. You don't have his phone number. He may even be dead. Or married to some fifty-year-old. Anyway, I can't take you to the airport."

Comforted for the moment, she returns to her room. I shut my door and turn out the light, knowing she'll soon forget the unlocked door, the daydream, love, and me.

Curiously, I've dreamed of my own mother of late, dead so young. Mama is always beautiful, dark-haired. I notice the pronounced widow's peak in the middle of her forehead, which I coveted as a child but did not inherit. It went instead to my firstborn, and I was glad. My mother's face is not my face, but her body is my body, long and slender, broad in the hips. She wears the plain little pastel suit and scarf I had her buried in. She holds her hands toward me, her aspect grave and accusing. As if I had been stripped and thrust suddenly into a snowdrift, I realize that she is not dead, that she has been there in her house waiting to hear from me. I want to beg forgiveness, but I shrink away, knowing that she cannot forgive me. She too was Athena's lady. Love was fidelity, supper on the table, ironed handkerchiefs for Daddy's pocket. Love was what passed between parent and child. Sister and sister. Sex, alas, was always tarnished, always suspect, a nuisance, something you did because you had to. It left wet spots on your clean sheets, tore the blanket from its moorings, was a threat to the innocence of children in the next room.

But I was looking for the pathway to beyond. "The world is flat," my mother said, but I would have it round.

Once, long ago, I saw Romeo and Juliet in a ballet, with two great dancers, Rudolf Nureyev and Margot Fonteyn. She looked like a bony child with her girlish chest, long legs, her tutu and ribbons; he was powerful in doublet and tights that proudly displayed his musculature, his sexuality — a grand male bird. Yet she was even more the athlete than he, as muscular, as powerful, balancing on the very tips of her toes, and he was just as vulnerable to injury as she was, the half-second lapse in timing that might mean disaster, a broken back or leg. Examined at close range, both pairs of feet would exhibit deformities, the brutal punishment this art inflicts on the body. How like real love it seemed to me at the time. In fact, Margot Fonteyn was twenty years his senior, was faithfully married to a paraplegic, whom she tended, and Rudolf Nureyev was a homosexual. But bending and swaying in each other's arms, leaping and twisting, they were the image, the personification of love, two creatures yearning for union, a union neither of them could know. Here was the ancient heresy in the flesh, mocking the notion of marriage, mocking the love that cares only for respectability and order. The threadbare old liebestod. Yet in my time this heresy has died and gone to its grave, deprived of meaning not by the triumph of orthodoxy but by its death.

Perhaps love is memory only, a mnemonic device, a window on illusions, a secret for the mind's eye.

After they had drunk the magic potion, Isolde and Tristan made love. But if you read the true old version of the story, you find a strange ending. In fact, the lovers in this wicked medieval poem (sung for centuries at castle hearths, the source of all rebellion) did not die young. Tristan took Isolde to Cornwall as he was meant to do, and she married King Mark, as she was meant to do, and reigned as queen. No doubt she ran the household, arranged state dinners, and went to mass. All this time, though, she and Tristan remained lovers. They lied, sneaked around, cheated, had close calls; they endured death threats and hardship. The love potion imprisoned them, or maybe it was God himself, playing games.

In his sorrow Tristan finally went off to Brittany, across the Channel, and married another woman. She too was called Isolde, which must have been the equivalent of Tiffany or Ashley in its day. He did whatever knights do, and eventually was mortally wounded in a tournament. "Ah," said he, on his deathbed, "I must see my darling once more." So he sent a white-sailed ship to bring the true Isolde to him; the ship was to return with black rigging if the queen refused to make the journey. Isolde II knew what to do. She watched through the window, and when the white sails billowed on the horizon, she told her husband they were black. Thus Tristan fell back in his bed to die, and when his true love ran into the bedroom, they had just enough time to die in each other's arms.

But the strangest part was yet to come: King Mark commanded that the bodies be brought home and buried on opposite sides of a church. And what should happen next but that two trees sprang up, one from each coffin. They grew until their branches intertwined, interlaced, twisted into a wild tangle over the roof. King Mark chopped them down. He prayed against those trees, called down the curse of God upon them. But no matter how many times he pruned them, they did the same old forbidden thing right on the roof of the church. The love potion operated beyond the grave.

I intend to travel to Cornwall to find this pair of trees. I'll locate them first on the map of love, the *carte de tendre*. It cannot be far from Camelot, which I'll also search for. And when I've found the church and the unrepentant trees, I shall water them and harvest a few leaves for myself. Then I'll set out for Brittany in a ship with white sails. Perhaps my true love will be waiting for me in France.

ACKNOWLEDGMENTS

I have been fortunate in the patience and skill of my critics and readers up to this point. Zane Kotker, author of four novels as well as other books, has seen every draft at every stage and provided expert editorial advice and constant encouragement, as always. (Without her, I could never have been a writer at all.) My friends Anna Bodine and Karen Meehan each read with attention and heart, advising me wisely on larger issues and catching scores of errors. I am grateful to my daughters, Katharine Miller and Elizabeth Tomkievicz, for their comments; this manuscript cannot have been easy reading for them. Brett and Robert Averitt, Michael Goldman, and JoAnn Kobin read drafts at various stages and offered valuable counsel. Huguette Martel not only read and advised on the manuscript but brought me back in touch with the French language, thereby reviving earlier days and forgotten emotions for me. Lilyan and Irwin Glusker read an early draft, and their words of encouragement stayed with me. The late Senator J. William Fulbright of my home state devised the program that financed my year in France. This book is certainly the result of that sojourn. (None of these people, and certainly not the Fulbright Commission, is to be blamed for whatever shortcomings and errors may lie herein.)

Janet Silver at Houghton Mifflin has been at once the most sympathetic and most demanding of editors. Liz Duvall, senior manuscript editor, brought her magical skills to this typescript as she did to *The Bookmaker's Daughter*. Lois Wallace, my literary agent, calmed my anxieties and cheered me onward as she has unfailingly done for two decades.

I have sought help in my bookshelves and in the library as well as from my friends. In addition to the authors named in the narrative (those universal companions of humanity such as Tolstoy and Flaubert and Charlotte Brontë), I should like specifically to thank Fenton Johnson for his essay "Wedded to an Illusion: Do Gays and Lesbians Really Want the Right to Marry?" (*Harper's Magazine*, November 1996), an illuminating comment on heterosexual marriage that came at just the right time. Richard Bernstein's *Fragile Glory* (Knopf, 1990) also appeared exactly when I most needed to read a book like his. Tony Judt's *Past Imperfect: French Intellectuals, 1944–1956* (Berkeley, University of California Press, 1992) helped me recall the atmosphere of the late 1950s in France. The biographies of George Sand by Curtis Cate (Houghton Mifflin, 1975) and by André Maurois (*Lélia*, translated by Gerard Hopkins, Harper Brothers, 1953) have been sourcebooks for me for many years. The late Frederic Grunfeld's brilliant articles on Chopin and on the troubadors have stayed in my mind since they appeared in *Horizon* magazine in spring 1969 and summer 1970, respectively. I drew inspiration from the magnificent new translation of the Flaubert-Sand correspondence by Francis Steegmuller and Barbara Bray (Knopf, 1993), which brings the English-speaking reader into intimate contact with two great literary souls of France, both of them, needless to say, experts on love. I hope Dan Hofstadter will accept my thanks for the pleasure and the ideas I derived from *The Love Affair as a Work of Art* (Farrar, Straus, and Giroux, 1996), surely the best book about nineteenth-century French literature and love I have ever encountered. Andrea Dworkin's *Intercourse* (Free Press, 1987) was immensely helpful — a brilliant and original work. Finally, Denis de Rougemont's *Love in the Western World* (Pantheon, 1956) set me thinking many years ago about the dangers and delights of romantic passion. He warned against passion's ancient mythology, saw it elevated to alarming new heights in American film and song, prophesied it would be our ruination. Sad to say, this grand and learned work, so pertinent for contemporary life and love, is now out of print.